This Volume is an extremely evocative book, revealing a fascinating ancient template of truth that became distorted and used in the creation of ideological designs, and events against the public.

It shows how Abrahamic stories of sacrifice have different original meanings.

The Twelve Tribes of Israel never really existed. Know the true meaning of the Kaaba its stone and what Muhammad set in motion. How the original Zodiac came from the Hidden Matrix. What the very Elite have kept from mankind. How Pope Pius IX planned to usurp original purpose of America, evidenced by what Brumidi created through the Apotheosis of Washington.

Hidden knowledge used in creating the original Twin Towers also established their purpose, and the plan of 9/11 in all the detail. Inside are details never known of the Holy Land. How Racism is rooted in the misuse of the universal truth. How Kircher adapted and made a truth into a lie to favor the Catholic Church. A book compacted, full of earthshattering revelations, worth sharing. Ultimately, we have an expose of true crime that has never been revealed before.

1111 FACTOR

THE HIDDEN MATRIX

CROWN CODE

ROYALTY, RELIGIONS, AND ELITE SECRETS IN PLAIN SIGHT

VOLUME 2

BARON GABRIEL ESPINOSA AND

BARONESS JAN DE AVALON-ESPINOSA

11:11 FACTOR, THE HIDDEN MATRIX, Volume 2 Copyright © 2020 by Dr. Gabriel Foster Espinosa and Dr. Jan de Avalon-Espinosa. All rights reserved. Printed in the United States of America. No part of this book may be reproduced or utilized in any form or by any means, electronic or mechanical, including photocopying, recording, or by any information storage and retrieval system, without permission in writing from the publisher, except in the case of brief quotations embodied in critical articles and reviews. For information address Barony Books, 1701 California Street, Suite 1080, Denver Colorado 80202

All rights reserved. All Moral rights are held by Baron Gabriel Foster Espinosa to all visual art, graphs and or charts contained herein in perpetuity. (1) Independently of the author's economic rights, the author shall have the right to claim authorship of the work and to object to any distortion, mutilation or other modification of, or other derogatory action in relation to, the said work, which would be prejudicial to his honor or reputation.

First Edition

Library of Congress Control Number: 2020919143

Copyright © 2020 By Baron and Baroness Espinosa

Copyright © 2020 By Baron and Baroness Espinosa BB5063 ESPI

Barony Books website: https://www.baronybooks.com

Espinosa, Dr. Gabriel Foster, Dr. Jan de Avalon-Espinosa

> **11:11 Factor, The Hidden Matrix, Volume 2/ By Dr Jan de Avalon-Espinosa and Dr Gabriel Foster Espinosa**
> **ISBN: 978-1-7353513-6-0 (pbk)**
> **ISBN: 978-1-7353513-7-7 (ebook)**
> **Includes bibliographical references and index.**

1. PERSONIFIED PATRIARCHS. 2. SECRET OF SARAI. 3. STORY OF SACRIFICE. 4. THE TRIBES. 5. WHAT SET IN MOTION. 6. ZODIAC CONCEPTION KEY. 7. ELITE COMFORT ZONE. 8. SECRETS OF THE APOTHEOSIS. 9. OWL KNOWING. 10. THE SECRET OF 9-11. 11.SECRET OF ISRAEL. 12. The stations. 13. THE OTHER SIDE OF GENESIS Racism Root.

Dedication

To my beautiful wife Jan, Baroness of Minster Lovel who has given me absolute moments of true inspiration and love like none can. Her specialness has surely influenced my mind, my essence and most of all tugged at the strings of my heart. Thus, through this work, the world shall become better for it.

CONTENTS

FOREWORD..*8-9*

INTRODUCTION..*10-14*

ONE- PERSONIFIED PATRIARCHS 15

TWO - SECRET OF SARAI..31

THREE - STORY OF SACRIFICE..35

FOUR - THE TRIBES..37

FIVE - WHAT ISLAM SET IN MOTION... 47

SIX - ZODIAC CONCEPTION KEY...57

SEVEN - ELITE COMFORT ZONE 67

EIGHT - SECRETS OF THE APOTHEOSIS......................................83

NINE - OWL KNOWING..99

TEN – THE SECRET OF 9/11...109

ELEVEN - SECRET OF ISRAEL 121

TWELVE -THE OTHER SIDE OF GENESIS-RACISM ROOT......147

ABOUT AUTHORS..163

NOTES   165

FOREWORD

I have known Baron, Rabbi, Dr. Gabriel Espinosa for over 10 years, we met in Midland Texas. Gabriel is a Polymath and Mathematical Epigraphist, he introduced me to the Hidden Matrix Formula, he referred to it as the Pattern and Totalities at the time, and from that moment, I was hooked on the information he disclosed. I became a student to him and wanted to learn everything from the Formula. I would simply gaze upon it for hours, allowing my mind to drift, to comprehend beyond the actual Pattern details, and into the invisible world. I cannot find the words to express how fortunate I feel, to have met Gabriel, and having the opportunity to understand the hidden secrets of the universe, through the Formula. Gabriel is a genius, no matter what you ask of him, he will explain the forces in nature as energies of Light going into Matter. He can create charts revealing the mathematical equations of hundreds of Architectural and Land designs, created by those in ancient and modern times, who have utilized information from the Matrix Formula, not always for the good of the people. Gabriel says he can 'see' into the unknown worlds and bring to life those hidden mysteries for all to understand. I have recently been introduced to Gabriel's wife Baroness, Dr. Jan de Avalon-Espinosa and discovered, that she has worked in many Metaphysical fields as an expert in Auras, Energy, Esoteric and Spiritual subjects for over 40 years. They have brought their own uniqueness and expertise together, to create a masterpiece for the betterment of all humanity.

1111 Factor Crown Code is a mind-blowing, illustrative, and enlightening book.

-Joel Arevalo Midland Texas USA - Cosmic Consciousness

I have known Baroness, Reverend, Dr. Jan de Avalon-Espinosa for over 22 years, she is a brilliant mentor, tutor, and friend.

I was a student of Jan's 20 years ago, at her Metaphysical Reiki School in Norwich, Norfolk, UK… After the incredible energetic Reiki course, I went on to take many other courses in Metaphysical, Spiritual and Esoteric subjects with her. I have witnessed so many amazing experiences with energy in Jan's classes and her Meditation Lessons. She has incredible insight into Esoteric subjects, a profound knowledge as an intellectual. I believe that her intuitive perceptions, are from another domain of existence. Jan taps into the universal knowledge and 'senses information' beyond this world, as revealer of the unseen realm. She also teaches Ancient Magick by utilizing her innate talents to encourage others, to raise their consciousness to a higher level. I remember the day when she was introduced to Baron, Dr. Gabriel Espinosa, she was ecstatic, and overwhelmed because at long last she would have a Mentor to open her mind, to a different type of awareness, as the Creation Formula, Hidden Matrix. Together as a couple they are awesome, creative, powerful, and dedicated to revealing ambiguities, mysteries, and a truth beyond man's own intelligence. They offer the world an opportunity to understand the foundation source of universal realities, focusing on how the Elite, Royals and Religions have abused the knowledge, that was meant for all mankind and not a select few.

1111 Factor Crown Code is an illuminating, evocative and exemplification of higher intelligence and knowledge.

-Gudi Grange Norwich Norfolk UK

NLP, Hypnotherapy, Reiki/Karuna Master, Rev. Minister, Healer, Energy Worker, Metaphysics, Spirituality, Esoteric, Cosmic Consciousness.

INTRODUCTION

With our world noticeably changed since a 55-year-old individual from Hubei province who in China on November 17, 2019 may have been the first person to have contracted COVID-19, according to the South China Morning Post. Reality is we do not know. Pointing the finger, blaming others as the erroneous claim, that it started in Wuhan, China in the Hubei province a month later in December 2019 is of no help.

Coronaviruses are a group of related RNA viruses which have ribonucleic acid as its generic material that cause diseases in mammals and Birds. In humans and birds, they cause respiratory tract infections that can range from mild to lethal. Notable human diseases caused by RNA viruses include the common cold, influenza, SARS, Covid-19, Dengue Virus, hepatitis C, hepatitis E, West Nile fever, Ebola virus disease, rabies, polio, and measles.

The universe has various ways at combating diseases and keeping balance. Whether we like it or not, there is cause and effect, whereby those means used by nature become more noticeable. Not only are there increasing natural phenomena, which are not limited to earthquakes, tsunami's, fires and more, it appears that humanity is facing a precipice, that could lead us all into the abyss. In modern day by our perceptions, we consider ourselves highly advanced and having the answers to life. Yet the question remains, just as civilizations past, which I'm sure they too considered themselves advanced, is what the cause of such setting as we find ourselves in, and can we do something to change the curve from a downward spiral, to that which gives all humanity a fighting chance against what nature will bring? We must ask the question, what truly was the cause that led to the destruction of past civilizations, and are we next in line toward the same fate?

The inability of mankind to defend itself from known viruses and others which in no doubt will manifest, as a direct result of the state of consciousness mankind operates by, is without doubt already begun.

It is an interesting fact, that no matter where we look, there are clues left behind, which leave us without doubt, that a great secret has been used from the beginning. Within this Volume are

15 short chapters, that summarize and touch on those elements that have influenced life as we know it. The use and or misuse of a universal truth will become evident.

It is up to all mankind, to realize the depth of the conspiracy, deceit that we have endured, through religious and royal right. Let us now unite as a global people, and advance past those nefarious practices, and embrace that deeper truth which can bring humanity into alignment with universal purpose and existence.

We can no longer wait, nor can we allow this issue to be solved by our children, as chances are, they may not have that opportunity at making correction. We must stop fighting each other due those ill influences which has shaped our world experience. My purpose is to shed light upon that which is meant for all to know, and all to incorporate as themselves toward that enlightened existence, by the light of universal truth.

Please do not ignore this opportunity for a better world. Yes, in the process, there will be growing pains. Yet the result is that toward preservation of the human species.

How has mankind erred, when we think ourselves highly advanced, yet we find ourselves on a precipice, seemingly in a downward spiral. We cannot ignore the past, if we are to have a future, especially when we recognize that we are a product out of the past, which is why it is especially important to consider, that all ancient scripts, written in the 'antiquities' and in those languages of that time, do not transliterate into English correctly. There is no evidence or record, of any ancient historical mysteries, or sacred knowledge and books written in English.

Therefore, in general these ancient languages, have difficulty in remaining unadulterated and precise when transliterated into English. More especially Aramaic and Hebrew.

Hebrew language and Alphabet are first as a 'number' expression, and then a letter. Many words and phrases cannot translate easily into English; however, the numbers never alter.

Therefore, I must be noticeably clear about the Christ story. The Christ returning, is to say that the truth of what the Christ is, shall be revealed again in modern times, and no longer hidden. The Christ was only ever known as Christus, and later changed to Christos. Its meaning is not that of a 'man', but that of the first thought, as expressed through the Creator. Therefore, the Creators first expression, as thought, was known as the Son or Sun.

The Creator being both Male and Female, by recognition of each other as the ONE, birthed the image, which was known as the Son, hence the trinity conception.

Religions have nefariously taken the truth and made it into a lie.

The Christus was known thousands of years before the Jesus/Christ narrative, came on the scene, it was borrowed and reused, from the Mithras account. We must look to Constantine for the error and deception, as he, with others, created the 'Jesus' birth story, as a political tool.

Again, please understand, that ancient knowledge was cloaked in lies, and ancient languages describing the true Christus meaning, was hidden in plain sight.

Hence, Christ or Christus returning is happening now, because I am revealing the absolute truth to you, concerning what the Christ or Son is, and not who they made the Christ or Son out to be.

Christ, Christos is referring to the CHRISTUS that has nothing to do with any religion, especially the Christian Religion, which ran with the narrative and intermingled it with Pagan festivals to suit the calendar and philosophies they designed to control mankind.

"Knowing the truth will set you free"

Throughout the years, just like many of you, I was experiencing events, where the results had a direct or indirect effect on my life. Individually, each even seemed to be separate, yet there was a sameness, that in my mind was systematically keeping everyone as slaves to a system, a system which by its parts appears unrecognizable. After careful consideration to the facts presented to me, it became truly clear, that we were dealing with types and images. It was by these types and images reflected throughout history, that all humanity has been conditioned and controlled. Everyone, in their own way are now experiencing effects, which is presented in what we know as 'the world today'. My journey into the "awakening", has given me insights into real life situations, that we as humanity must attend to before we forfeit the future for our children and families.

How it began, I was born at Hotel Dieu in El Paso Texas in 1963, in 1987 it was permanently closed, and demolished in 2003, the first school I attended was called St. Patrick's Cathedral an (Elementary)School, the address is 1111 North Stanton, El Paso Texas. It was 1111 that would become tantamount in my discovering the universal truth and developing the Great Secret, which I call "The Hidden Matrix" and "Crown Code". In 1983; my mother took me to visit her father's old ranch, in Indian Hot Springs Texas, where she was born. My Grandfather was J.D. Foster of Ingersoll Rand, he had developed the ranch into a health resort back in the 1920's, with some very wealthy business partners.

I found it intriguing that in order to get to Indian Hot Springs Ranch, we would travel via Farm to Market Road 1111, this got me thinking, my elementary school address was 1111 N. Stanton, and now Farm to Market Road 1111. Was this a coincidence or was there a deeper meaning? Besides my grandfather's elite friends J.D. Rockefeller, the Vanderbilt's, there were several High Society visitors that would stay for long weekends. Even the President of the United States, William Taft made a stopover to enjoy the spa and curative waters.

Was there something else that drew these rich and famous people to the (IHS) 1111 ranch?

Behind the ranch buildings I noticed an old sway wooden bridge, with two large posts at the end of the bridge, and another two the same across into Mexico, the viewpoint and angle produced an abstract 1111, (by posts each end of the bridge). Immediately I thought of 1111 Stanton Road, Farm to Market Road 1111, and now the bridge posts 1111. Was this a message hidden in plain sight?

There had to be a purpose why 1111 was so prominent in my life.

Through-out the eighties, 1111 would randomly appear, on receipts, phone numbers, license plates, and other strange observations. It was apparently popping up everywhere I went, I noticed 11:11 on the flashing digital clock at home and work, it seemed to be telling me something about my experiences with 1111, I needed to discover something about this number?

On August 16th and 17th 1987, an event closely coincided with an exceptional alignment of planets, in the Solar System, it was called The Harmonic Convergence and the world's first synchronized global peace meditation. At this exact time, I was working in my office in the Coronado Towers 6006, N. Mesa El Paso, [Coronado means Crowned or Crowned One]. I was on a quest to discover the truth about 1111.

I experienced a positive recognition deep inside myself, but did not realize until 15 years later, when a sudden and compulsive urge from within, compelled me to develop a mathematical formula an algorithm, using the 1111 code/key.

This was the redeveloped Creation Formula, in ancient times the Pattern and Totalities, now I renamed it The Hidden Matrix and Crown Code. I realize now that my time at the Coronado Towers was preparing me for the mystical and divine experience of the true 'Crowning by the Pleroma'. An authentic King was Crowned.

Now I am a Dr. of Theology and Divinity, a Rabbi, Polymath and Mathematical Epigraphist, and I needed to redeem myself from the errors of history. Much is at the root of what ails the human condition, yet through my extensive research over the last 30 years, I have uncovered unbelievable yet astounding evidence, of a universal truth, that is there for all to know.

The uniqueness of what has been developed, far surpasses any work done before, in relation to how certain stories and concepts developed in the antiquities, to what we know today.

In this volume, secrets are revealed, which when originally implemented became part of those errors which have cursed the future of mankind. From the invention of Abraham, the promised land, and the Ark of the Covenant, to what the virgin concept became out of source material known as the Pattern and Totalities, known today as the Crown Code. Mankind can now grasp just how civilizations have been fooled into accepting an imposter of truth, which has altered and incarcerated the consciousness of mankind.

ONE

PERSONIFIED PATRIARCHS

1. WHOSE YOUR DADDY? – PERSONIFIED

Aside from being a physical being, one must understand, that ends were met, to instill likenesses of the Hidden Matrix, as enhancements within the narrative of the human experience. Here you will understand how a General of Royal lineage could incorporate a narrative although different from reality, expressed a must accept narrative amongst royals for everyone. Understand, if they did not agree, their lies regarding their god's foundation would have been revealed. That, they did not want. Thus, what developed has influenced that path of mankind since. As other developments were strategized, the Hidden Matrix became more so used as a Crown Code of security.

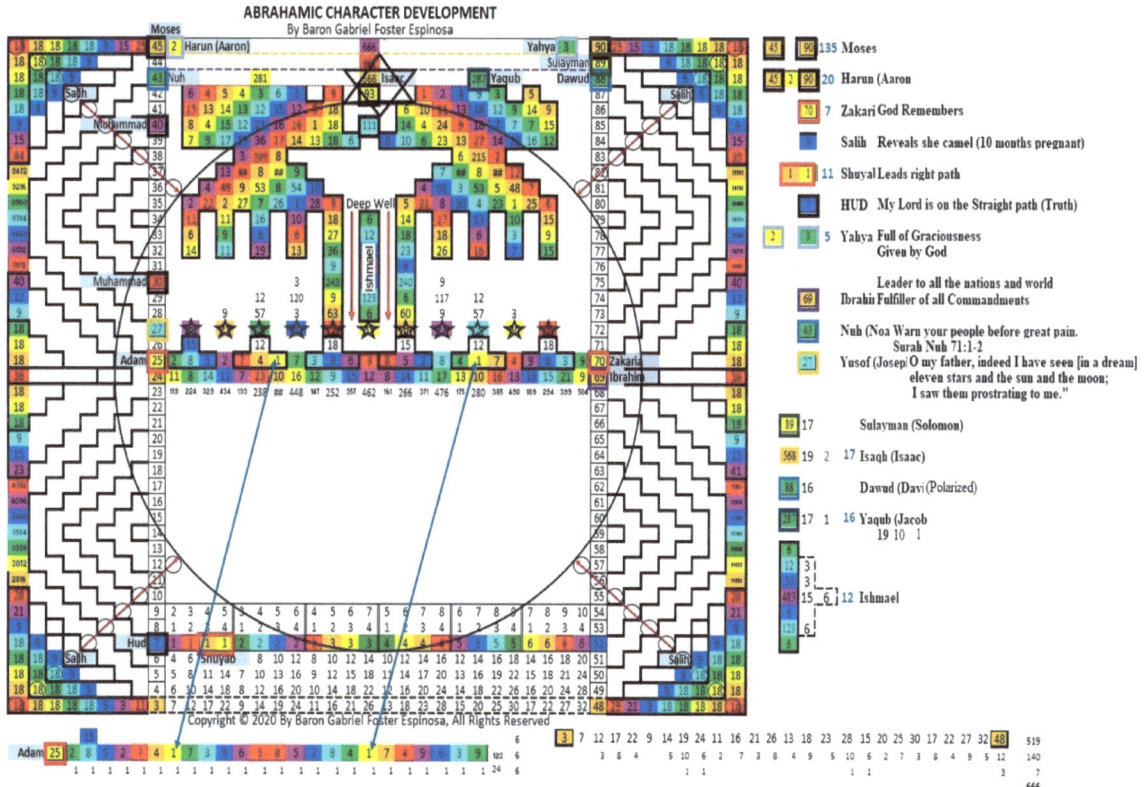

Exhibit 1: Abraham Character Development

Beginning with Ibrahim (Abraham), we can understand that the concept of Ishmael, not only referred to cosmic development, Ishmael's coordinate refers toward those building blocks infused into creation, out of the Matrix Code as source to the Word of God, which is at the root of, and to every human likeness universally.

1.1 Ibrahim as Leader

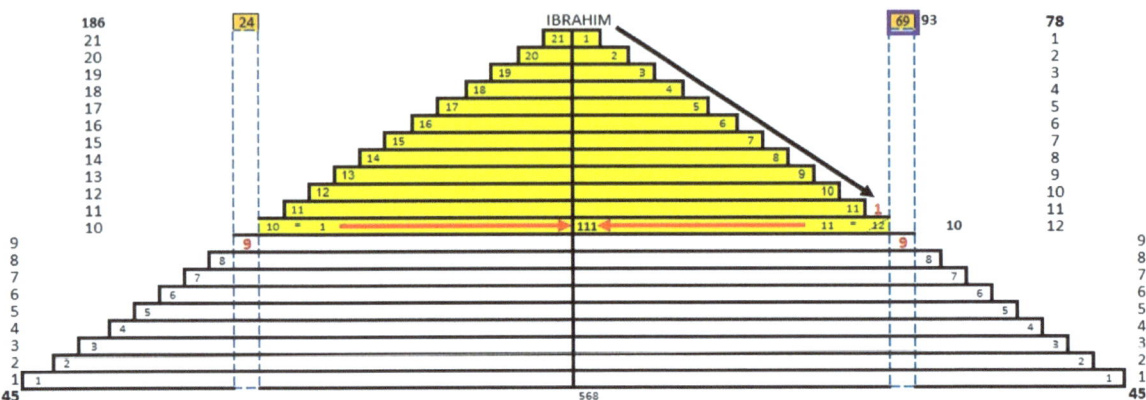

Exhibit 2: Ibrahim as Leader 568 at 69

Ibrahim at 69 horizontal right guide centers, became the leader as that pinnacle coordinate essence.

By Matrix Code establishment, Ibrahim from base, fulfills each side of the Matrix square by ascending upward fulfilling each step to the top, stopping, and standing as upon the capstone of a pyramid. In doing so he is fulfiller of all Matrix commandments. Here Ibrahim reveals that 111 within 1111. 69 and 24 united equal 93. 93+9+9 becoming 111 as recognized. 69 being half of the whole, is interpreted as 6+9 as 15. The 21 becomes 3 as under 93 and is united with the 1 to its right and the 1 produced from 12 in creation of the 11 representing 5. Together 15.5. 111 x 93 establishes 10,323/15.5 for 666. 45 +186+ 45+186+111 less the 5 = 568

1.2 Adam as first human likeness

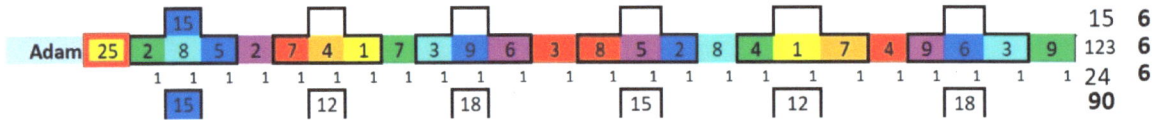

Exhibit 3: Adam as the first human likeness

Adam as the first in development, after center guide is at 25, where-after its row totality (soil) is taken from earth equaling 123 polarized to 6. 15 which creates the first three, and one square group bonding, is that gathering up polarized to 6. Which is typified as to say Adam was created on the sixth day, of the creation week.

The number of squares occupied are 24 for 6. Side by side the number of a man, being 666 (Congealed Blood) is understood. The 90 realized, reveals the Countenance level upon the Matrix Code.

1.3 Moses mentioned 135 times in Quran

Exhibit 4: Moses mentioned 135 times in Qur'an

Moses here by those top guides 45 and 90 is as that cap, when added together establishes that cap point essence of 135. Therefore, the Quran was designed to have Moses mentioned 135 times. As exterior to the core ascending numbers themselves, establishes Moses? as the younger brother.

1.4 Harun (Aaron) mentioned 20 times

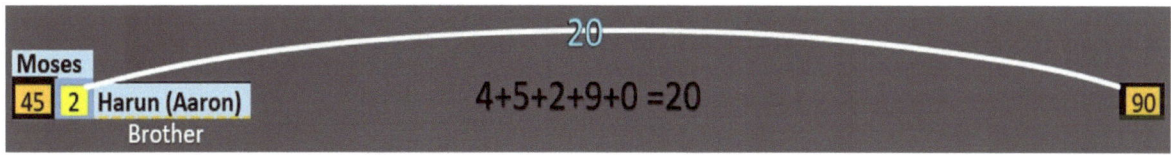

Exhibit 5: Essence 20 of Aaron the older brother

Harun (Aaron) connected to guide square 45, as the older 2, is united by polarization, giving instruction for 45 as 4 plus 5 for 9 plus 2 and 9 plus 0 of 90 revealing 20. The number 20 becomes the number of times Harun is mentioned in Quran.

1.5 Zakaria mentioned 70 times in Quran

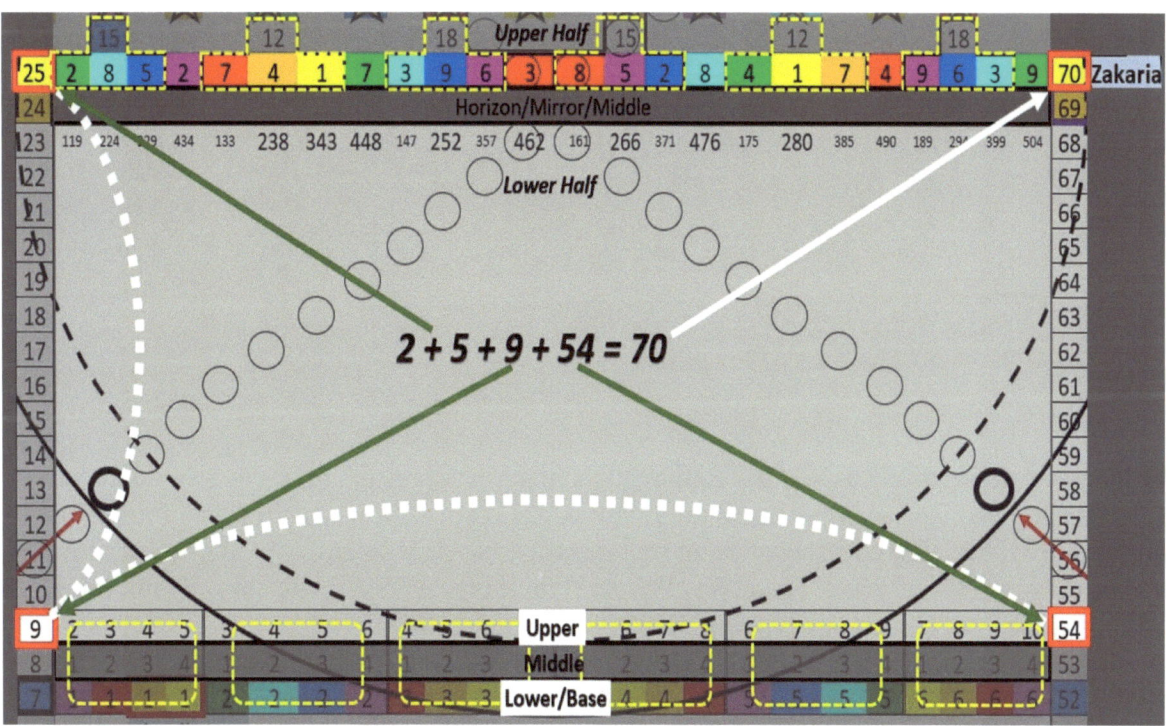

Exhibit 6: Zakaria God remembers by Baron Gabriel Foster Espinosa

Zakaria at right column guide 70, sits on the other/upper side of 69. As origin to the name, Zakaria developed its attributes of the former first six clusters 3rd level, at guide square 54 its corresponding opposite guide number 9 and 70's partner guide number of 25 as 7. In concert, they total 70, which became that remembrance of 70, thus God remembers, and is mentioned 70 times in Qur'an.

1.6 Man of Promise

Exhibit 7: Salih 9 and The Man of Promise

Salih has the description "as you were among us a man of promise," refers to the countenance of the Matrix, that face as previous photo 27b. It is this reality, as to what the 'Son' means and is upon the Matrix. Clarity of what Salih represents, rings clear to any Muslim, whereas truth defines usage. Thus, "And to Thamood [We sent] their brother Salih. He said, 'O my people, worship Allah; you have no deity other than him,"[Quran 11:61]

The Prophet Salih is described as having wisdom, purity and goodness (as in the Hagia Sophia designate) "O Salih, you were among us a man of promise before this. Do you forbid us to worship what our fathers worshiped? And indeed, we are, about that to which you invite us, in disquieting doubt." [Quran 11:62]

They merely wanted to worship the same gods as their fathers had, which is what is experienced today. Each following the other, with no reason, no proof, and no thought. Like sheep!

1.7 Idea of the Camel

They tried to discredit him, by giving him what they thought an impossible task. They asked him to let a unique "she-camel" emerge from the mountains.

The Arabic absolute divine strategy, was in establishing a beast as developed previously, as the bull, a male goat, a ram, and what Ibrahim at Genesis 15:9 added, being a turtledove and a pigeon

Exhibit 8: Rock split producing the She-camel by Baron Gabriel F. Espinosa

Here by Matrix eye of the beholder, Allah granted the Prophet Salih this great miracle and unique she-camel, appeared from the direction of the mountain. They also demanded that the she-camel be 10 months pregnant. 9 as foundation to the eighteens, being the corners upon the Matrix, provide direction to coordinate rationale. Which is why Salih is mentioned only nine (9) times in the Quran.

Prophet Salih replied: "Look now! If Allah sends you what you have requested, just as you have described, will you believe in that which I have come to you with and have faith in the message I have been sent with?" They answered: "Yes." So, he took a vow from them on this, and then prayed to Allah, The Almighty, to grant their request. Allah ordered the distant rock to split asunder, to bring forth a great ten-month pregnant she-camel (Bactrian Camel).

When their eyes set on it, they were amazed. They saw a great thing, a wonderful sight, a dazzling power and clear evidence!

Several of Prophet Salih's people believed, yet most of them continued in their disbelief, stubbornness, and going astray. Allah, the Almighty, said in the Noble Quran (what means): "And We gave Thamood the she-camel as a visible sign, but they wronged her." [Quran 17:59] And (what means): "And certainly did the companions of al-Hijr (628) [i.e. the Thamood] deny the messengers." [Quran 15:80-81]

As seen upon the Matrix Code as given by God, the chart has ten (10) yellow circles from central divider which stops between red 11 and yellow 11. The subliminal message is that creations impregnation is established by that union at Cayan, point at 11 and 11.

1.8 Leading to Right Path

Exhibit 9: Shuaib leads to right path by 11.

Shuaib 11 leads to the right path. It is not a surprise that Islam in its design chose to use associations that lead one toward the right path. Once the revelation of what 11 is to 11, as revealed by God through Gabriel, mankind as a whole can sway away from paths of error, which have condemned mankind to a lie.

Exhibit 10: Hud establishes the straight path.

Hud 7 establishes that the straight path as 1111, is that which establishes truth so pure, as to be salvation of mankind, being its universal properties.

1.9   Yahya Full of Graciousness

Exhibit 11: Yahya being full of Graciousness of 5

Yahya as 2 yellow and 3 green in between top 45 orange and 90, represent that full of graciousness known of the developers to Islam, as the great secret to the virgin of Christianity, more specifically a subliminal reference Catholic intercessory prayer, which is recited as "Hail

Mary, full of grace, the Lord is with you. Blessed are you among women, and blessed is the fruit of your womb, Jesus. Holy Mary, Mother of God, pray for us sinners, now and at the hour of our death. Amen"

Yahya here and then, as that hidden in plain sight methodology, which is to say Yahya became defined as full of Graciousness, as well as Given of God.

1.10 Nuh (Noah's) Instruction

Exhibit 12: Nuh pair instruction of 43.

Nuh (Noah) at 43 tells of development influence. In development to the Quran, hidden truths were peppered through-out, not as a means to deceive, but done so as a way of preservation regarding that influence of the Matrix Code, used in development of the Noah story in Judaism. Thus, prior to the worldwide flood, instruction was that Noah was to take one pair, a male and a female, of each kind of animal into the ark.

The later instruction not revealed through Nuh, was from between Matrix guide levels 29 and 74. You shall take with you of every clean animal by sevens, (the quantity of numbers between 29 and 74) a male and his female; and of the animals that are not clean (9 and 6) two, a male and his female; also of the birds of the sky (as seven blank squares to either side bound by the 9 and 6 instruction, extending to the 9 and 6 stars of Yusof.), by sevens, male and female, to keep offspring alive on the face of all the earth" Gen. 7:1-3

1.11 Yusof, The Sun, the Moon and Eleven Stars

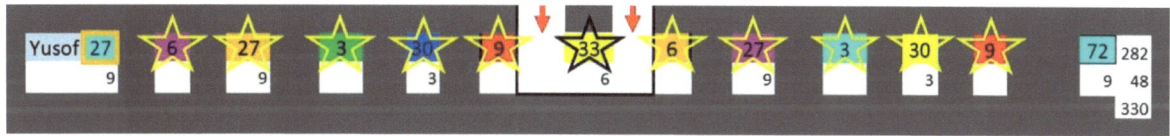

Exhibit 13: Yusof at 27 and the Dream

Yusof 27 (Joseph) (Sura 12: verse 99 - 101) - The Fulfillment of Yusof's dream - the sun, the moon, and eleven stars. (The sun represents male and the moon female energy forces in nature)

Yosef recalling a dream to his father, saying "O' My father I have seen [in a dream]. Eleven stars and the sun and the moon. I saw them prostrating to me."

The 33 at center represents the 33 lunar cycle years, as well as when the sun is clearest "The sun enters at the 30th degree but is not totally clear until the 33rd degree. (as the secret 33rd degree of Freemasonry) Thus, in astrology, the sun officially transitions into a new sign of the zodiac, at the 33rd degree, as it is of a certain size as well. Therefore, they said in the Bible that the ministry of Christ begins at 30 and finishes at 33, it is all symbology.

This reference would have been unmistakable to anyone aware of the secrets of astrology. The eleven stars represents 10 divider lines upon the Matrix, in creation of the zodiac parts, seen at Photo 32: Zodiac Coordinate Secret.

The ten divider lines are fanning outward at left and right, like wings. At center is that vertical unified color two columns, extending from bottom of Matrix to top of Matrix. In total there are divider 11 lines.

The proper interpretation considers that at center, coordinate between guide numbers 24 and 69 is that point of distinction, thus the 11th lines becomes two, as 11 and twelve. This secret would not be possible without the Matrix Code, as revealed through Yusof's dream.

Thus, it is true that the people come out of the dullness of the heart, where their ears have become heavy with lies, and their eyes heavy with illusions, which have caused blindness.

Truth as designed, now blossoms as revealed herein, setting within all mankind, that they should clearly perceive with their eyes, hearing truth with their ears, and understand with their heart, for healing them. That they may awaken from the deep sleep and the veiled illusion of lies to a higher state of consciousness and truth.

1.12 Sulayman Son of David

Exhibit 14: David 16

Dawud (David) at right guide 88 (polarized to 16) symbolized coordinate level to the assumption as leader as what Ibrahim at Photo 29b represented. 568 here became location from where Solomon would be birthed, thus becoming the Son of David.

1.13 Attributes of Sulayman

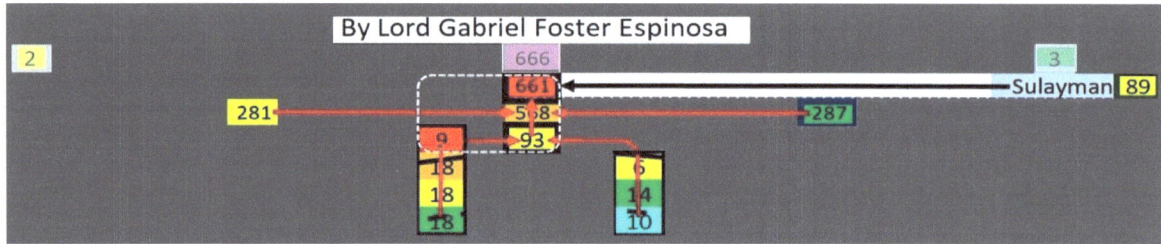

Exhibit 15: Sulayman the prophet/King

Sulayman, here follows the former level 88, we know became foundation to David. Firstly, in the Holy Koran, the emphasis was laid on Sulayman's role as a Prophet, whereas in the Holy Bible he is portrayed as a King.
And to go with the notion of a prophet, Sulayman was endowed with supernatural powers such as the power to move wind. Which is to say, That the character unites 281 and 287 in a side to side motion, whirling upward with 93, as per Matrix Code mandate.
In reference that he is a King, we have that 661 or 13 expression, being those twelve surrounding the central thirteenth. Thus, Sulayman was thirteen when he became King.
The wisdom attribute is conceived by the calculation in achieving 661. Solomon according to the Quran, died at 53 years old. By polarization, which defined the extent of Solomon's life, we see from the Matrix Code, within the white dashed area four numbers.
The column numbers are added as 6+6+1, 5+6+8, and 9+3 revealing that agreement number opposite guide 89 of 44. The right and left lower flanked column squares consist of seven

squares. The number 9 as that outward coordinate, as in Salih, provides fulfillment of expanding (four corner) mandate of the twelve (12). Thus 44 adds 9 for 53, as that numerical foundation to the age of Solomon at the age of his death

1.14 Ishaq mentioned 17 times in Quran

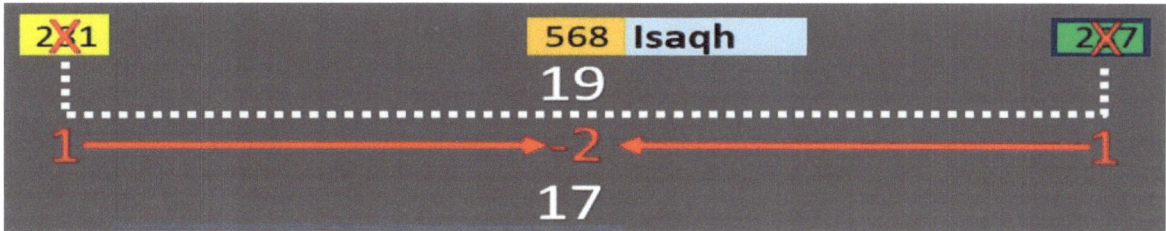

Exhibit 16: Ishaq mentioned 17 times in Qur'an

1.15 Yaqub mention 16 times in Quran

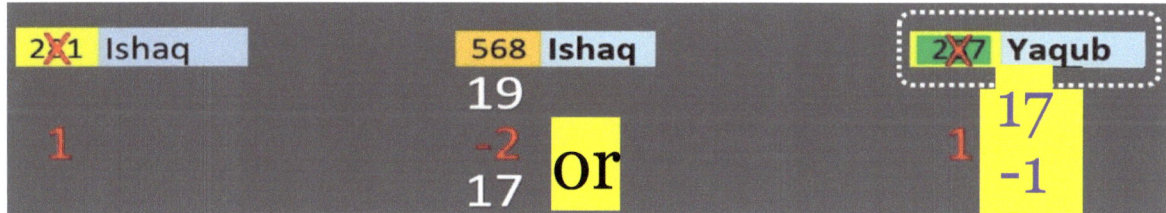

Exhibit 17: Yaqub mentioned 16 times in Quran.

The Prophet Ishaq had two sons and they were twins, named Ishaq and Yaqub, also known as Jacob in English, who was loved more by their father. For this reason, Ishaq envied his brother. When Allah (s.w.t.) chose Yaqub (AS) as prophet, Ishaq became so enraged that he threated to kill his brother. So Yaqub, (AS) decided to flee.
He found a place to rest and placed a stone underneath his head.
He dreamt about a ladder which connected the earth to heaven, with angels coming down to inform him about his future generation would be from his land. Now he was happy so he promised Allah (s.w.t.) that if he returned to his family, he would construct a mosque and donate a portion of his property. Before leaving the place, which is Jerusalem, he put some oil on the stone, so that he could recognize it later when he returned.

1.16 Yaqub dreams of Ladder

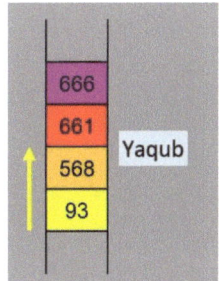

Yaqub and his dream of a ladder, was conceived by the ascending qualities of Crown Code development. The 93 unites with the 568 which produces 661. The key here is that 661 merges with the 2 and the 3 at level 40 to produce 666.

Exhibit 18: Yaqub Dream Ladder

1.17 Ishmael mentioned 12 times

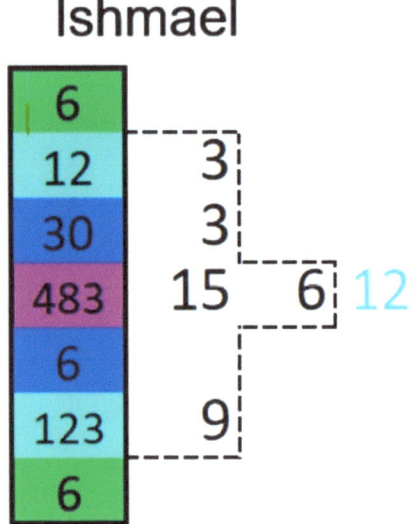

Ishmael, here, utilizes the coordinate to Matrix Code in total sum association of the numbers seen upon Photo 27: Jesus Christ and Virgin Secret at B "Birthed seen from in between A those virgin squares. Thus, Ishmael consisting of twelve squares including polarized numbers equal 12, is mentioned 12 times in the Quran.

Exhibit 19: Ishmael is mentioned 12 times.

1.18 Muhammad mentioned four times in Quran

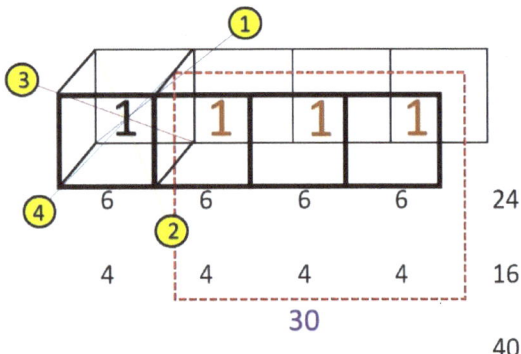

What is truly genius was the usage of 4 times mentioned in the Quran of Muhammad. To say Muhammad was the final prophet would be incorrect, as it does not allude to this author. Yet in the details we understand what was understood of truth.

Exhibit 20: Muhammad Four Toward Revelations

From the beginning the truth has been known. That 1111 being that 'seed' revealing universal truth, gives insight to that inner essence established by the one. Primarily before anything could become, a field or area must be established, so that anything or everything could ensue.

The first square having four corners expresses itself, through that crossing, reaching to the other side to the foreground square, creating a cube having 6 sides. Thus, the first cube essence is 6 plus 4 for 10. By Matrix certainty, the next three cubes fulfill the first cube four-part expression as 40, where the 111 is later revealed at guide level 40, between the mountains or hills upon the Matrix. But first 30, as those three cubes is then recognized. This becomes the reason why Muhammad is described as beginning to seek solitude, in the hills around Mecca at thirty (30) years old.

1.19 Muhammad 3 days in Cave

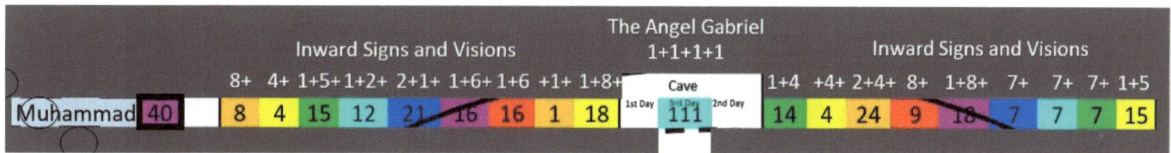

Exhibit 21: Muhammad Cave and Inward Visions.

In accord with the Matrix Code, Muhammad is described as meditating in a cave at his fortieth (40) year. While in the cave the experience in accord with Matrix Code, development the 111 is understood to reveal itself by inward revelations.

What we must remember is, that as universal mind, the Matrix Code is the divine message for all creation. How it was applied to the human experience, dictated other options. Through-out the annals of time, without doubt nefarious development ensued. Yet, the underlying truths which are immovable, will always remain.

Above you see at guide level 40, eighteen numbers flanked around 111 (which by Matrix process does not exist yet) but will manifest in the blank squares area. The Blank squares became that cave where Muhammad became described as, remaining for three nights. Thru which those eighteen numbers, instead of revealing the 1111 Key to truth, became expressed as visions and strong inward signs. The three blank squares between the eighteen numbers, became expressed as those three nights where Muhammad experienced the signs and visions. Then the Angel Gabriel being the actual 1111, understood at Exhibit 39: in Volume 1: Gabriel's wings and soles of his feet Secret, appeared to Muhammed and commanded him (Qur'an 96:1-3) Proclaim in the name of thy Lord and Cherisher, who created man out of a clot of congealed blood. Proclaim and thy Lord is most bountiful.

1.20 Islamic Secret of 1111

Here we must ask since we know the Matrix Code, what exactly was he to proclaim? It becomes obvious that the proclamation is the 1111, which Gabriel established. Whether, the truth of 1111 was intended to be revealed later, is unclear. What is certain, is that elements and salient details to the Matrix Code, had been used in the development of Islam.

The inclusion of Muhammad being consumed for 23 years, where, in stages the Quran was revealed becomes even more so telling, especially knowing that the angel Gabriel represented the 1111, of the Matrix Crown Code, who was described as verbally revealing the Quran from God to Muhammad gradually over that period, until his death.

Allah says (interpretation of the meaning): Quran: 17/106: "And (it is) a Quran which We have divided (into parts), in order that you might recite it to men at intervals.

At next page can be seen coordinate to what became known as the 99 names of Allah. The square at upper left of name grid, has Allah coordinated to green 119, with 29

This is the root to the Name and its true meaning.

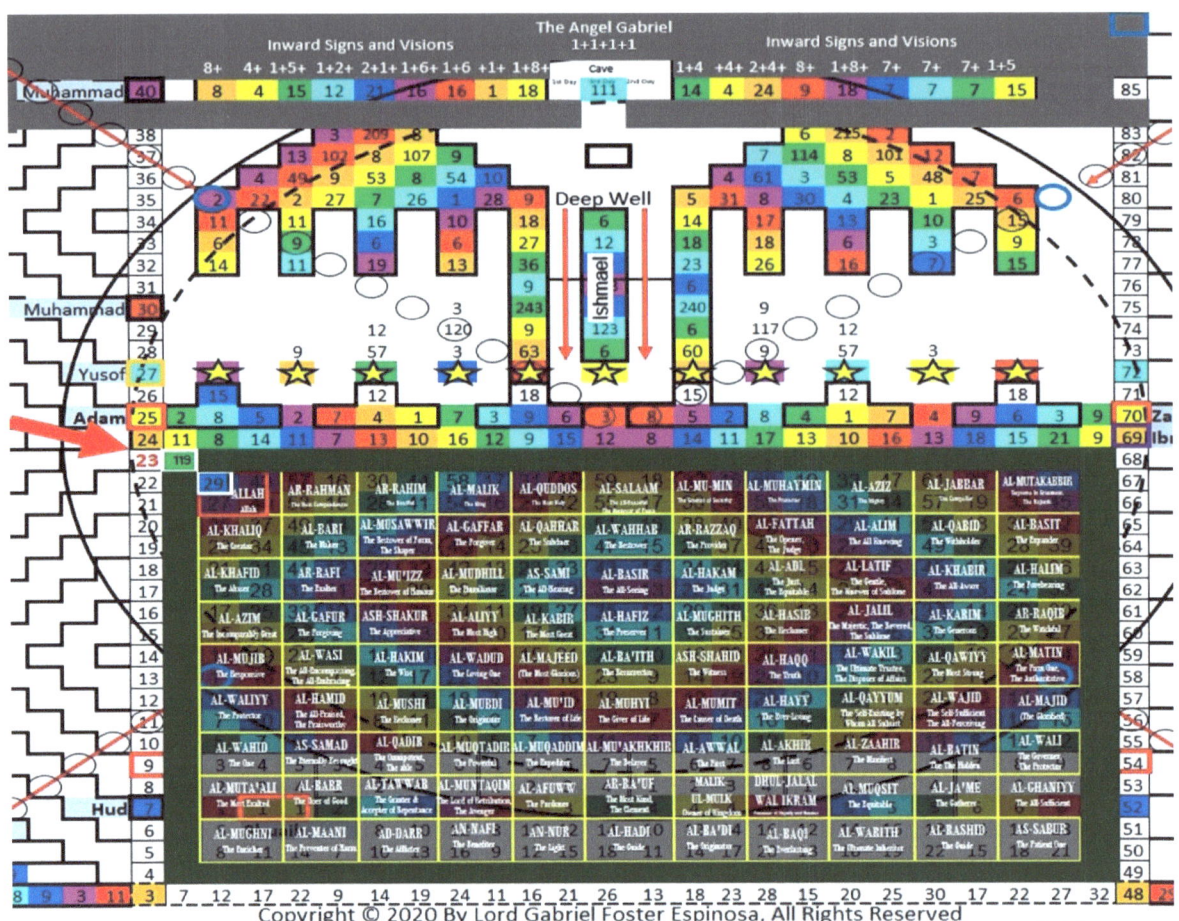

Exhibit 22: 99 names of Allah Conception Grid

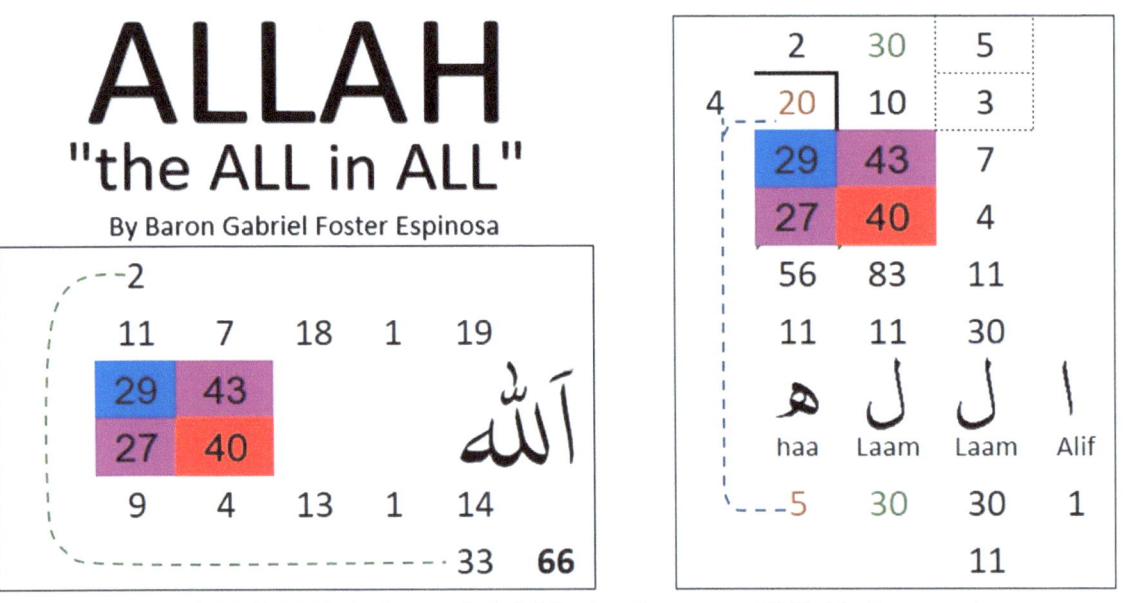

Exhibit 23: Allah the All in All

The usurpation of "the Truth", does not make the result a fact. Although Allah "the All in All" assumes the 1111 truth, it does not provide truthful evidence.

The Matrix Code as the word of God in its original form, explains past, present, and future complexities and mysteries of the universe. Whereby, through words alone they cannot. Thus consider:

To define God, we need to grasp the reality, that it existed by itself before the universe became. How would we, know that God really exists? By what means does truth absolute become?

By the Matrix Code, what the Son is, who is full, complete, and faultless becomes realized. The Matrix Code came through that creation as man, presently as me. What is now revealed herein, is that form and manner whereby, it is possible to know God with certainty.

Without such revelation, God cannot truly receive honor from anyone, who does not have path to that which reveals God himself, in his ineffability, hidden and invisibility, that they can marvel at him mentally.

It is in such, as he existed by himself, with those parts in which exists in his own manner and form with greatness as witnessed by you, herein of the Matrix Code.

In knowing truth, it is possible for those to see him and speak about that which they know of him. Knowing that he is incomparable, yet they can comprehend him, as the Architect of the universe by the blueprint/template herein.

Granted, all those creations from the beginning, which in modern day now include Zoroastrianism, Judaism, Christianity and Islam, contain that loftiness about them, due to the fact, that they speak about him and see him only unto themselves. He becomes manifest when truth is revealed. Thus, while mankind is in such imposed state, by not knowing.

The admirations and dispositions of all those previously mentioned, since they are of the word, are mental offspring, all influenced by Matrix Code knowledge, which had been unknown to the people.

Globally, we would not require religious voice or spirit, mind, and word, as expressed by all ideologies. It is not a requirement outside the Matrix Code, where the almighty is present. What the Son (Countenance upon the Matrix Code) becomes, by what the pattern reveals.

Therefore, what has been developed to date, are but traces of that deeper truth of him, according to the ability of each who strive to glorify him.

The Matrix Code countenance understood in the proper way, is the first one, the man, of the father. I now unite all the names created through religions, without falsification, as exhibited herein. Proving and Absolute truth.

It is through the Matrix Code, that Gods mind becomes that form of the formless, that body of the bodiless, the face of the invisible, the word of [the] unutterable, the mind of the inconceivable, that fountain which flowed of him, root of that planted, that providence of those for whom he providentially cares, true god of those who exist, a light to those whom he illuminates, being revelation of the things which are sought after, as that eye of those who see, that wisdom of those he made wise, power to those of its witness, being that assembly whom he assembles, that breath of those who breath, as that life of those who live, and that love of those he loved, all in unity mixed with the Totalities, existing in the single one.

He can never be called by a single name yet is understood in a unique way by the root of the Totalities.

The Matrix Code is neither divided of its body, nor separated by the names which have been given to its parts, as in previous examples.

For it is by that practice, that truth was usurped, as he is one thing, then by others another thing.

The Truth of the Matrix Code does not change and does not morph into other beings, as contrived by minds not connected. Universal truth does not, nor cannot be one thing in time and alternative at another. What the Son is, is wholly himself of the Matrix Code, to the most extreme.

It's like saying, that if someone else as myself, would establish the Totalities (Matrix Code) at any time, at any place in the universe, that he is each and every one of those Totalities forever at the same time, being what all of them are, as connection to the Father as the Totalities, being knowledge for himself as each and all properties and powers as numbered and beyond what is known, being innumerable and inaudible, as by God outside human comprehension.

Innumerable and indivisible of the Matrix Code, are the possibilities, when holding to the revelations and principles established by His Totalities.

It is by the 1111 as that single name, that the All in All was understood. It is him of the Matrix Code as the Matrix Code, which brings all into being, whereby all life which exist through their individual properties, become united in that single name (1111). Because the stories represent those parts as understood of the Matrix Code (Preserved Tablet) it is not surprising that the Quran would include the Injeel, the Torah and other books which were conceived through Matrix Code usage. The reality is, the universal language of the Matix Code, being the first Language, later spawned those base languages, Hebrew, Arabic, or all others.

It is now certain by what is revealed in this book, that through-out the centuries, every messenger added to the narrative we now understand, as the Abrahamic design.

TWO

SECRET OF SARAI

2 WHAT WAS THE TRUE MEANING OF ISRAEL?

Stele Discovered in 1896 in Merneptah's mortuary temple in Thebes, by Sir Flinders Petrie, which has the campaign in Canaan of 1207BC. A portion of line 27 reads: Canaan is captive with all woe. Ashkelon is conquered, Gezer seized, Yanaom, made non-existent; Israel is wasted bare of seed." The phrase "wasted, bare of seed" is formulaic, and often used of defeated nations – it implies that the grain-store of the nation in question has been destroyed, which would result in a famine the following year, incapacitating them as a military threat to Egypt.

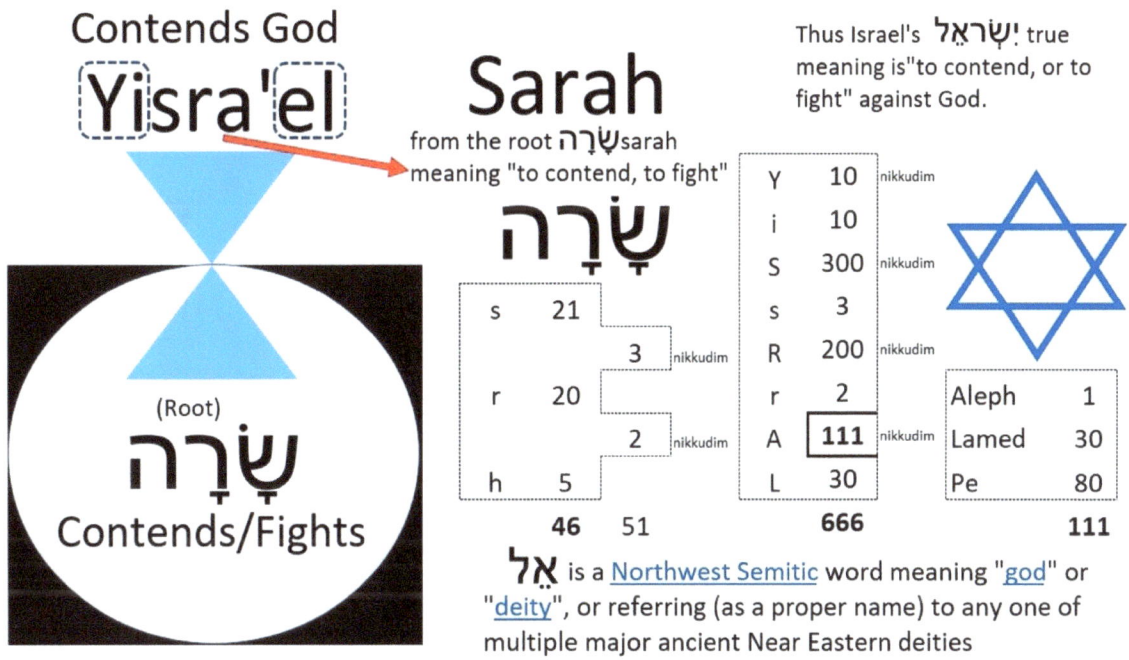

Exhibit 24: Contending God

2.1 Daemon Est Deus

From the Hebrew name (Yisra'el) some have surmised that it means "God contends", from the roots שָׂרָ meaning "to contend, to fight" and א meaning "God".

When considering Daemon Est Deus Inversus, in English. Daemon Est Deus Inversus (Latin), Daemon is divinity inverted; more commonly, the Devil is God inverted. An ancient Hermetic, and later Qabbalistic, aphorism referring to that polar power, which is required by the equilibrium and harmony in nature.

Which is to say, that those parts as defined have an inverted nature about it. In the Old Testament, Israel (who was formerly named Jacob; see Genesis 32:28) wrestles with an angel.

As seen previously, what is defined as the Angel Gabriel, or the Ark of Gabriel, which assumes that ancient truth of the Matrix Code core.

In other words, that which is written in the inside (at eight flanked squares on either side of guide number core) that struggles and even battles that expressed on the outside (beyond core guide development).

By Matrix Code core understanding, as expressed at Photo 29 f: Zakaria God remembers, the outer area takes on the mirrored expression, as that four-corner root expression in existence, as what is referred to as the four corners of the earth.

Please note, the Lord says, Israel is my firstborn son. Within the narrative a secret is revealed. One which answers the question regarding the firstborn.

The contention and fighting which was conceived from within the circle, defined those energies in the creative process, in archetype. In other words, that described, never represented what is in the physical world. And those of the antiquities understood that.

Moses allegedly lived in 1600 BC when there was not even written language in existence, thus how was Genesis written?

Language developed around 400 - 600 years later. Before this, it was Egyptian hieroglyphics.

So, let us get to the heart of the matter, which has caused so much chaos on this planet.

2.2 Abraham as the Expression of the Invisible

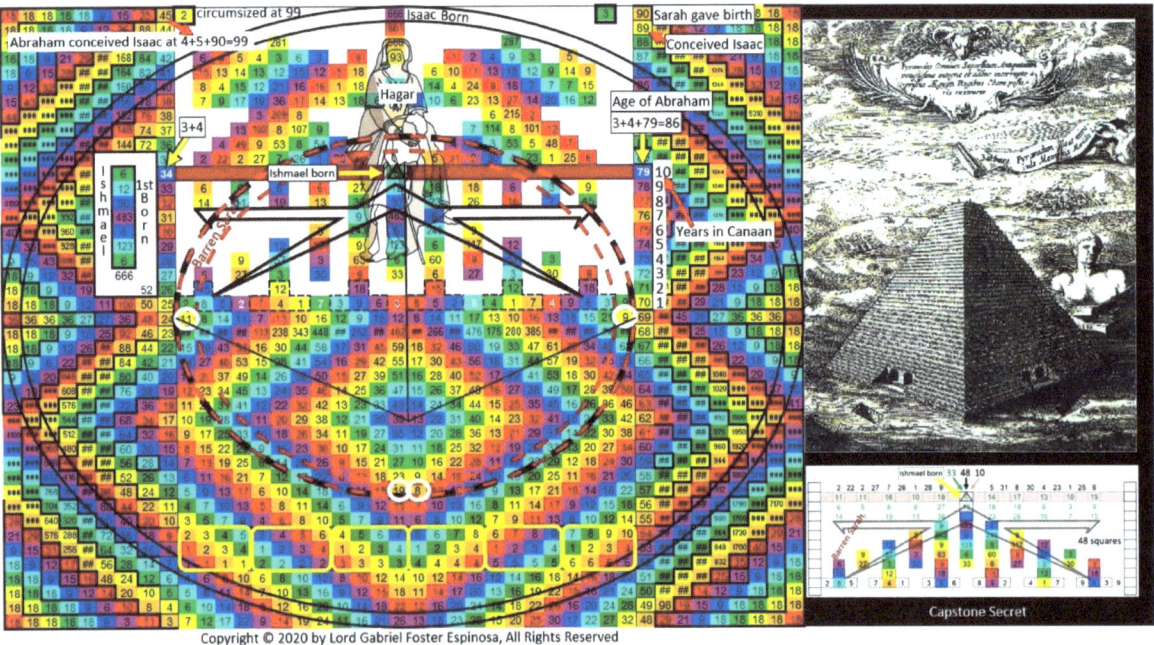

Exhibit 25: Ishmael, Isaac, and the Capstone Secret

Regarding Abraham/Ibrahim, the Matrix Code here by myself, provides an underlying understanding to the creative process. Abraham/Ibrahim became an expression of the invisible essence toward matter. From centre and upward begin that between guide 25 and 70. Base by the six ascending pillars equal 33, a key number also indicated by the lower extensions, of the Canaanite symbol, pointing to 15 and 18 which also equal 33.

The six clustered sets reveal 90, as an ascending goal within the operations to creation. What is achieved, would be those formative building blocks of life. Here, numbers unite and in ascent creating a pyramid likeness, in the process. In total there are 48 squares establishing 483, as the whole unifier, meeting up with 30. The 3 of 483 ascends upward and is multiplied by the next level flanked parts of 10 producing 30, that location where previous Photo 21, showed the Sojourning and Rounds, of the great pyramid.

The 480 remaining at the top of pyramid, recognizes the factor of 10, thus 480 is divided by 10 for 48. At centre, the 30, 12 and 6, are added together representing that ascended 48 which is foundation to which is the TRUE secret of the capstone. Notice there are 33 green numbers, by this display in concert with the founding ascending pillars sum of 33. Thus, as a treble by expression, we interpret that as 3 plus 3 at each result, as triangle we have the 666-creation number.

Humanity has not been served well by the elite. The absolute lie of the 666 narrative as dark and evil, is the opposite to the true creation story. The 666 number is the Light expression before manifesting into matter.

The first left and right inward squares give coordinate to the cosmic womb (That circle of promise). Notice that the upper cross point of the circle, has no numbers. That is because this is where those energies in blueprint stage, are developed, thus nonexistent yet. Different than what was previously established at Photo 27: Jesus Christ and Virgin Secret, here the Matrix Code became a different narrative. Instead of the Virgin concept, the Character of Sarah is given, where she is defined by the blank square coordinate, as still 'barren'. Sarah's name total of 51, must be deducted from the ascending goal of 90, with result being 39. Thus, Sarah was barren and had to wait 39 years for God to fulfil His promise to give her a child.

It was ten squares at right guide column from center, which became used to represent those 10 years Sarah waited in Canaan for Gods promise (Matrix Code process) to be fulfilled. The symbol of Canaan simply represented this knowledge.

In the meantime, in consideration of pyramidal ascension, as from the four corners, the story included that Sarah gave him (The Matrix Process) to her Egyptian handmaiden, Hājar (previously the virgin coordinate), to wed as his second wife. Ascending upward, the capstone coordinate appears, serving a dual meaning, which became both the conception and birth location.

At Capstone coordinate we have guide numbers 34 and 79. Here we must remember that the left guide is first where the right is second. For interpretive purposes, the left is polarized to one result, and the right-side guides as whole numbers. 34 becomes 7, which is added to 79, which became the age (86) of Abraham when the capstone (Ishmael) became (was born).

Notice the bust at right engraving next to the pyramid? The personification to the 666, is what transpired, at the birth-spot of Jesus, here became Ishmael birthed from between the legs of Hajar(Hagar) As a reminder, Gods messengers announce that barren Sarah would give birth to Abrahams second son, Isaac, described as also to be a prophet.

The larger outer circles coordinated, with the four corners, represent that point prior to reverse transfiguration. The smaller of the two aligns with 89, the age Sarah conceives.

The outer circle aligns with 90, which becomes defined as the age Sarah gives birth to Isaac. Isaac just like Ishmael represent the 666 totals. Therefore, the second son born to Abraham.

Here, Sarah represents those parts in pre-matter as understood by Matrix number revelations, to the archetype creative process.

Again, the characters were never meant to be recognized or understood in the physical world but were meant to be used as tools in learning the cosmic truth of Creation.

For Abraham, the 90 is added to the 4 plus 5 for 99, as his age at the conception of Isaac. Which also became the age of his circumcision.

These Biblical narratives are simply a way of describing the creative forces in nature. Numbers on the Matrix Code where given 'names' to create a storyline as a way of expressing the Truth of the Forefathers and the creation process. Therefore, the secret was hidden in plain sight.

THREE

STORY OF SACRIFICE

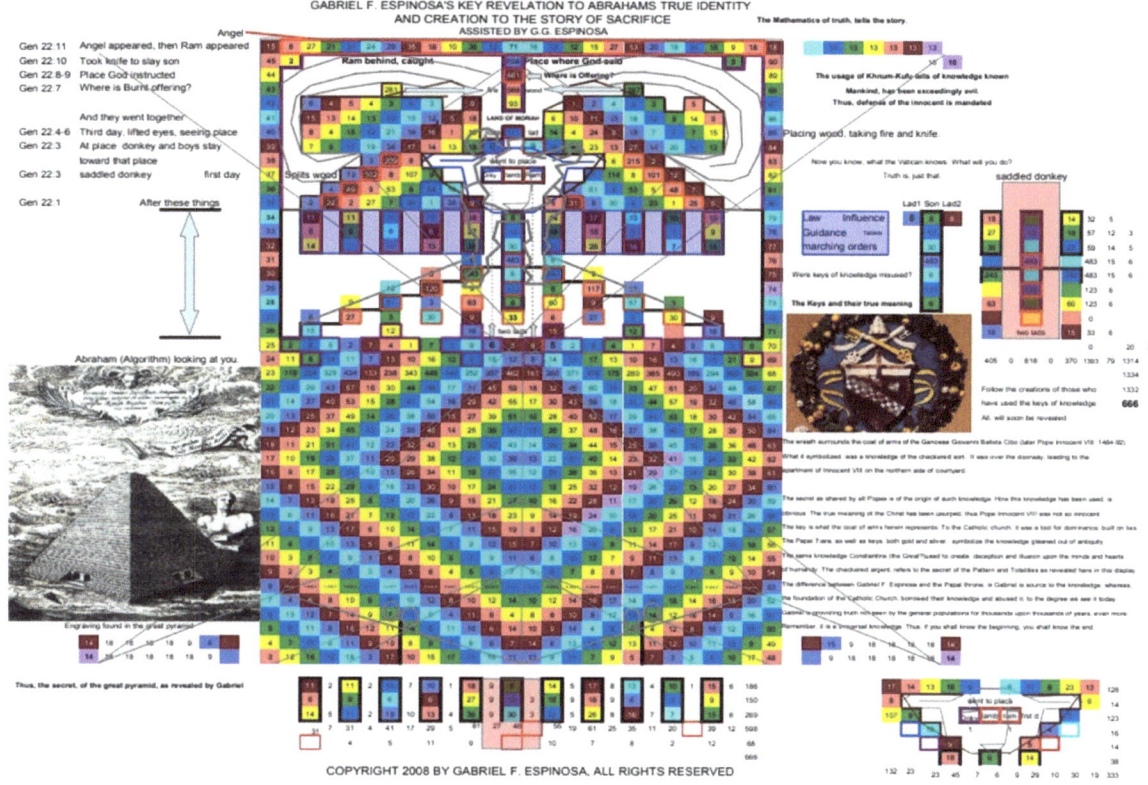

Exhibit 26: Creation of the Story of Sacrifice

21 Story Development Beginning at center to include guide levels 28 thru 34, Abram as the formula, referred to this part as his son (Isaac) The instruction became in Genesis 22:2 "Take now your son, whom you love, Isaac, and go to the land of Moriah see above as the triangle between guide numbers 35 through 44.

As an overall descriptive, Abram (the Crown Code) encompasses the eye of the beholder concept.

At guide level 25 the six (6) and the eight (8) expresses the ascending qualities of the pattern development. Thus, Abram rose early in the morning and saddled his donkey (those squares without number); and took his two young men with him and Isaac. Remember the Isaac squares represent a equal 666. The splitting of the wood became that expression of the widening area of blank squares, the first day.

The third day, meaning three squares up, Abram raised his eyes and saw the place from a distance.
Naturally in succession, the next level dictated what the story would unfold. Abram said to his young men (the 6 and the 8 of pattern development) "Stay here with the donkey, and I and the lad will go yonder, and we will worship and return to you"

This is where the numbers 6 and 8 remain [as the two young boys personified], in formula development. At the next level, the 111 appears, which is converted to symbolize the wood Abram took and laid it on his son Isaac, taking the fire and the knife walking on together (Genesis 22:4-6)

The next level, the square space is empty (no number) this is where the personification takes on the character of Isaac.

And Isaac spoke to Abraham his father and said, "My father!" And he said. "Here I am my son." And he said, behold, the fire (yellow square) and the wood (orange square), but where is the lamb for the burnt offering?" (symbolic of the red square) (Genesis 22:7)

Abram as the pattern as the Crown Code said, "God will provide for himself the lamb for the burnt offering, my son," So the two walked on together. (Genesis 22:8)

At the purple square which is the sum of 666, became described as "Then they came to the place of which God had told him; And Abram built the alter (four corner foundation) arranged the wood, and bound his son Isaac, laying him on the alter on top of the wood. (Genesis 22:9) Then Abram stretched out his hand and took the knife to slay his son. (Genesis 22:10)

At the top of the Formula, which was held secret, the level which created boundary to the core became personifies as the angel, thus, it was written. The angel of the Lord, caused breath of life from heaven to fall upon Abram, causing him to become Ab-ra-ham] and said, "Abraham, Abraham!"

And he said, "Here, I am." And he said, "Do not stretch out your hand against the lad, and do nothing to him, for now I know you fear God. (Genesis 22:11-12)
Here the developers of the above story, converted that wing reference of the Egyptians into and angel that provides the new offering.
Upon boundary development, a visual not seen before is realized.

Which brought about the following:

Then Abraham raised his eyes and looked, and behold, behind him a ram caught in the thicket by his horns; and Abraham went and took the ram, and presented him as a burnt offering in the place of his son. (Genesis 22:13) I need not say anymore. You get the picture.

The effect of misuse of the great secret, has undoubtedly influenced ideological practice, and result wherein sacrifice has been instituted as means of psychological control over the masses by implementation.

Beginning with Buddhism, in the Jataka collection are stories of the Buddha's previous births accounts of his self-sacrifices, which alludes to the pattern reference.

Yet in China it had existed, that human sacrifice associated with the death of a ruler, was employed, as a means at having the former ruler accompanied by those who served him during life. Various methods and inclusions by different civilizations have been noted.

Japan, Greece, and as understood at the creation of the Sacrifice story.

FOUR

THE TWELVE TRIBES

4   Origin of the Twelve Tribes

The ancient Egyptians geographical significance related to Crown Code associated relativity. Thus, the black land, as that field toward creation in Matrix understanding, became represented as the fertile land for growing crops and so forth, due to the rich layer of black silt deposited each year after the Nile flooded.

The "red land" represented the barren desert (Mystery) that protected Egypt on two sides. Both deserts in the ancient Egyptian Elite mind, were symbolic of what became in later development, in the banks of Ulai story, discussed in part 1, about Daniel.

By conceptual literary license, the expanding revelatory emanations of what the Crown Code established, as discovered by Hebraic minds. As they adapted cosmic understanding of Egypt, and Samaria.

Incorporating the Twelve-part reality of the Crown Code, by personifying an imaginary race of people, is unacceptable.

The twelve (12) tribes of Israel became developed as Reuben, Simeon, Judah, Issachar, Zebulun, Benjamin, Dan, Naphtali, Gad, Asher, Ephraim and Manasseh, all relate as sons and grandson's names out of Jacob, from which biblical tradition holds the 12 tribes descend, according to the Jewish Virtual Library.

Their development, using the Matrix Code (Pattern and Totalities), we understand the process used in their creation. Biblical reference to the 12 Tribes in the Book of Numbers, states the population of each Tribe, yet the truth remains and never will change, that the Results of the Census of the 12 Tribes of Israel. from the Book of Numbers 1:1- 34 is a census of the numbers to each grouping, and not to a physical population at all.

The numbers become NAMES that describe forces in nature, Light energies as calculated and understood of the Matrix Code (Pattern and Totalities).

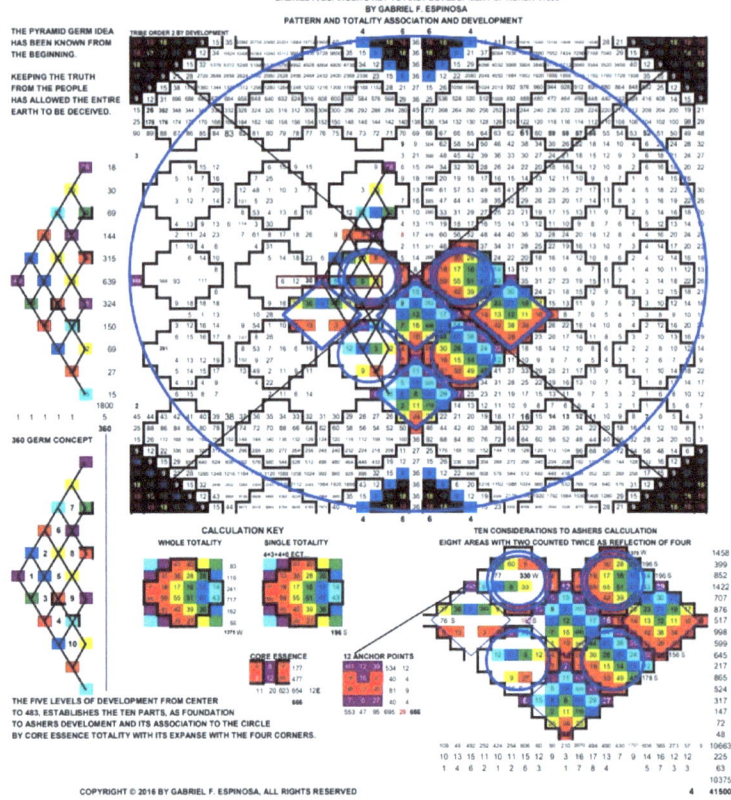

Exhibit 27: Development of Asher 41500

Beginning at centre we have Asher with eight (8) blue sections, incorporating seventeen (17) total considerations for 41500.

Directly opposite upper area, are eight green sections having eleven (11) considerations for - Zebulun total of - 57400

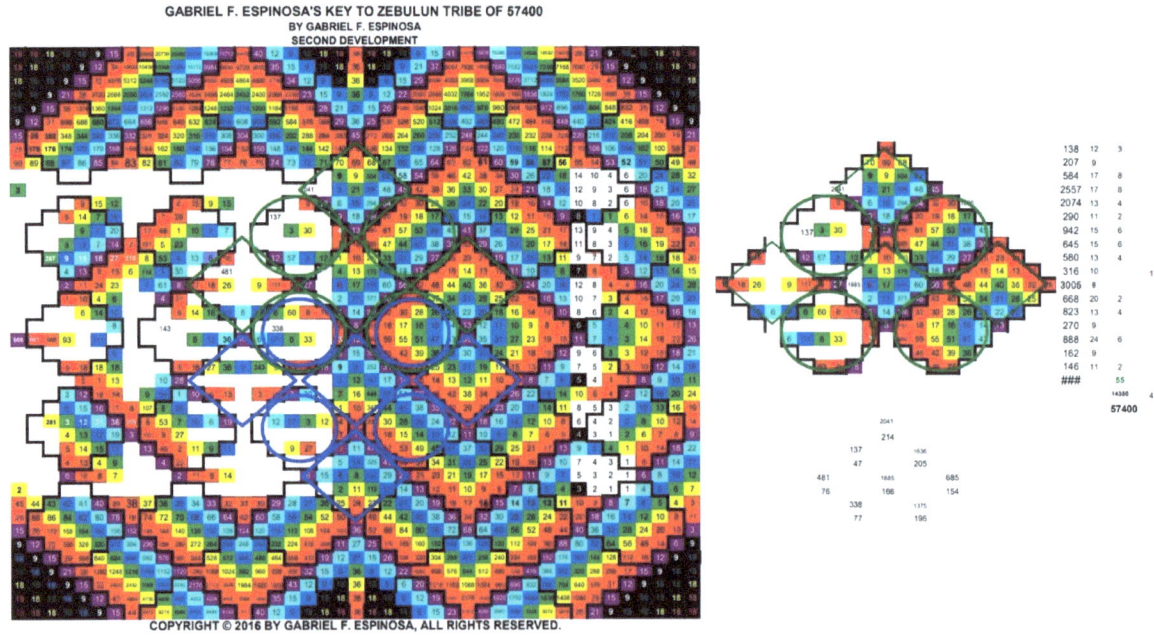

Exhibit 28: Development Sequence of Zebulun

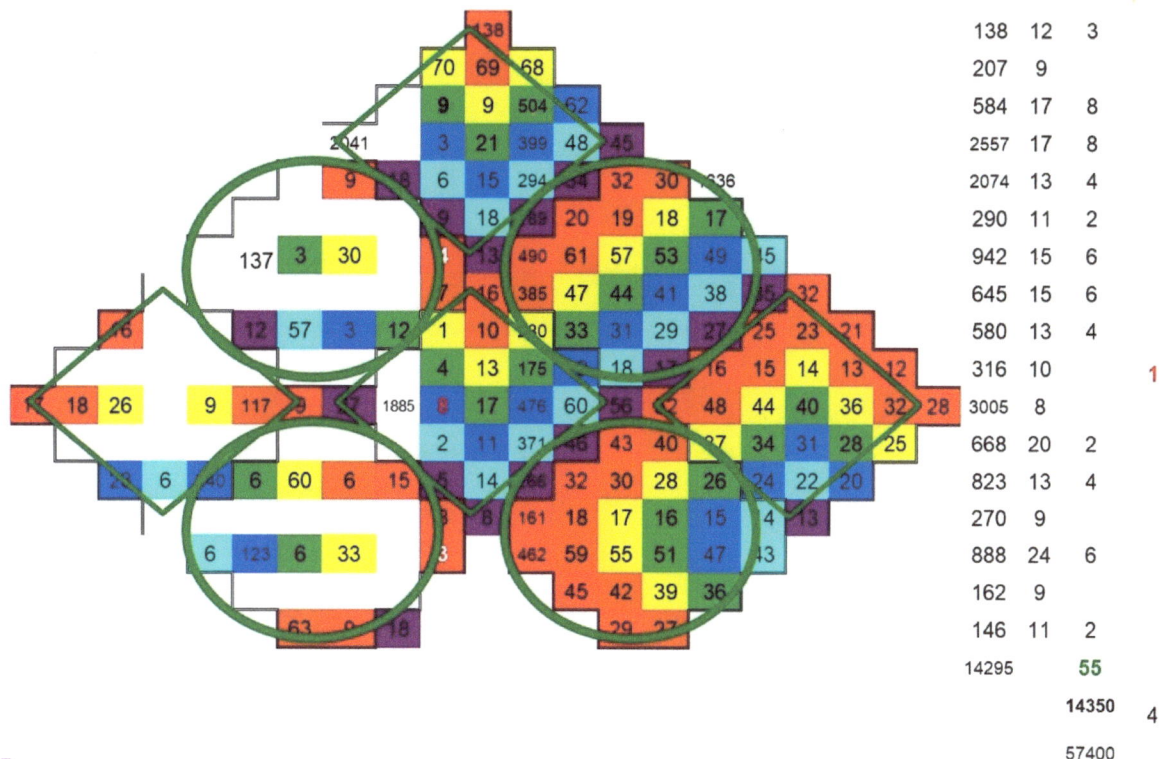

Exhibit 29: Development Result for Zebulun 57400

Below incorporates side to side expansion qualities, including the upper left and right blue circle sections. Here Simeon collectively has Ten (10) blue sections and twenty (20) consideration to its sum of 59300.

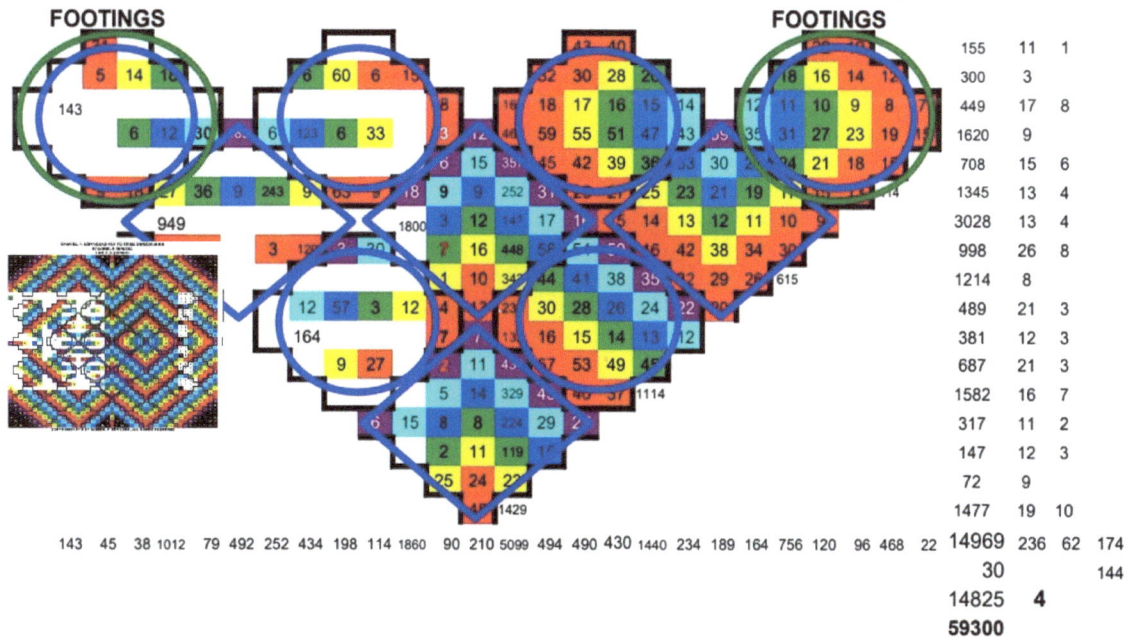

Exhibit 30: Development Result for Simeon 59300

Zebulun previously shown evolves into Issachar, its lower two circles are as unfolding arms expanding outward, where its hands grasp Simeon's expanded qualities having eight (8) sections, and fourteen (14) considerations providing foundation to Issachar's census number of 54300.

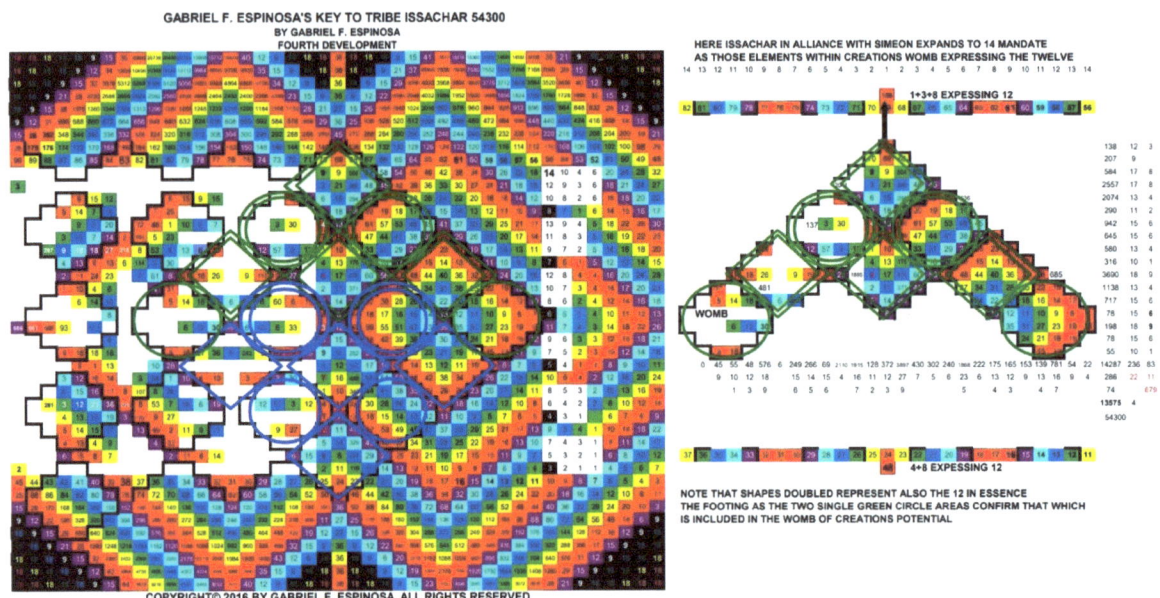

Exhibit 31: Development Sequence of Issachar

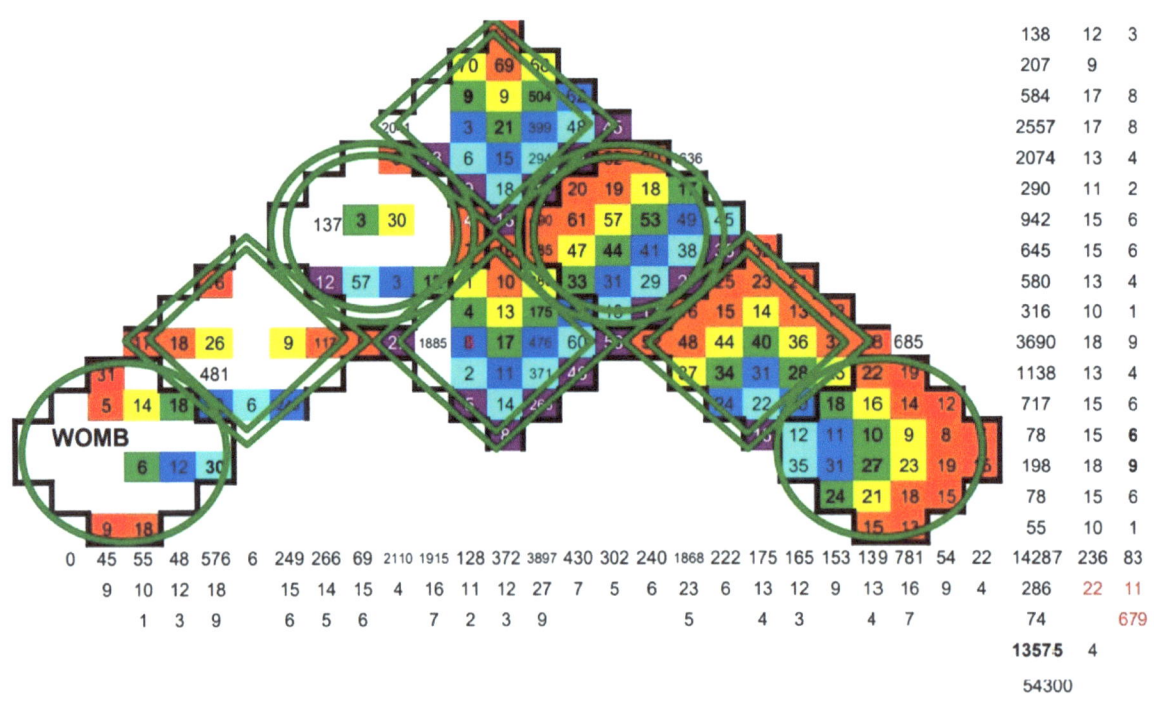

Exhibit 32: Development Result for Issachar 54300

Next, Rueben expands from those efforts of Simeon, reaching further to calling Benjamin in union. Rueben also solidifies both itself and Benjamin centrally becoming 12 sections in the census as 46500.

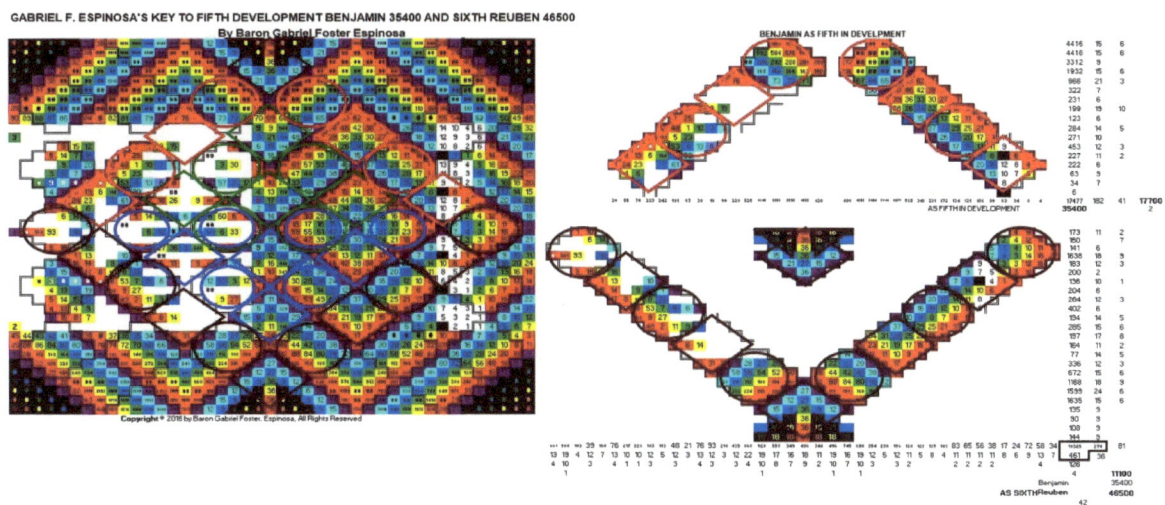

Exhibit 33: Development Sequence of Reuben and Benjamin

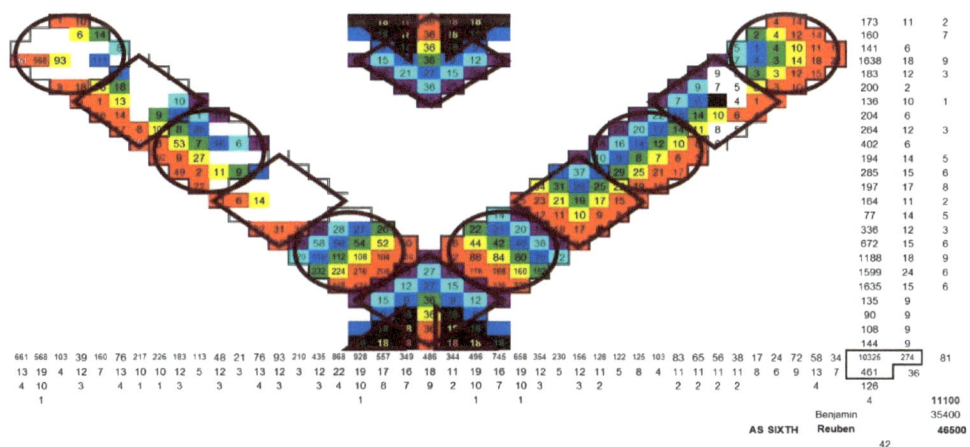

Exhibit 34: Development Result for Reuben

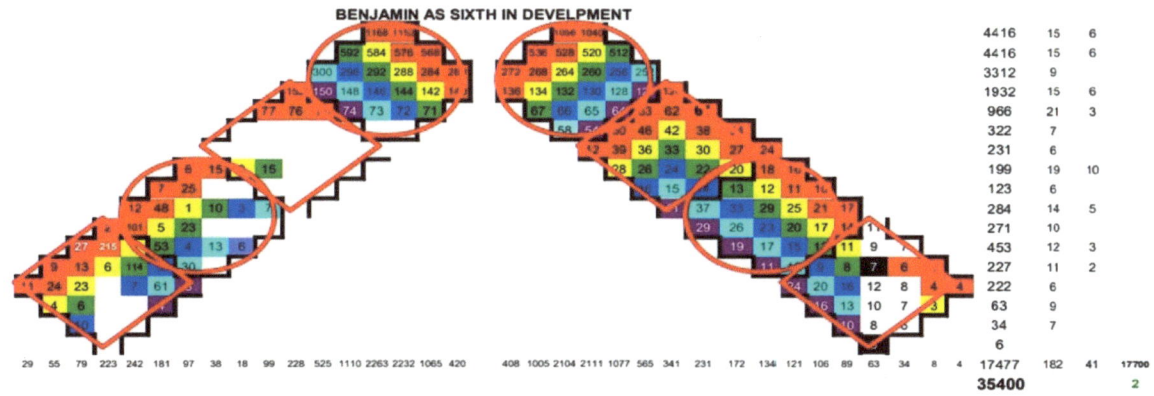

Exhibit 35: Development Result for Benjamin

Benjamin as sixth becomes by those outstretched arms supported by Issachar. In agreement Benjamin has eight (8) sections producing 35400 for the census.

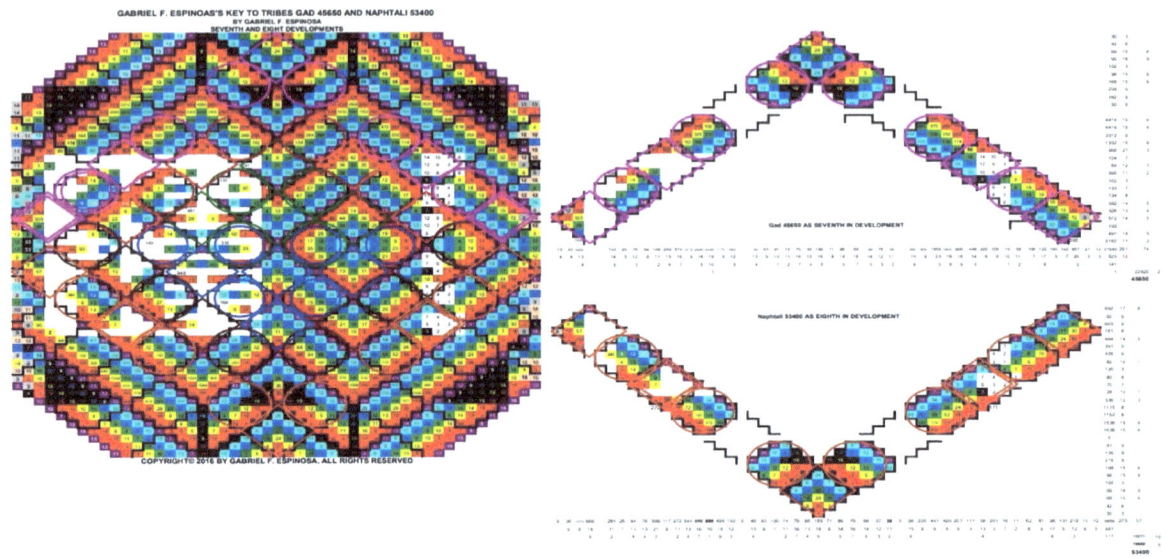

Exhibit 36: Development Sequence of Gad and Naphtali

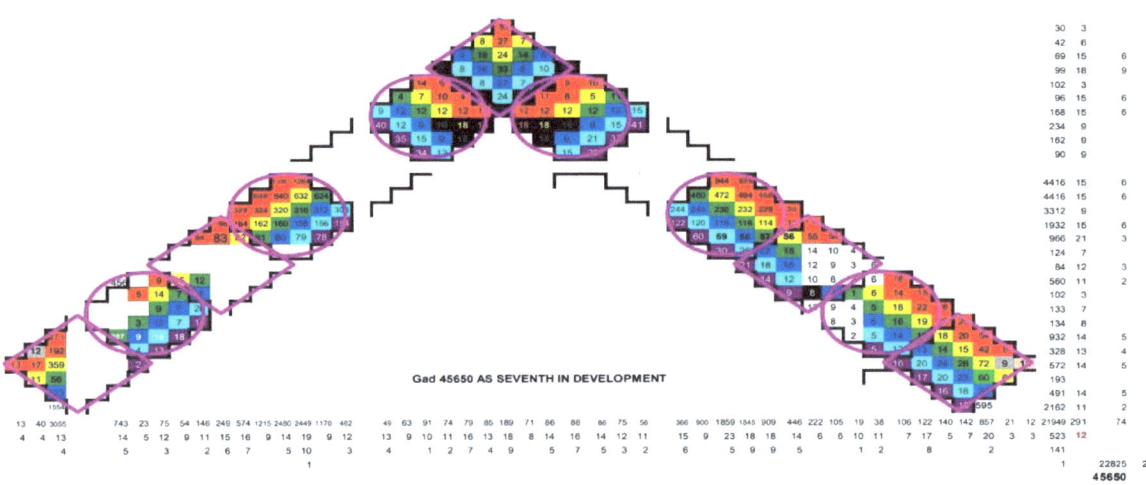

Exhibit 37: Development Result for Gad

Naphtali after seeing the success of Gad, and the grace bestowed upon Gad, Naphtali uses the same strategy in achieving it number. Naphtali has eleven sections, with a total of 13 considerations for its census number of 53400.

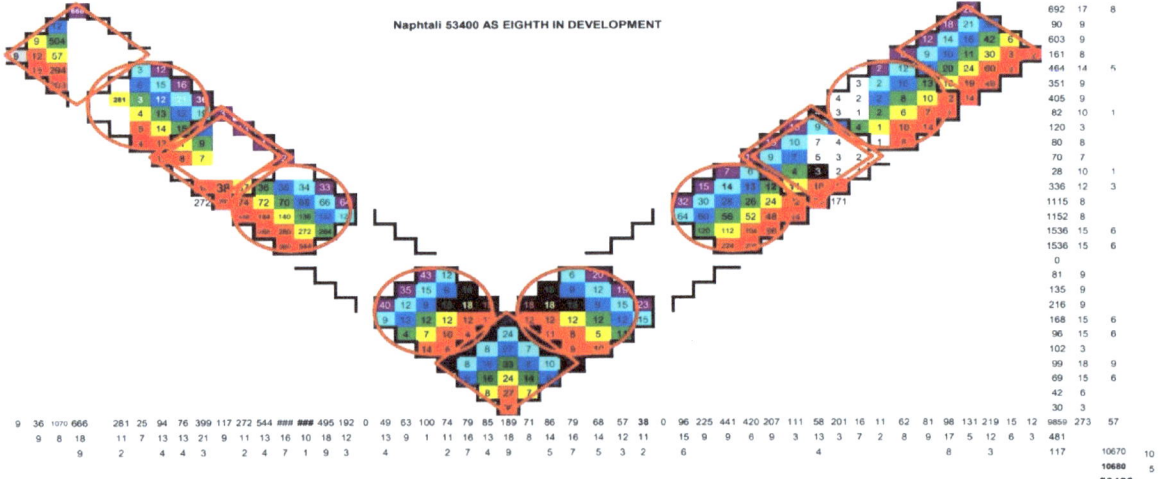

Exhibit 38: Development Result for Naptali

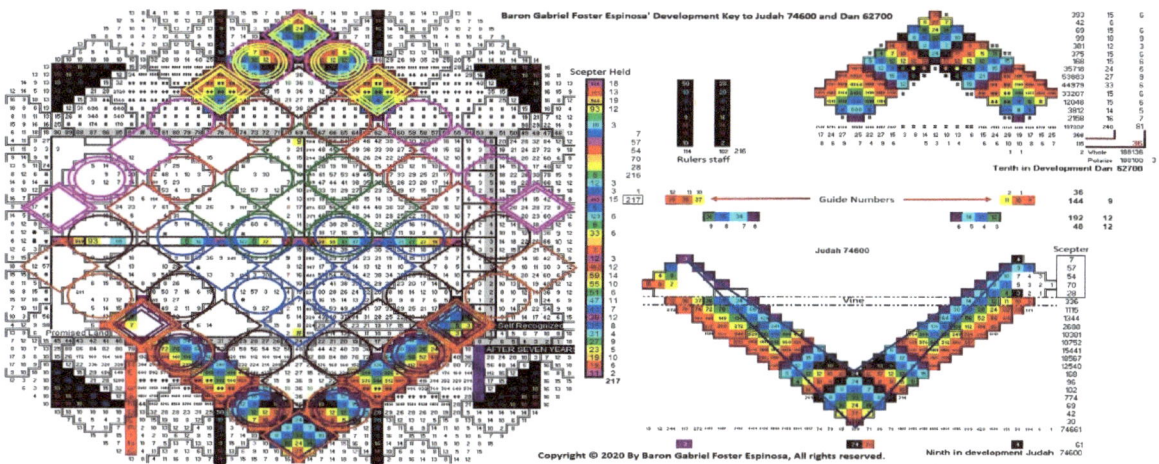

Exhibit 39: Development Sequence of Judah and Dan

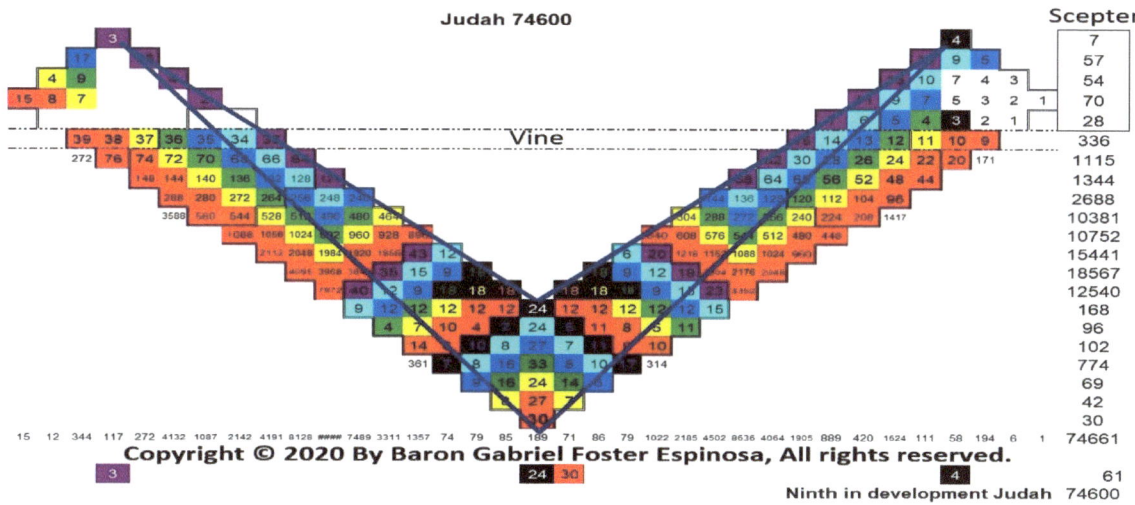

Exhibit 40: Development Result for Judah

Dan assisted Gad in number, sojourning the outer areas together they prosper. Having 14 considerations, there five assemblies became stronger. In total they concentrated for Dan to having 62700 at census.

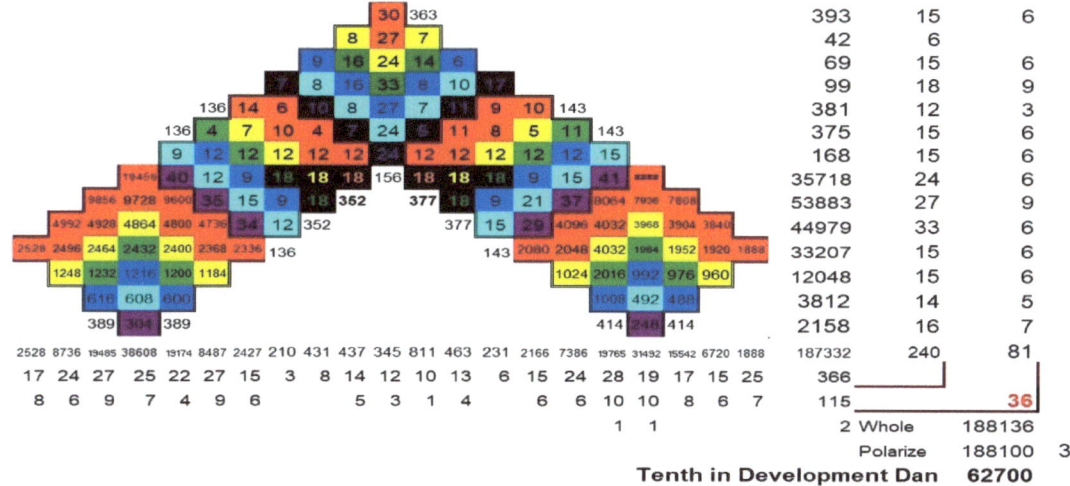

Exhibit 41: Development Result for Dan

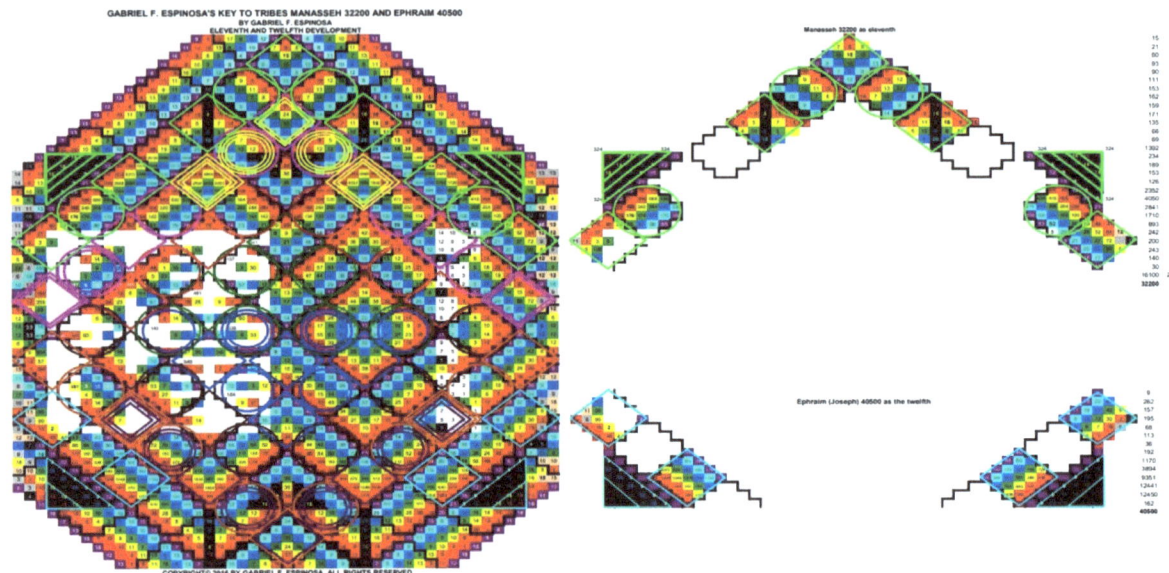

Exhibit 42: Development Sequence of Manasseh and Ephraim
Manasseh having eleven sections, employs 17 considerations, making up for any deficiency, that its total remains at 32200.

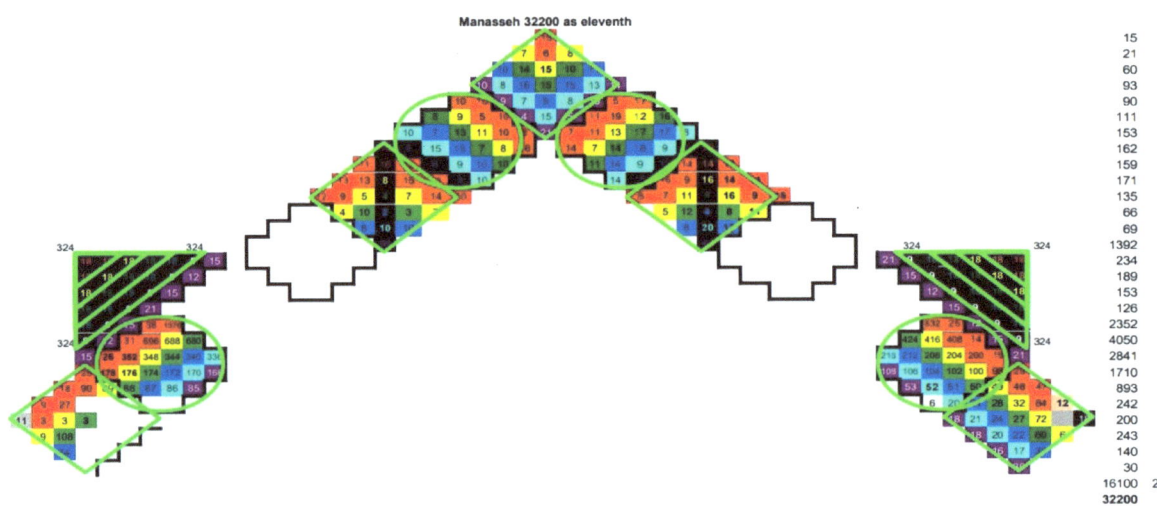

Exhibit 43: Development Result for Manasseh
Ephraim has six (6) sections, with eight (8) considerations to the number of 40500 of the censuses.

Exhibit 44: Development Result for Ephraim (Joseph)

Collectively, each Tribe as conceived, originally provided insight to the energetic resonance from the Core of the Crown Code. Asher – 41500 introduces itself to-Zebulun total of – 57400. Simeon 59300 and Issachar 54300 hold together. Benjamin supported by Issachar agrees to the force created with Simeon. Benjamin holds 35400 for the census. Helping Expand efforts of Simeon, Rueben solidifies itself and Benjamin centrally contributing 12 sections in the census as 46500. Gad stretched its resources to assist Rueben establishing its dominion. Gad receives material and Grace two-fold to number 45650 for the census. Naphtali follows Gad example to number 53400 at the census. Judah concentrated its numbers reaching and establishing its kingdom number of 7400. Dan made effort to having 62700 at census. Ephraim 40500 of the census unites with Manasseh total of 32200 for 72700 representing the four-corner essence.

Exhibit 45: Development Scheme of All Tribes

FIVE

WHAT ISLAM SET IN MOTION

5 Beginning in 610 AD, what Muhammad developed became attributed to being receiving from Almighty God (Allah) through Gabriel (Matrix coordinate) who recited to Muhammad, piece by piece, sentence by sentence, in small and large portions over a period of 23 years, what would become the Quran. Fourteen years after Gabriel first appeared, Muhammad the god's devotees fought against followers of the Islamic prophet Muhammad during the Battle of Badr in 624 AD. After Muhammad entered Mecca in 630, he removed the statue of Hubal from the Kaaba along with the idols of all the other pagan gods.

While Mohammad, the Kaaba and the Islamic religion seems to be very well documented in religious sources, I regret to say that there are few authentic Historical sources of Mohammad and Mecca."

"All the facts point to the historical argument that Mecca was constructed in the 4th century A.D. This does not in any way take away from the purpose of the development.

5.1 Development

The Kaaba did not exist until the 5th century AD when Asa'd Abu Karb built it, while the black stone did not arrive until the late 5th century (likely from Yemen). During those 1-2 centuries before Muhammad, the Kaaba became populated with 360 idols, dedicated to Arabian Star Family and jinn-devil worship, so the black stone was not likely ever considered a lingam or shiva either.

5.2 The Story

Muhammad was born around the year 570 CE to the Banu Hashim clan of the Quraysh tribe, one of Mecca's prominent families. His father, Abdullah, died almost six months before Muhammad was born. According to Islamic tradition, Muhammad was sent to live with a Bedouin family in the desert, as desert life was considered healthier for infants.

Amongst pre-Islamic Arabs, people classified themselves according to their tribe, their clan, and then their house/family. There were two major tribal kinds: the Adnanites (descended from Adnan, traditional ancestor of the Arabs of northern, central and western Arabia) and the Qahtanites (originating from Qahtan, the traditional ancestor of the Arabs of southern and south eastern Arabia).[1][2] Banu Hashim is one of the clans of the

Quraysh tribe,[3] and is an Adnanite tribe. It derives its name from Hashim ibn Abd Manaf, the great-grandfather of Muhammad, and along with the Banu Abd Shams, Banu Al-Muttalib, and Banu Nawfal clans comprises the Banu Abd al-Manaf section of the Quraysh.

5.3 Nobel Secrets Infused

The House of Abdul-Muttalib of Banu Hashim comprised nobility in pre-Islamic Mecca. This was based on their hereditary duty to act as stewards and caretakers of the pilgrims coming to Mecca to worship at the Kaaba, the sacred shrine that in Islamic tradition was built by Ibrahim (Abraham) and his first-born son and heir Ismail (Ishmael) was a Monotheist site of worship.

5.4 Business Grew

With time, the Kaaba had come to be occupied by some hundreds of idols. Visiting of these idols by the different tribes caused traffic which added considerably to the wealth of the merchants of Mecca, which also benefited from its position astride the caravan routes from Yemen (Arabia Felix) up to the Mediterranean markets.

It was into the House 'Abd al-Muttalib of Banu Hashim of Quraysh that Muhammad was born. At the age of 40, his establishment of Islam set him at odds with the established powers in Mecca. His membership of the 'top house, of the top clan' (in terms of prestige and power) was a factor (according to Islamic tradition) through which God kept him safe from assassination during the early years of his mission, as a number of his uncles would not countenance any such insult to their so-called clan honor.

After 13 years, the Muslim community of Mecca migrated (made Hijrah) to the city of Yathrib (which subsequently became known as Medina), to avoid their often-murderous persecution by the non-believers of Mecca. With the conquest of Mecca, the city was captured by the army of Islam.

5.5. The Purge

The Kaabah was cleansed of idols and became the centre of pilgrimage for Muslims, once again the centre of pure Abrahamic monotheism. (It is illegal for non-Muslims to enter an area designated surrounding the city of Mecca).

5.6 Controlling Families

The two major lines of descent of Muhammad are those of his two grandsons, Al-Hasan and Al-Husain, born of the union of his daughter Fatimah and his cousin and son-in-law Ali. Muhammad besought the love of the Muslims on his grandsons; thus, their descendants have become spiritual aristocracy among the Muslims.

The descendants of the Banu Hashim are known by the titles of Sayed, Sayyid, Syed and Sharif.

In the 19th Century CE, to try to resolve the confusion surrounding the descendants of Muhammad, the Ottoman Caliphs attempted to replicate the Almanach de Gotha (the tome listing the noble houses of Europe) to show known and verifiable lines of descent.

Although not 100% complete in its scope the resulting Kitab al-Ashraf (Book of the Sharifs), kept at the Topkapı Palace in Istanbul is one of the best sources of evidence of descent from

Muhammad.[4] The Alids (the term given to the descendants of Muhammad via his daughter Fatima and Ali) lines of descent produced many once, current (and future) reigning dynasties across the Islamic imperium, amongst these stand:

1.^ Reuven Firestone (1990). Journeys in Holy Lands: The Evolution of the Abraham-Ishmael Legends in Islamic Exegesis. p. 72.

2.^ Göran Larsson (2003). Ibn García's Shu'ūbiyya Letter: Ethnic and Theological Tensions in Medieval al-Andalus. p. 170.

3.^ Al-Mubarakpuri, Safi-ur-Rahman (2002). The Sealed Nectar (Ar-Raheeq Al-Makhtum). Darussalam. p. 30. ISBN 1591440718.

4.^ http://asfa-widiyanto-scholarly.blogspot.com/

5.7 Bedouin Union

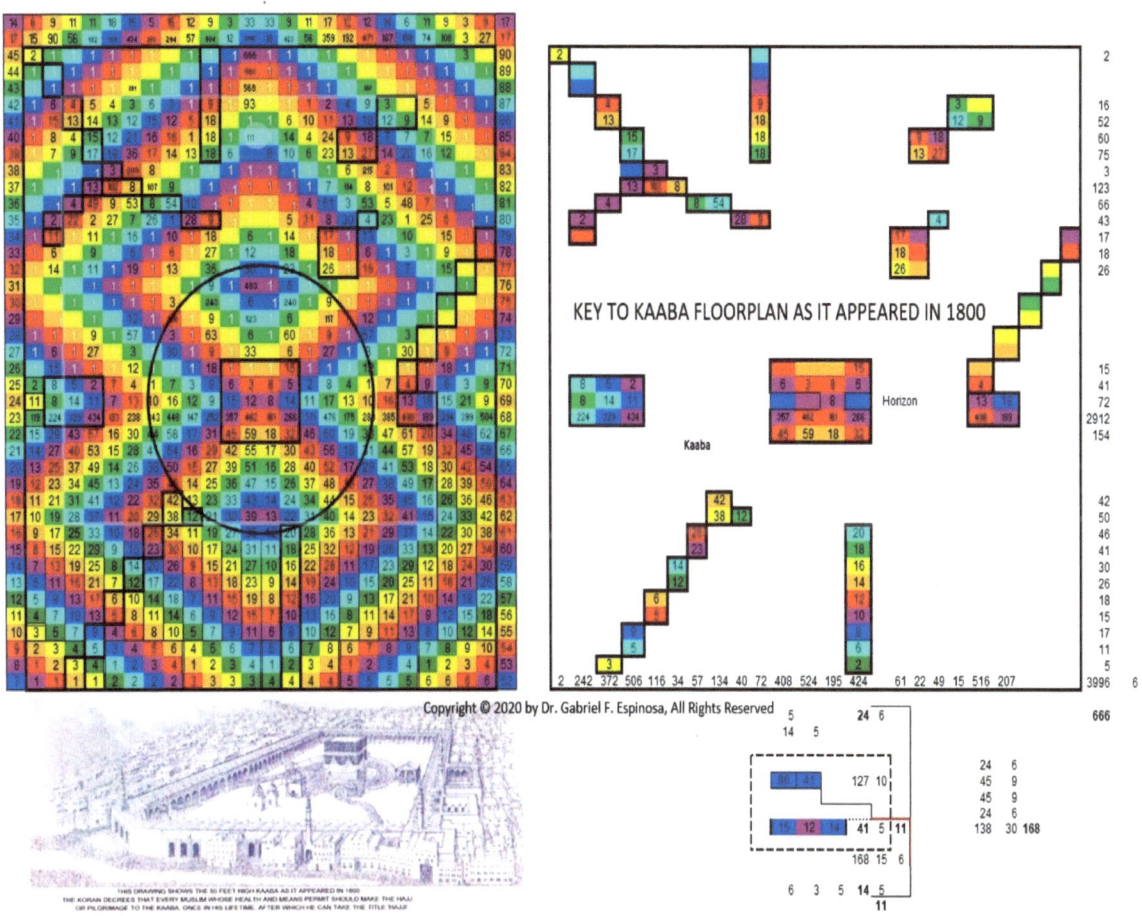

Exhibit 46: Kaaba 1800's

In this exhibit is the floorplan as the Kaaba appeared in the 1800's. The Kaaba has been demolished and rebuilt several times in the course of its history, originally only four walls, when it was first built.... or by whom is still unclear.

5.8 The House of Saud

Muhammad ibn Saud ibn Muhammad ibn Muqrin Al-Maridi (Arabic: محمد بن سعود بن محمد آل مقرن آل مريدي; died 1765), also known as Ibn Saud, was the emir of Ad-Diriyyah and is considered the founder of the First Saudi State and the Saud dynasty, which are named for his father, Saud ibn Muhammad ibn Muqrin (died 1725).[1] Ibn Saud's family (then known as the Al Muqrin) traced its descent to the tribe of Banu Audi and Hanifa tribes but, despite popular misconceptions, Muhammad ibn Saud was neither a nomadic bedouin nor was he a tribal leader. Rather, he was the chief (emir) of an agricultural settlement near modern-day Riyadh, called Diriyah.[2] Furthermore, he was a competent and ambitious desert warrior.[2]

5.9 The Agreement

The initial power base was the town of Ad-Diriyyah, where he met Muhammad ibn Abdul-Wahhab, who came to Ibn Saud for protection.[2] Muhammad ibn Saud granted him entry into Diriyah. They formed an alliance in 1744 which was formalized by the wedding of Muhammad bin Abdul-Wahhab's daughter to Abdulaziz, son and successor of Ibn Saud. Thereafter, the descendants of Muhammad bin Saud and the descendants of bin Abdul-Wahhab, the Al ash-Sheikh, have remained intricately linked.

Ibn Abdul-Wahhab provided Ibn Saud with the military backing for the House of Saudi. helped establish the House of Saud among other forces in the Arabian Peninsula.[3]

1. ^ Pike, John. "King Abdul Aziz Bin Abdul Rahman Al-Saud". Retrieved 12 July 2016.

2. ^ Jump up to a b c McHale, T. R. (Autumn 1980). "A Prospect of Saudi Arabia". International Affairs. 56 (4). JSTOR 2618170.

3. ^ Jump up to a b Historical Memorandum on the Relations of the Wahabi Amirs and Ibn Saud with Eastern Arabia and the British Government, 1800-1934. Qatar Digital Library: British Library: India Office Records and Private Papers. 1934. p. 2.

Muhammad ibn Abd al-Wahhab was a religious leader and theologian from Najd in central Arabia who founded the movement now called Wahhabism.[2][3][4][5][6] Born to a family of jurists, Ibn 'Abd al-Wahhab's early education consisted of learning a fairly standard curriculum of orthodox jurisprudence according to the Hanbali school of law, which was the school of law most prevalent in his area of birth.[1]

5.10 The Strategy

Despite his initial rudimentary training in classical Sunni Muslim tradition, Ibn 'Abd al-Wahhab gradually became opposed to many of the most popular Sunni practices such as the visitation to and the veneration of the tombs of saints,[1] which he felt amounted to heretical religious innovation or even idolatry.[1]

Despite his teachings being rejected and opposed by many of the most notable Sunni Muslim scholars of the period,[1] including his own father and brother,[1] Ibn 'Abd al-Wahhab charted a religio-political pact with Muhammad bin Saud to help him to establish the Emirate of Diriyah, the first Saudi state,[7] and began a dynastic alliance and power-sharing arrangement between their families which continues to the present day in the Kingdom of Saudi Arabia.[8]

The Al ash-Sheikh, Saudi Arabia's leading religious family, are the descendants of Ibn Abd al-Wahhab, and have historically led the ulama in the Saudi state,[9] dominating the state's clerical institutions.[10]

1. ^ Jump up to: a b c d e f g h i j k l m n Laoust, H., "Ibn Abd al-Wahhāb", in: Encyclopaedia of Islam, Second Edition, Edited by: P. Bearman, Th. Bianquis, C.E. Bosworth, E. van Donzel, W.P. Heinrichs.

2. ^ Moosa, Ebrahim (6 April 2015). What Is a Madrasa? UNC Press Books. p. 97. ISBN 9781469620145.

3. ^ White, Jonathan R. (1 January 2016). Terrorism and Homeland Security. Cengage Learning. p. 252. ISBN 9781305886940.

4. ^ Hubbard, Ben (10 July 2016). "A Saudi Morals Enforcer Called for a More Liberal Islam. Then the Death Threats Began". The New York Times. ISSN 0362-4331. Archived from the original on 15 December 2016. Retrieved 16 December 2016.

5. ^ Asad, Talal (3 February 2003). Formations of the Secular: Christianity, Islam, Modernity. Stanford University Press. p. 222. ISBN 9780804747684.

6. ^ goston, Gábor A.; Masters, Bruce Alan (21 May 2010). Encyclopedia of the Ottoman Empire. Infobase Publishing. p. 260. ISBN 9781438110257.

7. ^ Hourani 1992: 257–258

8. ^ Nawaf E. Obaid (September 1999). "The Power of Saudi Arabia's Islamic Leaders". Middle East Quarterly. VI (3): 51–58. Archived from the original on 6 August 2011. Retrieved 23 June 2011.

5.11 Before Islam

Before advent of Islam, the four walls of the Ka'aba (cube) were associated with the four regions of the known world (Syria, al-Iraq, Yemen and "the West"). The Ka'aba major axis is aligned to the star named Canopus in the south. The minor axis is aligned towards summer sunrise and winter sunset, the furthest limits of the moon at solstices. As a pre-Islamic observatory whereby, solstices were derived, and Canopus was observed as a primary navigation star. To understand why Canopus was used and not Sirius, is simple.

In Greek mythology, Canopus or Canobus (Greek: Κάνωβος) was the pilot (navigation star) of the ship of King Menelaus of Sparta during the Trojan War. Canopus is described as a handsome young man (countenance of Matrix, the face on the pattern) who was loved by the Egyptian prophetess, Theonoe, but never reciprocated her feelings.

According to legend, while visiting the Egyptian coast, Canopus was bitten by a serpent (Uraeus) and died. His master, Menelaus, erected a monument to him at one of the mouths of the River Nile, around which the town of Canopus later developed.[1][2]

Also named for Canopus is Canopus, the brightest star in the southern constellation of Carina (the keel of the ship Argo), and the second-brightest star in the night sky, after Sirius.

In Greek mythology, Theonoe (Ancient Greek: Θεονόη) was a character in Euripides' play, Helen—daughter to the Egyptian king, Proteus, and sister of Theoclymenus, the current king of Egypt. Her name means "divine wisdom," coming from theós 'god' and nóos or noûs 'mind.'

Thus, as founding reference, Canopus was used at the Kaaba.

5.12 Abrahamic Religions Agree

Jewish and Islamic traditions agree (They both are all derived out of Matrix development) and that Ibrahim (Abraham Aveinu) being the attributed builder of this "altar" from which the heavens were observed, took advantage of a more ancient coordinate of Matrix Code revelations. The Metsamor observatory comes to mind.

5.13 Door of the Kaaba

Exhibit 47: KAABA Door King Abdulaziz Secret by Baron Gabriel Foster Espinosa

As a modern example of knowledge, Islam needed to reveal, due use of the Gabriel coordinate truth, as that likeness of Gabriel in original form Muhammad referred. Ibn Saud

Abdulaziz ibn Abdul Rahman ibn Faisal ibn Turki ibn Abdullah ibn Muhammad Al Saud, usually known within the Arab world as Abdulaziz and in the West as Ibn Saud, was the first monarch and founder of Saudi Arabia, the "third Saudi state". Knowing the push toward establishing the State of Israel, which was eventually proclaimed, on May 14, 1948, in Tel Aviv, by Jewish Agency Chairman David Ben-Gurion. Establishing the first Jewish state in 2,000 years. Instead of abiding by Muhammad's origin intent of revealing the great secret, in 1944, King Abdulaziz had the commissioned door which coordinated with the 'Secret of Gabriel' installed.

Abdulaziz, in his own way set the ground at revealing truth, by use of the 666 secret. Knowing that the Hidden Matrix core reaches 45 squares, being foundation to what becomes the boundary of the four corners (Kaaba), upon the Hidden Matrix, he decided to use 46 as that hidden point to the other side. The sum of the door is 30636. The key number to the other side is 46 as per chart revealing a 666 gateway.

As a way of establishing that hidden secret and meaning to the Kaaba, the coordination as a symbol the concept of the stone was used by Muhammad, as a means at establishing universal knowledge which would inevitably be revealed by Gabriel. It is a truth held by all Abrahamic ideologies.

5.14 The Stone

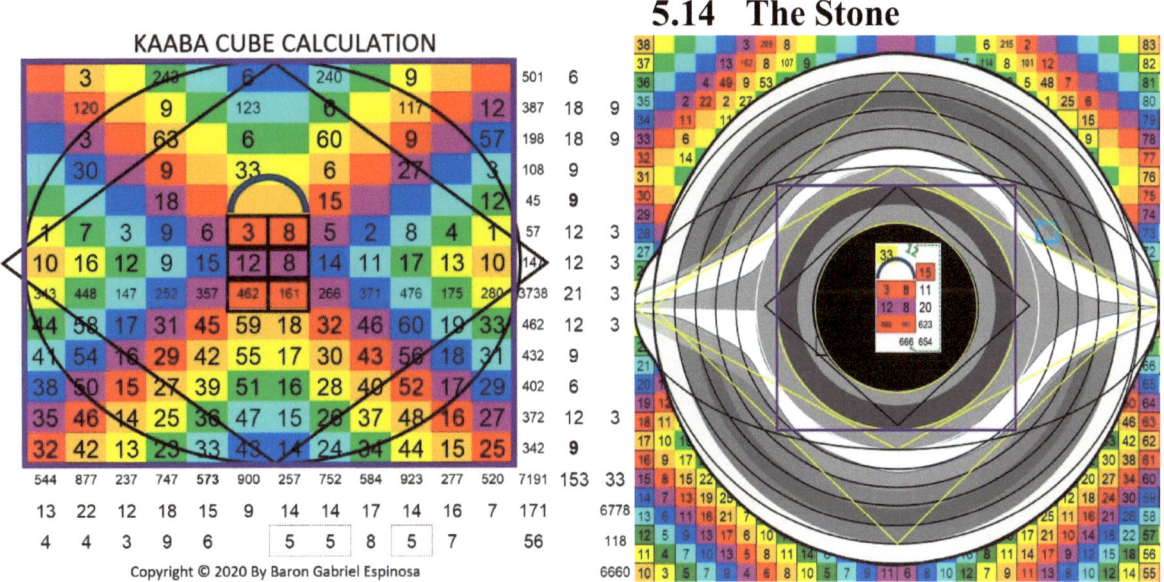

Exhibit 48: KAABA Central Essence and Stone Container by Baron Gabriel Foster Espinosa

The reason tradition holds that it dates to the time of Adam and Eve, source to the story, which is the crown code. The solidarity of Crown Code, should have been understood as what the Crown Code represents to all people of the earth, yet what it became did not reflect what Muhammad represented, as a symbolic gesture to the underlying truths held within the great secret of Allah.

Exhibit 49: Stone covering and Hajj development

5.15 Conceiving the Hajj

To use the Hidden Matrix in the development of Islam, Muhammad personified parts and process as did the Jewish and Christian versions. Here, the concept was to overtake the Jewish version with one of their own.

Thus a route was established as one following a path fulfilling the footsteps of the prophets Ibrahim and Ismail in their path to the sacrifice, only instead of Isaac, we have Ismail, and instead of a Ram Ibrahim is sent a white, big eyed sheep with horns in replacement of Ismail which was sacrificed instead.

The route includes

Mount of Mercy, which is visited before the beginning of Hajj.

Al-Masjid Al-Haram – Makkah (The Holy Mosque built around the Kaaba),

Day one: Put on the *ihram*. Make the intention for the hajj and go from Mecca to Mina before noon.

Day Two: Go to Arafat by noon, pray Zuhr and Asr together

Three: leave for Muzdalifah at sundown. Pray Maghrib (Sunset prayer) and Isha (evening prayer) together and rest for the night, Collect pebbles for *rami*.

Al-Hash'ar Al-Haram -Muzdalifah (is between two mounts of Muzdalifah where pilgrims imitate the prophets supplicating with their own),

Day three: Before or after fajr; head off to Mina. Perform rami (Throwing stones at Satan) on the Largest Jamrah only.

Jamarat – Mina (represent the three locations where Ibrahim pelted Shaytan/Satan with stones when he tried to dissuade him from sacrificing his son Ismail),

Cut/shave your hair, remove ihram, offer an animal sacrifice, and go to Mecca to perform tawaf-i-infadah.(circumambulates round the Ka'bah for seven rounds and prays two rak'as of Taw) Return to Mina and stay for another 2-3 days performing rami on all three Jamrah (smallest to largest) each day.

Five: Head of to Mecca and perform tawaf-i-wida (Farwell tawaf) before leaving.

Granted, causing acts toward fulfillment of parts of the Hidden Matrix, is commendable, yet to keep the Pattern and its Totalities from the people in creation of a God spring and using the same as what Abrahamic design hold, is nefarious at minimum.

SIX

ZODIAC CONCEPTION KEY

As a way of going back in time, foundation to what became shared the world over, in their own way, as in the twelve tribe development seen and understood by the following chart out of the Hidden Matrix are synonymous to the Zodiac.

Knowing that upon the Hidden Matrix, twelve fixed parts were revealed, which by the evidence was in no doubt understood by ancient civilizations, even by those we have no knowledge of. It is not surprising of all those developments in likeness to that truth.

Exhibit 50: Zodiac Conception keyt by Baron Gabriel Foster Espinosa

6. The fixed parts which become planes or areas to each house, are determined by their sectional cause. The following are examples of what types became developed in satisfying what each of the twelve parts related to in time.

6.1 The Field Dweller as Aries

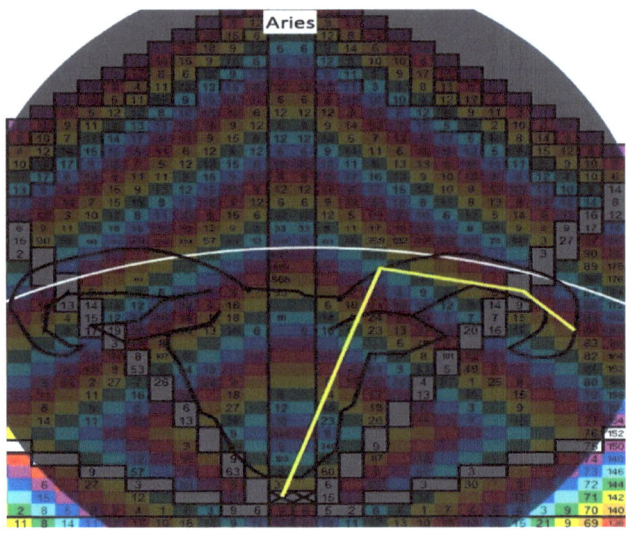

Exhibit 51: Aries Coordinate Secret by Baron Gabriel Foster Espinosa

The upper half of centre vertical column parts here, as first equal 6010. Note 6010 polarizes to 7, which can be compared to completion, whole, the first week, here we are satisfied with it being the first of fanning procession becoming Aries, as that hook over Pisces, as one of the constellations of the zodiac, becoming by Matrix guide, located in the northern celestial hemisphere. Prior to the Ram as conceived of the Matrix perception, ancient Sumer referred to the blank area's essence as the "Field Dweller"

6.2 The Lady of Heaven as Pisces

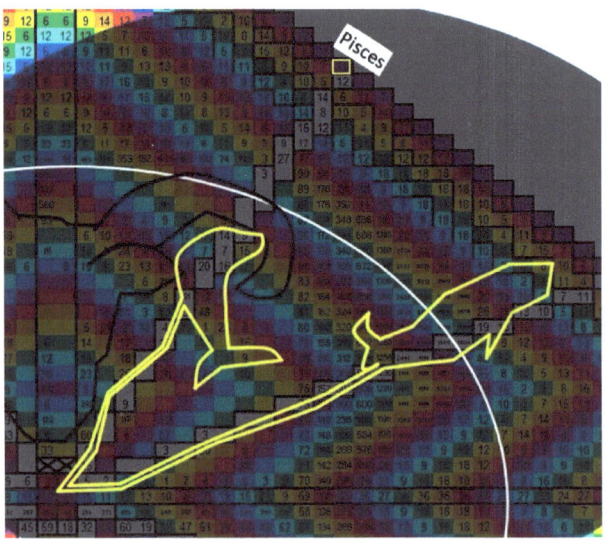

Exhibit 52: Pisces Coordinate Secret by Baron Gabriel Foster Espinosa

Pisces (Simmah) originates as that manifesting out of "The field dweller" (Aries) united by those part dividers of Matrix unifying as by a fish cord or ribbon into Aquarius, understood as the Anunitum holding the Northern fish of Pisces as The Lady of Heaven was the patron goddess of the city of Akkad. She was closely affiliated to Inanna-Ishtar, who as the 'Syrian Goddess' was envisioned holding her sacred fish and dove.

Pisces used to be referred to as the first constellation of the zodiac. This is because the Sun appears against the backdrop of Pisces during the northern hemisphere's spring equinox, which was previously considered the start of a new year.

6.3 Lord of the Waters as Aquarius

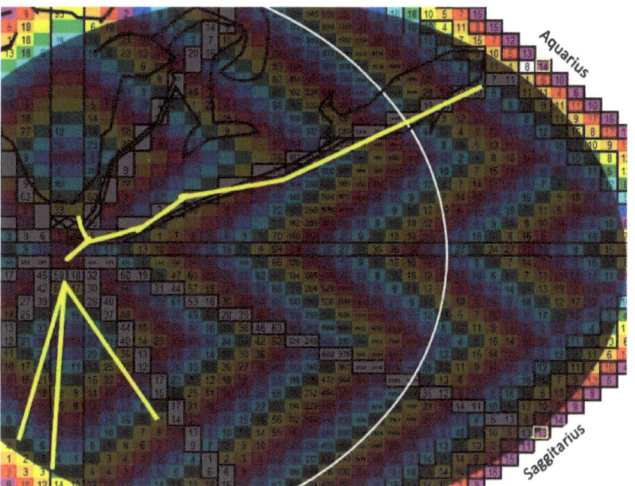

Exhibit 53: Aquarius Coordinate Secret by Baron Gabriel Foster Espinosa

Aquarius (Sumerian Gu "Lord of the Waters") at the backdrop Pisces is a constellation of the zodiac, situated between Capricornus and Pisces. Its name is Latin for "water-carrier" or "cup-carrier" due to the path of the sun which follows part dividers from Aquarius through to Gemini, the likeness of a cup is perceived. Contained within becomes the representation of water where the fishes of Pisces enter. The Water Bearer Aquarius.

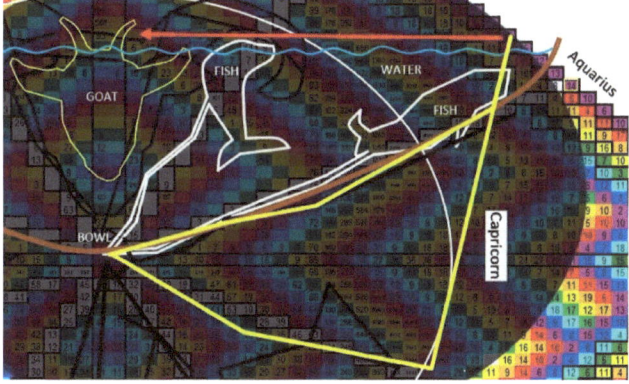

6.4 Suhurmash as Capricorn

Exhibit 54: Capricorn Coordinate Secret by Baron Gabriel Foster Espinosa

Capricornus (Sumerian Suhurmash) is one of the constellations of the zodiac. Its current name is Latin for "horned goat" or "goat horn" or "having horns like a goat's", and it is commonly represented in the form of a sea-goat: a mythical creature that is half goat, half fish. This is founded upon origination coordinate. Note that Capricorns upper curve coincides with Aquarius cup/bowl. Being within the water with fishes of Pisces, the goat is merged becoming expressed as that half goat half fish likeness.

6.5 The Grandfather as Sagittarius

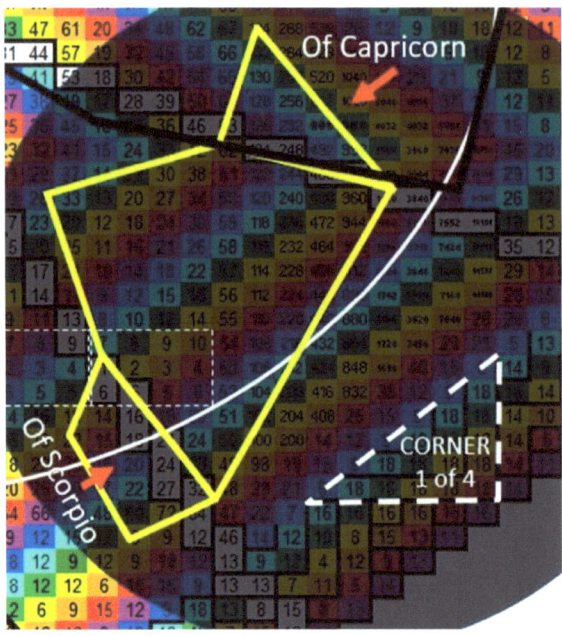

Exhibit 55: Sagittarius Coordinate Secret by Baron Gabriel Foster Espinosa

Sagittarius (Sumerian MUL.PA.BIL.SAG [pa.bil.sag] (The "Grandfather [Pabilsag (a defender god)] ;) one of the constellations conceived of Hidden Matrix. Current name is Latin for the archer, As a stylized arrow. Sagittarius as a centaur pulling back a bow, is due its extensions as one extending into Capricorn and opposite with the other extending into Scorpio, which became bows.

The concept of a centaur is due the coordinate to the corner, which is one of four upon the hidden Matrix. Likened to a beast with four legs. It lies between Scorpius and Ophiuchus to the west and Capricornus and Microscopium to the east.

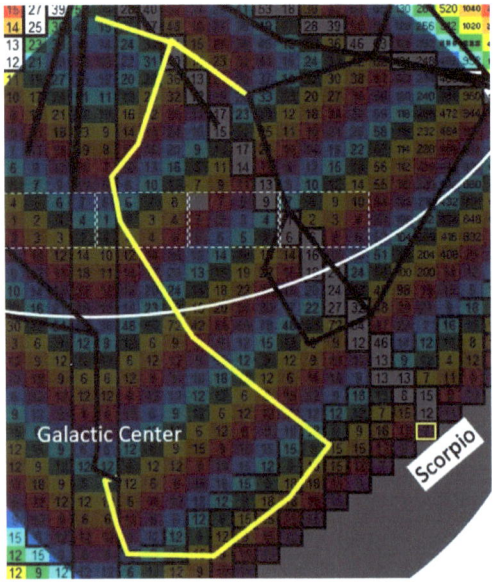

6.6 Which Claws and Cuts as Scorpion

Being near centre of the Milky Way Scorpio (Sumerian Girtab, "Which Claws and Cuts") is one of the constellations of the zodiac. Current name is Latin for Scorpion. An offshoot to Sagittarius its constellation predates the Greeks.

The Clawing and Cutting, prior to its name of Scorpio, signified the attracting and unifying force (that hooking shape) toward centre of Matrix coordinate. The cutting characterization is understood by Matrix parallel central double column squares.

Exhibit 56: Scorpio Coordinate Secret by Baron Gabriel Foster Espinosa

By interpretation, that column is separated, thus cut to represent two halves of Matrix grid.

It appears between Libra to the west and Sagittarius to the east. It's a large constellation in the southern hemisphere, near the centre of the Milky Way. Its association is to the Galactic Centre 168.

6.7 Scales of Heaven as Libra

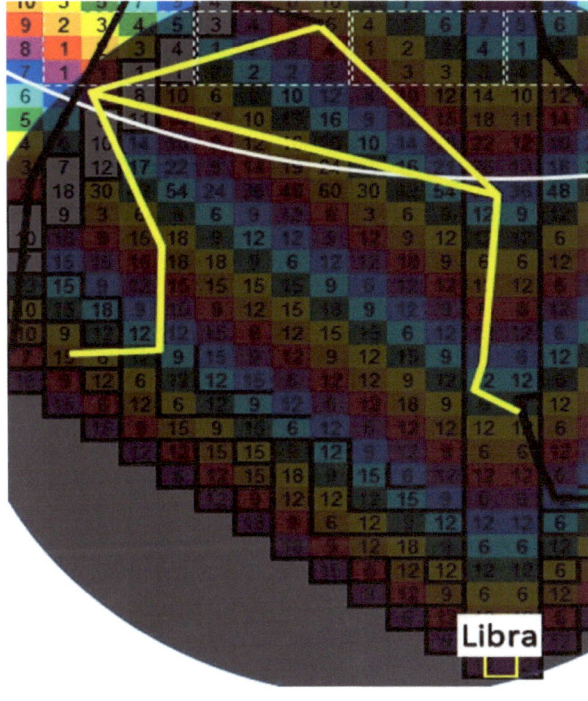

MUL.ZIB.BA.AN.NA [zi-ba-ni-tum] (The "Scales of Heaven [The balance];" later to be one of the 12 ecliptic constellations.) (Greek zodiac: originally "the Claws" (of the Scorpion) but the Romans later (re)introduced Libra (the Scales).)

Libra (Sumerian Zibaabba "Heavenly Fate") is a constellation of the zodiac. Its name is Latin for weighing scales, echoes Zibaabba origin.

Lying between Virgo to the west and Scorpius to the east, it consists of reference to the centre sum of 6 at top, 6 of two fold from guide numbers 7, 8 and 9 levels second column as two fold (1 and 2) and (3) and 66 at right. The left descending arm connects 18, 12 and 15 for 45.

Exhibit 57: Libra Coordinate

The right descending arm below and outside the white circle periphery unites 66, 12 and 12 for 90. Both the Left and right descending arms represent the two guide columns upon the Hidden Matrix. The 6, two-fold and 66 holds the creative column squares of 45 at left, and 90 at right, weighing result in creation.

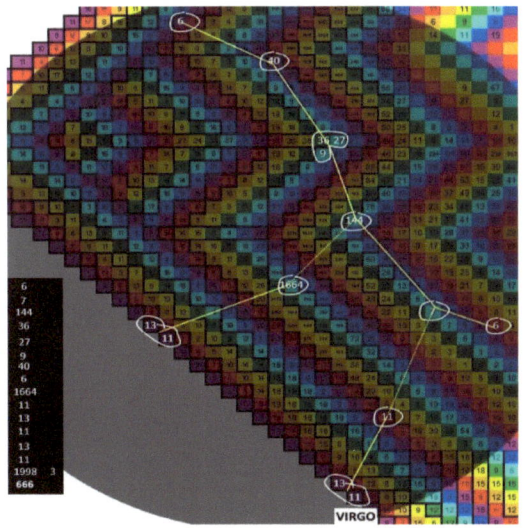

6.8 The Maiden Virgin as Virgo

Virgo represents the essence of what 11:11 provides. Starting at right 6 atop Libra scales, 7 is fulfilled, which continues to 144. In total 36, 27 and 9 bring together the 72 of the first instruction. reaching 40 the virgin holds the 111. The two at base found the 48, is polarized to 3. 1998 is divided by 3 for 666

The Sumerians described her as holding a stalk of corn, which represents the 72 squares of the first six clusters. Also, Absin – "Her Father Was Sin", The Maiden Virgo MUL.AB.SIN [ab.sin] (The "Furrow [The barley-stalk];" [or Spica]

Exhibit 58: Virgo Coordinate Secret by Baron Gabriel Foster Espinosa

6.9 The Lioness as Leo

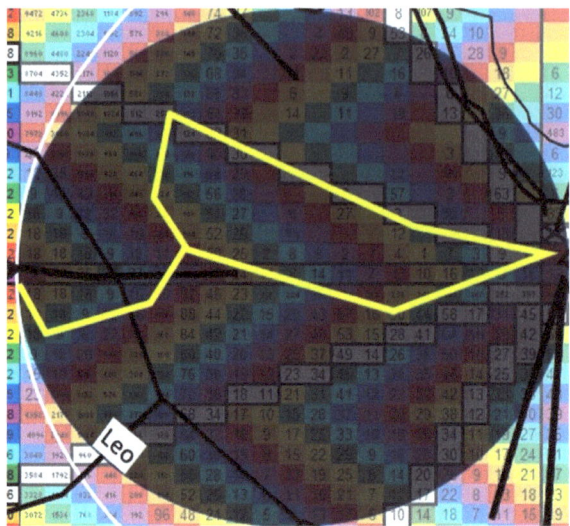

Exhibit 59: Leo Coordinate Secret by Baron Gabriel Foster Espinosa

MUL.UR.GU.LA [ur.gu.la] (The "Lion;" [or Lioness], later to be one of the 12 ecliptic constellations.) (Greek zodiac: Leo (the Lion).)
Originally, aligned to the circle at four corner coordinates, a Lion by conception is perceived, thus having a prominent mane.
The female on the other hand, represents the circular coordinate within the four corner Matrix expression. This attribute became likened and later developed as the Sophia, which represents recognition to the number 666.

6.10 Dub – "Pincers, tongs", the crab Cancer

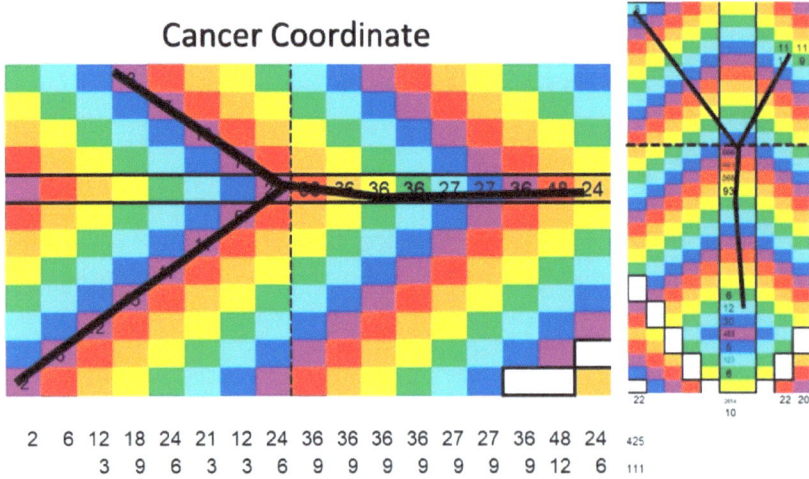

Originally conceived as to express the insertion of 111 upon Matrix Core. That insemination revealing the relationship of 666 to 111. Cancer Coordinate establishes constellation order as 10 mandated of Core reference, the relationship of 111 to 666 is seen by the outer left 22 and outer right number 22 and 20 polarized to 10.

Exhibit 60: Cancer Coordinate Secret by Baron Gabriel Foster Espinosa

The central descending extension from vector reveal 2654 which funnels in 10 for 2664. The three extensions of constellation represent that 111 of 1111. Thus 2664 is divided by 4 to establish 666 in agreement with the lioness of MUL.UR.GU.LA [ur.gu.la]

6.11 The Great Twins as Gemini

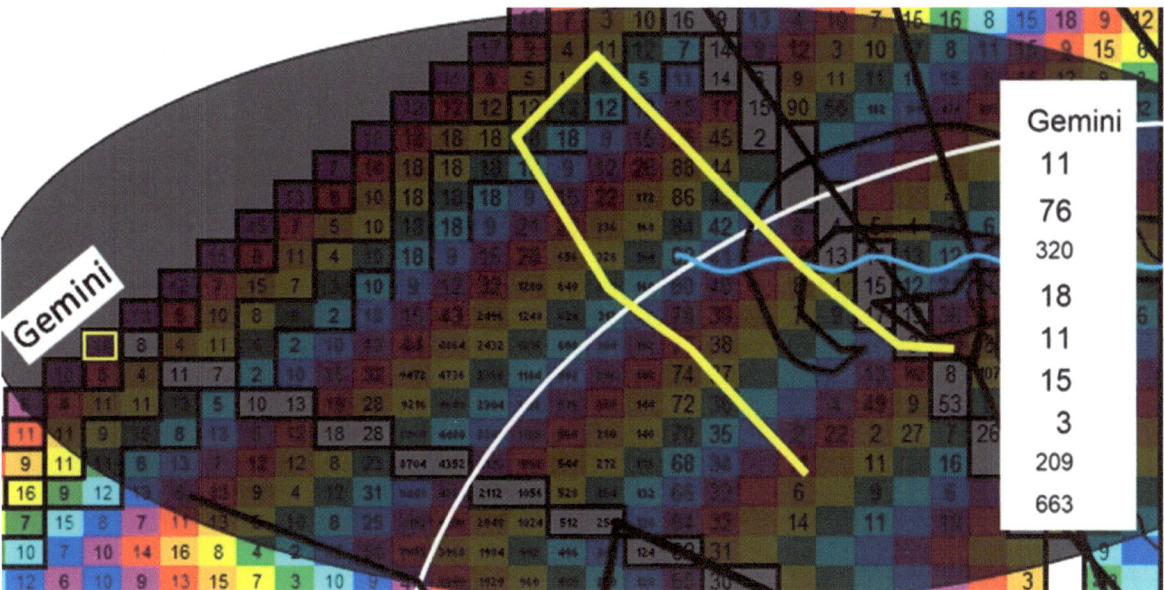

Exhibit 61: Gemini Coordinate Secret by Baron Gabriel Foster Espinosa

MUL.MASH.TAB.BA.GAL.GAL [mash.tab.ba.gal.gal] (The "Great Twins;") was conceived as that last part into the waters before MUL.GUD.AN.NA [gu4.an.na] (The "Bull of Heaven [the bull of Anu];" later to be one of the 12 ecliptic constellations. (Greek zodiac: Taurus (the Bull).

The narrative attributed to the gods were established to reflect the numerical association to those expressive parts to The Hidden Matrix. The upper connector bringing together 11 and 18 express 29. 29 polarized is 11, thus 11 as a carbon copy needed inclusion to represent 11:11 of Matrix Foundation. In total the conceived shape to Gemini represented the connected twin number of 663 understood by boundary to the Zodiac explained later. Matrix parts personified, became cast of Greco-Roman deities by the authors.

As one half, 11 became in one narrative, personified as Zeus (swan), with counterpart 11 becoming Tyndareus. Knowing that 1111 produces those four corners (Four children) upon the Hidden Matrix.

The circle upon the square became Queen Leda, which undoubtably represented that womb whereby both Zeus and Tyndareus made their deposit, both impregnating Leda. The four children born to Leda were the two brothers Castor and Pollux, and two sisters, Helen and Clytemnestra; Castor and Clytemnestra were considered to be the children of King Tyndareus, whilst Pollux and Helen were the offspring of Zeus the pair by design were inseparable. In Greek mythology they were referred to as the Dioscuri (Dioskouroi), and in Rome they were Gemini.

6.12 Guanna – "Heavenly Bull" as Taurus

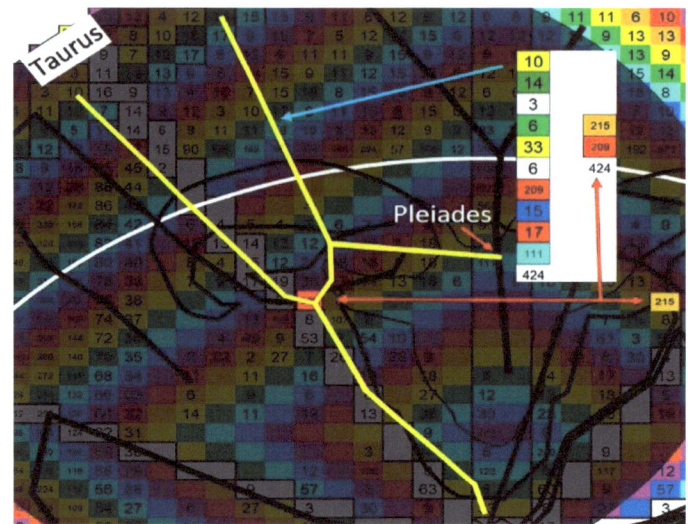

Exhibit 62: Taurus Coordinate Secret by Baron Gabriel Foster Espinosa

The Polarized numbers of the collection are 1, 5, 6, 11, 6, 8, 3 which total 40, significant to the crossing, here revelation of the Pleiades.

According to Greek mythology, the constellation Taurus commemorates the god Zeus changing himself into a beautiful white Bull to win the affections of the Phoenician princess Europa. After Europa hopped onto the Bull's back, the Bull swam across the Mediterranean Sea, taking Europa all the way to the Island of Crete.

That religion which grossly indulged the self-love and vanity of the Egyptians, easily found favor, and took root in the minds of the people.

6.13 Zodiac Conception Code

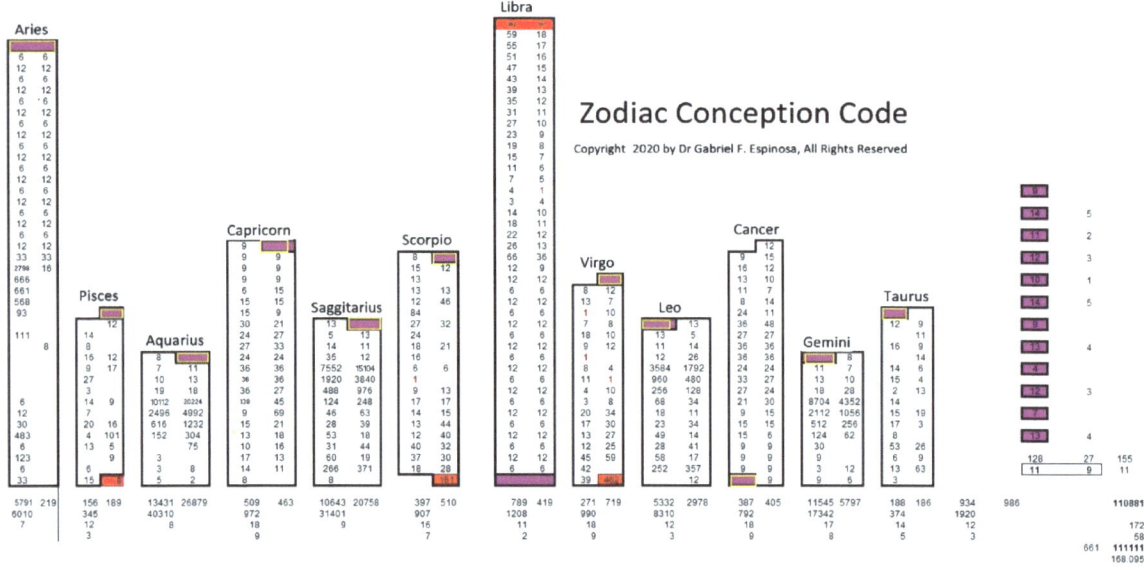

Exhibit 63: Zodiac Field Dividers, By Baron Gabriel Foster Espinosa

The universal code of 1111, and its expression of 111 establishes 111111.
The Key to Gemini being two manifest deducts two from its number of 663, showing 661.

Imagine a mirror image to this one, where one recognizing the other as potential within the cosmic waters. She sees his reflection becoming enamored.

111111 is the divided by the revelation of Gemini's 661, to reveal its unifying code of 168. Gemini's primary number of 663 as unified produces 111 or Three (3) for a total of 666 numbered squares that establish the 12 parts and surrounding border of the Zodiac.

6.14 Zodiac Divider Numbers

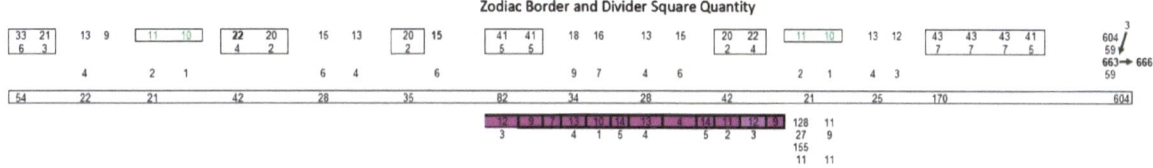

Exhibit 64: Zodiac Divider Totalities, by Baron Gabriel Foster Espinosa

6.15 Zodiac Divider Polarization Number

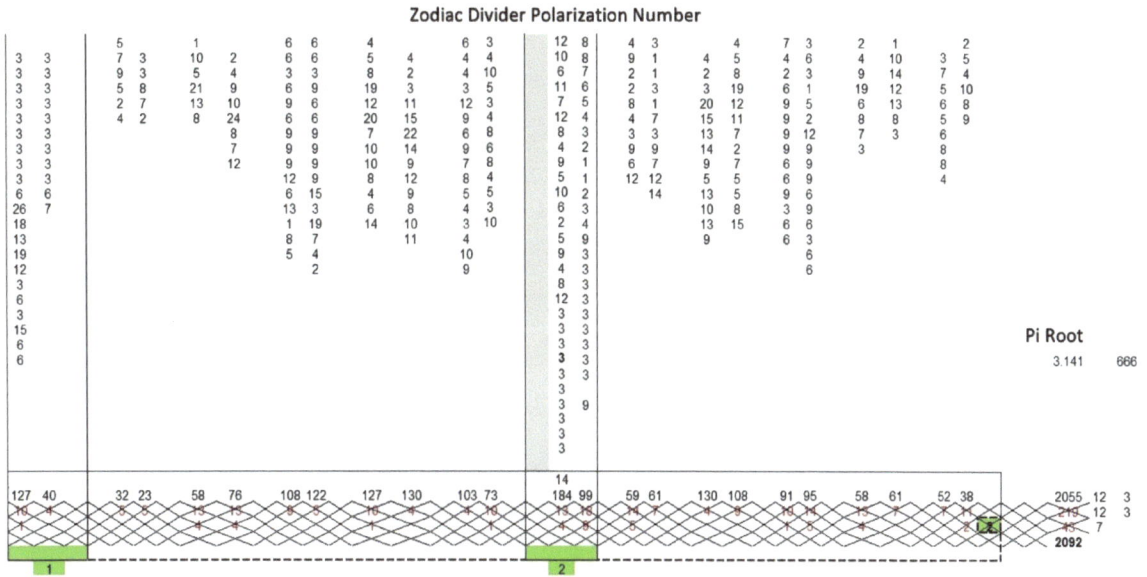

Exhibit 65: Zodiac Divider Polarization Number Pi by Baron Gabriel Foster Espinosa

The earliest legitimate reference to what we now know as Pi, belongs to Greek mathematician and genius, Archimedes. Yet by what is revealed here, it is more likely that Archimedes sought to match the ancient knowledge to detail of circle per "The Matrix Code"

SEVEN

ELITE COMFORT ZONE

7. Colgate's Secret

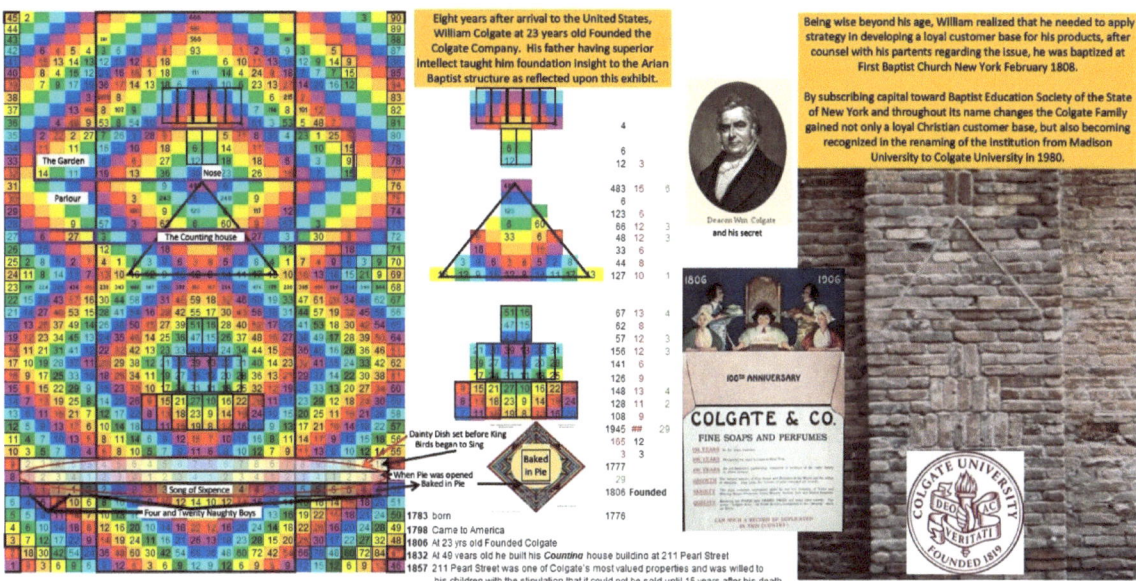

Exhibit 66: Pearl Street Founding Reference by Baron Gabriel Foster Espinosa

We must without influence hold on to truths universal, without false presentations. The recognition of Colgate to the higher truth, was without doubt that influence that inspired him. As one of the insightful privileged in America, he realized that a new dispensation had unfolded, which differed from his Arian understanding in union with Matrix knowledge. Arianism as a nontrinitarian Christological doctrine, holds that Jesus Christ is the Son of God, who was begotten by God the Father at a point in time, being a creature distinct from the Father, therefore subordinate to him, yet the Son (Countenance upon Matrix) is also God (i.e. God the Son) as a product thereof.

7.1 Arius Factor

Arian teachings were first attributed to Arius (c. AD 256-336), a Christian presbyter in Alexandria of Egypt. The term "Arian" is derived from the name Arius; and like "Christian", it was not a self-chosen designation but bestowed by hostile opponents, and never accepted by those on whom it had been imposed.

Arius / Priest

Arius Born: 256 AD Ptolemais, Cyrenaica, Libya

Died: 336 AD Constantinople, Turkey

Written works: Thalia was a Libyan presbyter and ascetic, and priest in Baucalis in Alexandria, Egypt. His teachings about the nature of the Godhead in Christianity, which emphasized God the Father's uniqueness and Christ's subordination under the Father, and his opposition to what would become the dominant Christology, Homoousian Christology, made him a primary topic of the First Council of Nicaea, which was convened by Emperor Constantine the Great in 325.

7.2 Colgate Knew

This brings us to what Colgate must have realized. The implications to what Constantine had brought about, as I said before Colgate as one of privileged insight, realized that a new dispensation had unfolded by Americas opportunity, which was different than before.

Enlightenment lost against Emperor Constantine in 325.

Bibe of the University of Oregon wrote about that time: Arius and the Nicene Creed Published on November 9, 2015 Author: biby@uoregon.edu

During this time in the history of Christianity, one of the biggest topics under debate in the church was the topic of the Trinity and the relationship between God the Father, the Son, and the Holy Spirit.

The church argued that the Trinity was three equal entities, the Father, the Son, and Holy Spirit, creating one fully divine being. Arius and his supporters had a different view on this. Thus, The Thalia was created and circulated by Arius and his supporters after he broke with the Bishop of Alexandria. The word Thalia means "festivity."

7.3 In Minds of men

In the beginning of the Thalia, Arius comes across rather hot headed. He claims that he has been taught by "participants in wisdom, skillful, taught by God" (158). He is claiming that his teachers, the one who passed this information on to him, were taught and instructed by God. He goes on to say, "having learned from God, I myself know wisdom and knowledge" (158). For the rest of the poem, the reader might look at Arius in a different light thinking that he received this information from God, so then he must be right.

My only concern about that is that his opponents too, could claim the same thing. Arius seems to think he is positively right on the subject.

Arius made the claims that the Father is superior to the other two parts, the Son, and Holy Spirit. He claims that the Son, was less than the Father. He said, "the Father is essentially foreign to the Son, because he exists unbegun" (159).

When considering what Arius understood, we must recognize, that his knowledge was different than most, in fact one could consider it Theosophical in nature.

The word stems from the Greek words "theos" (God) and "sophia" (Wisdom) and refers to the "Wisdom of the Gods." "This Divine Wisdom" the Hidden Matrix.

According to tradition, This Divine Wisdom, was brought to earth during humanities infancy, via a superhuman race, whose leaders were remembered as gods, where after legendary heroes of mythology were established.

First lessons in science, art, and philosophy were recognized of the Hidden Matrix, by these beings who laid the foundations for world culture. It is said that the Divine Wisdom was taught openly to the first human races. Some surmise that it was during the time of the fourth, or Atlantean race, that it became hidden from the majority.

Helena Petrovna Blavatsky, in the following words explained why the secrecy: She wrote:
The first, semi-divine, pure and spiritual Races of Humanity . . . had the "truths of God," and lived up to them, and their ideals. They preserved them, if there was hardly any evil, and hence scarcely a possible abuse of that knowledge and those truths. But evolution and the gradual fall into materiality is also one of the "truths" and also one of the laws of "God." And as mankind progressed, and became with every generation more of the earth, earthly, the individuality of each temporary Ego began to assert itself.

It is personal selfishness that develops and urges man on to the abuse of his knowledge and power. And selfishness is a human building, whose windows and doors are forever wide open for every kind of iniquity to enter man's soul . . . Hence the necessity of gradually taking away from man the divine knowledge and power, which became with every new human cycle more dangerous as a double-edged weapon, whose evil side was ever threatening one's neighbour, and whose power for good was lavished freely only upon self.

Those few "elect" whose inner natures had remained unaffected by their outward physical growth, thus became in time the sole guardians of the mysteries revealed, passing the knowledge to those most fit to receive it. (Collected Writings, 14:40-41) Thus from those days were established the Mystery Schools in which the Wisdom Teachings were preserved for the worthy. Chapter 1 Schools of Esoteric Teaching AN INTRODUCTION TO ESOTERIC PRINCIPLES. FOURTH EDITION A Study Course by William Doss McDavid.

With knowledge as those truths of God, that were usurped by evil, now having a chance at being shared with humanity once again.

Is it possible that Arius realized its truth, by what had taught him by "participants in wisdom, (Hidden Matrix) skillful in its interpretation, as revealed, thus taught by God? Knowing what the Hidden Matrix shows, understanding to Arius's claim, that his teachers, as the ones who passed this information on to him, were taught and instructed by God, would be correct, as its parts are divine and universally exact. Thus, by having access to and knowledge to the Hidden Matrix, he would go on to say, "having learned from God I myself know wisdom and knowledge".

Arius makes the claims that the Father is superior to the other two parts, the Son, and the Holy Spirit. He claims that the Son was less than the Father. He said, "the Father is essentially foreign to the Son because he exists unbegun" (159).

As known now, the reason for Arius that the Father is superior to the other two parts, the Son, and Holy Spirit, was that the father as all mind, exists outside the Hidden Matrix, which is what the Son is, as pre Hidden Matrix conception. The circumference upon the water of the Matrix is defined as the Holy Spirit.

Colgate in his wisdom, understood, the struggle of Arius, knowing that America being that renewed opportunity for humanity as what her founding fathers envisioned, that truth would eventually ensue upon this great land. Thus, his support of the Baptist Church in New York, as a way at weakening the stronghold the Catholic Church had upon the minds of Americans.

7.4 Pearl Street

It is no wonder that Colgate made effort to have a message written in stone at 211 Pearl Street, which speaks loud of the Hidden Matrix truth, destined for a time in the future, just as the founding of Colgate and Co, by the same as displayed through his brick exhibit.

As we become enlightened to the real reasons of our actions, and taking time in research, further than what some have required of us is paramount. Being American, is being part of the global body, which is not partitioned as superior or less than our brothers and sisters around the world, which has for far too long been promoted by ideological designs.

Knowing source to type and image of the divine, and how it has been used ushers in the age of awakening to the Universal truth, which America stands upon. It should not allow its light as upon the hill, to be extinguished by the nefarious actions of others. Standing upon truth, together as humanity is the greatest gift, we can give each other. It's time we make that stand.

7.5 Enlightened Men

Consider you are witnessing a scene in which a group of men are gathered in a room, discussing the beginning of the American Concept. "You look around to each as one by one interject ideas, perceptions… hearing their voiced opinions"

Being men of high intellect, men such as Charles Thompson, as congressional secretary from 1774-1789 through the revolution, and establishment of the Federal Government, and the man who made the final decision for the design of the great seal to The United States, now seen on the back of the one dollar bill.

The true meaning of that design can now be realized.

7.6 Americas Original Concept

The original conception idea, was that the Hidden Matrix Truth, unknown to most, yet would be revealed as a Landscape idea, on the virgin soil, laying down the foundations of a New World Idea, and the Architectural expression therein/thereon out of The Hidden Matrix Design... it would represent the manifesting, or materialization of the pattern and design, or the template/blueprint itself. But, most importantly this New World 'experiment' would not be bound by any religious tenant, or influence, that this America would be of absolute TRUTH as the Creator intended. An expression of the pattern as a 'living experiment' created by man....

Without realizing that the indigenous peoples already lived in such communities, of nonreligious influence, but by understanding and respecting the Spirit or Essence and Nature of the Creator. Yet, those who came here, destroyed the very Soul of that way of living, and took for themselves this sacred land and created a bitter truth, that we all must be accountable for, as we continue in the falseness we experience daily, which was not out of the pure intent, of an original perceived notion, of the American Dream.

Those efforts of men who envisioned that opportunity for a better world, could not go unnoticed.

It was by the insight of Charles James Fox, who became noted as an anti-slavery campaigner, whose father was Henry Fox, 1st Baron of Holland, Edmund Burke, whose work titled "A Vindication of Natural Society: or, a View of the Miseries and Evils arising to Mankind from every Species of Artificial Society published in 1756. It is a satire of Lord Bolingbroke's deism, confronting Bolingbroke in the sphere of civil society and government, arguing that his revelations against revealed religion could apply to all institutions. So right he was.

William Windham. and their friend Thomas Coke, that support of the American colonists during the American Revolutionary War grew. The insights held by many including these men, challenged the very foundation of the old establishments. George III king of Great Britain and King of Ireland understandably opposed their efforts.
Fox, who occasionally corresponded with Thomas Jefferson and had met Benjamin Franklin in Paris, shared the same insight and desire to forge a democratic institution.
It was Fox and his supporters that took up the habit of dressing in buff and blue, the colours of the uniforms in Washington's army, exhibiting their support of the American Revolution.

Little is known of Coke's early career in Parliament; he spoke relatively infrequently, and the parliamentary session was dissolved soon after his election. During that summer, however, he struck up a relationship with Charles James Fox, a soon to be famous Whig politician noted for his outspoken and flamboyant lifestyle. Coke later recounted that "When I first went into Parliament, I attached myself to Fox and clung to him through life. I lived in the closest bond of friendship with him." The period was one of economic stability and political calm under Lord North, which ended due to the American Revolution and resulting American Revolutionary War.

Coke was noted for his support of the American colonists; as a strong supporter of the 1688 Glorious Revolution and the resulting Bill of Rights 1689, he felt that the support of the espoused principles of justice and tolerance in Britain and overseas was his duty as a British subject, and saw no conflict between his position as a supporter of the colonists and his patriotism. After the Battles of Saratoga, it became clear that any victory in America would be long and expensive, and to raise funds King George III asked subjects to donate. In Norwich, a meeting was held in January 1778 for this purpose; it raised £4,500 in less than an hour. Windham and Coke attended this meeting, Windham making an impassioned speech pointing out that the campaign had so far resulted only in "disappointment, shame and dishonor", and that "peace and reconciliation with America" was the only option.[12] Windham, Coke and their supporters then withdrew to a nearby pub, where they drafted a petition to the king from "the Nobility, Gentry, Clergy, Freeholders and Inhabitants of the County of Norfolk". This was presented to Parliament by Coke on 17 February 1778, signed by 5,400 people from Norfolk. George III took this as a personal insult, and as a result disliked Coke until his death.

A mutual friend to in 1831, Coke's friend Earl Grey became Prime Minister; as a result, Coke's appearances in Parliament became more regular. He expressed delight at the Great Reform Act 1832, although he only spoke on the subject once, and chose its passage on 4 June 1832 as the appropriate moment to retire as an MP.[47] As the "greatest commoner in England", Coke finally accepted a peerage in July 1837 (having been offered one six times before), becoming the Earl of Leicester. He took no pleasure in attending the House of Lords, however, describing it as "the hospital for incurables".

Thomas Paine (born Thomas Pain) (February 9, 1737 [O.S. January 29, 1736] – June 8, 1809) was an English-born American political activist, philosopher, political theorist, and revolutionary. He authored the two most influential pamphlets at the start of the American Revolution and inspired the patriots in 1776 to declare independence from Great Britain. His ideas reflected Enlightenment-era ideals of transnational human rights.

Paine asserts that mankind was originally in a state of equality, and, therefore, present inequalities must have been brought about by some circumstance. Paine says that a common distinction that lacks any natural or religious basis, is the division between kings and their subjects. This distinction, unlike those between male and female or good and evil, is not one "of heaven," and Paine wishes to inquire into its origin and its consequences.

Originally, Paine says, there were no kings in the world. Then, the ancient Jews copied the custom from the "heathens" who surrounded them. This was a grave mistake, and Paine maintains that in establishing a king for themselves, the Jews sinned. Man is supposed to have only God ruling over him, and to introduce a king, who in ruling over the people is like a God, is a grave misdeed. Eventually, Paine says, the Jewish people asked the prophet Samuel for a king. Samuel attempted dissuade the people, but they insisted that they wanted to have a King like the other nations, and God assented, even though he thought it evil that the people should want someone other than God to rule over them.

Having considered the biblical origin of monarchy, Paine concludes that it is a practice begun in sinfulness. The many pages of scriptural evidence make it clear that God stands in opposition to monarchy. Paine moves on to attack the notion of the hereditary succession of the monarchy. Paine argues that, since all men are born equal, no man could have the right to establish his family as forever presiding over others. Even if a person deserves certain honors, his children may not deserve them, and that person has no right to pass those honors on.

Paine also observes that the recent kings of England have mostly been bad, which he says should indicate, even to those who favor hereditary succession, that the present line of kings does not exercise legitimate power.

Paine wonders where the power of kings originally comes from and decides that this power is always based on one of three things: election, random selection, or usurpation. **Paine says that if a king is chosen by election, this means all future kings should be chosen in the same way, and if the king usurped his throne, then the entire reign is illegitimate.** Any way you look at it, hereditary succession is not valid. Paine adds that hereditary succession brings other evils with it. **For example, people who see themselves as born into an elite existence are** often **"ignorant and unfit."** Lastly, Paine refutes the theory that hereditary succession reduces civil wars, as there have been at least eight civil wars and nineteen rebellions in Britain's history. *Monarchy and hereditary succession, Paine concludes have produced nothing in the world but bad governance and bloodshed.*

To the contemporary reader, Paine's slogging through mounds of biblical evidence might seem less interesting and less relevant, but in Paine's time, the bible shaped opinions on most matters. It was not uncommon to believe that kings ruled by divine right, and for this reason, many were hesitant to revolt against a King—after all, if the king's power was genuinely divine, a revolt against the king was akin to a revolt against God. Paine tries to undercut this line of thinking by attacking it on its own terms and presenting Biblical passages that reject the idea of a divinely appointed monarchy. In this case, Paine presents an arsenal of Biblical evidence to show that monarchy is neither a natural nor a preferable institution.

Of further interest is the question of what role the biblical arguments play in Paine's own thought. Is Paine's belief that the Bible abhors monarchy central to his belief that America should be independent, or does he merely include a biblical argument to counter opponents who based their ideas on the gospel?

Although he was raised a Quaker, Paine's political beliefs were decidedly secular. His conception of government, especially as presented in the first section of this pamphlet, is largely informed by abstract, liberal, and philosophical speculation, not by religious dogma. Furthermore, Paine generally opposed the mixture of religion and politics, as indicated by his response to the Quakers in the appendix to Common Sense. Still, Paine was acutely aware of the role the Bible played in the minds of his contemporaries, and it is to convince them that he includes the arguments of this section.

In arguing against hereditary succession, Paine exhibits a tendency to rely on a kind of logic known as a false dilemma, wherein only a certain number of explanations for a phenomenon are presented even though other explanations are just as likely.

For example, Paine says that the first king must have been chosen "either by lot, by election, or by usurpation," deliberately ignoring the idea that the king was divinely appointed, a possibility to which many of his contemporaries would have subscribed.

Thompson made a detailed history of the events that took place during the revolution, and of the men who were being celebrated as heroes across the country.

Although compelled to publish this history, he ultimately declined. "No, ought not, for I should contradict all the histories of the great events of the revolution ," "Let the world admire the supposed wisdom and valor of our great men." He said, "I shall not undeceive future generations." Source: Charles Thomson, as recorded by Dr. Benjamin Rush, cited in "Rulers of Evil," by F. Tupper Saussy, p.125

7.7 In the Revolutionary era, Thomas Paine

De marquis de Lafayette said, "A free America without her Thomas Paine is unthinkable." Source: "Inspiration & Wisdom from the Writings of Thomas Paine" by Joseph Lewis, p301

It is Thomas Paine who penned the pamphlet, "Common Sense". Which was the writing which brought about the Declaration of Independence.

In Fact, Thomas Paine wrote in Common Sense ", nothing can settle our affairs so expeditiously as an open and determined declaration for independence,"

The knowledge as shared by the founding Fathers to America, embraced an insight sorely needed upon the human stage. Benjamin Franklin a printer, convinced Thomas Paine to come to America, where his writing style could be used to its maximum potential. Which ultimately resulted in Paine writing Common Sense.

Paine also wrote "The Crisis" pamphlet series which were read aloud by George Washington to his troops.

7.8 Age of Reason Quotes

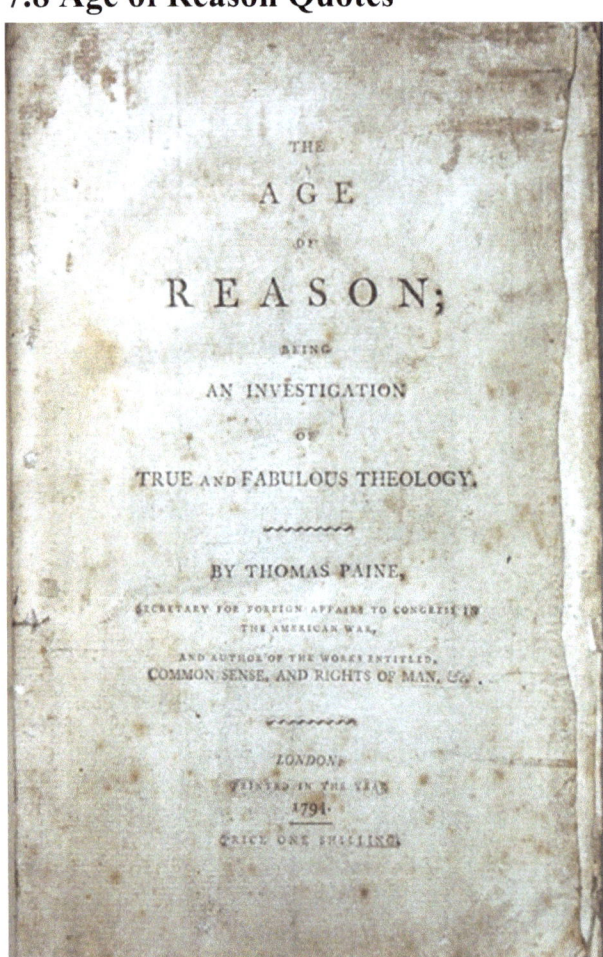

After the revolution was over, he published the entirety of his understanding of Christianity and The Bible, known as the Age of Reason. Wherein he wrote: "When I see throughout the greater part of this book (the Bible) scarcely anything but a history of the grossest vices ," ",and a collection of the most paltry and contemptible tales ," "I cannot dishonor my Creator by calling it by His name." Source: Thomas Paine, "The Truth Seeker Co., 1898 Edition, p.21

Believing in a God not of the Bible. By the evidence as afore mentioned and displayed within the Reports, can one come to agreement where Thomas Paine wrote:

"It is the fable of Jesus Christ as told in the New Testament, and the wild and visionary doctrine raised thereon, against which I contend." Even to agree, that "The story, taking it as it is told, is blasphemously obscene." Source: Thomas Paine, "The Age of Reason, "Truth Seeker Co., 1898 Edition, p.138

Exhibit 67: The Age of Reason Cover

He also wrote: "What is it the Testament teaches us? – to believe that the Almighty committed debauchery with a woman engaged to be married," ",and the belief of this debauchery is called faith." Source: Thomas Paine, "The Age of Reason, "The Truth Seeker Co., 1898 Edition, p.171

Paine also stated:

> "I do not believe in a creed professed by any church that I know of." "My own mind is my church."

Thomas Paine, "The Age of Reason, "The Truth Seeker Co. 1898 Edition, p.6

Since Paine knew source material as in "The Crown Code" and understood how the Divine knowledge was misused in development of the Bible, he wrote:
"it would be more consistent that we called it the word of a demon, than the word of God."
Source: Paine, The Age of reason, The Truth Seeker Co. 1898 Edition, p. 18

He stood by the fact as revealed herein, that Religion is a Fable and a fraud. One need not search long to grasp that George Washington, Thomas Jefferson, Benjamin Franklin, and others understood the philosophical reason the Hidden Matrix provided. Thus, we hold these truths to be self-evident, as established in the Declaration of Independence.

Upon the tombstone of Thomas Paine reads:

> *Thus, Paine's philosophical contribution, was equal to that of George Washington, in fact indispensable in bringing about the American Revolution.*

Paine was first to use the phrase "The United States of America".

7.9 Other Quotes

John Adams voiced that:

> *"When philosophical reason is clear and certain by intuition or necessary induction…." "…no subsequent revelation supported by prophecies or miracles can supersede it."*

Source: John Adams, as cited in "American Philosophy: An Encyclopedia." John Lachs, Robert B. Talisse, p. 164

As per the evidence as displayed through the Crown Code,
"The Christian theory is little less than idolatry of the ancient mythologists…" "…and it yet remains to reason and philosophy to abolish the amphibious fraud." –Thomas Paine, The Age of Reason.

Voltaire:

> *"Christianity is the most ridiculous, the most absurd, and bloody religion that has ever infected the world. "*

(Source: Voltaire. Cited in "Encyclopedia of Ethics." By Lawrence C. Becker, Charlotte B. Becker, Volume 3, p. 1771)

7.10 Original Intent

The reason for The United States of America as established and its founders refrained from claiming foundation on any religion, was in knowing the secrets not known to the masses. Thus, it was unanimously agreed to on the floor of the Senate, during the administration of John Adams for The Barbary Treaties 1786-1816

The Barbary Treaties 1786-1816

Treaty of Peace and Friendship, Signed at Tripoli November 4, 1796

ARTICLE 11. (Drafted by George Washington)
As the government of the United States of America is not in any sense founded on the Christian Religion,-as it has in itself no character of enmity against the laws, religion or tranquility of Musselmen,-and as the said States never have entered into any war or act of hostility against any Mehomitan nation, it is declared by the parties that no pretext arising from religious opinions shall ever produce an interruption of the harmony existing between the two countries.
https://avalon.law.yale.edu/18th_century/bar1796t.asp

7.11   Knowing Origins

John Adams ", ye will say I am no Christian; I say you are no Christians, and there the account is balanced." Source: John Adams, Letter to Thomas Jefferson, Sept 14, 1818
Thomas Jefferson

Thomas Jefferson Quotes

In a letter to General Alexander Smyth, on January 17th, 1825, Jefferson commented on the Book of Revelation. He said:

"It has been between fifty and sixty years since I read it and I then considered it as merely the ravings of a maniac" ", no more worthy nor capable of explanation than the incoherence's of our own nightly dreams"
Thomas Jefferson, Letter to General Alexander Smyth, January 17, 1825

He also wrote:
"And the day will come when the mystical generation of Jesus, by the supreme being as his Father in the womb of a virgin ," ", will be classed with the fable of the generation of Minerva in the brain of Jupiter. But we may hope that the dawn of reason and freedom of thought in these United States will do away with all this artificial scaffolding and restore to us the primitive and genuine doctrines,"
Source: Thomas Jefferson, Letter to John Adams, April 11, 1823.

Rev. Bird Wilson, D.D., LL.D., who was emeritus professor of systematic divinity in the General Theological Seminary of the Protestant Episcopal Church in the United States of America
In a controversial sermon to the unlearned, he preached in 1831 that

"…the founders of our nation were nearly all Infidels…" *"When the war was over , the Constitution was framed, and God was neglected."* *"He was not merely*

forgotten. He was absolutely voted out of the Constitution." "The proceedings, as published by Thompson, the secretary ... show that the question was gravely debated whether God should be in the Constitution or not ..." "... and after a solemn debate he was deliberately voted out of it....'

(Dr. Bird Wilson, as cited by J.E. Remsberg, "Six Historic Americans," p. 120)

He went on to say,

"Those who have been called to administer the government have not been men making any public profession of Christianity..."

Source: Dr. Wilson, as cited by John E. Remsberg, "Six Historic Americans"

The Revolution was not a Christian Revolution. Nowhere do Church leaders establish that it ever was.

In Fact, if they done so, they would have opened themselves to accessories to Fraud. Measures were taken July 4th, 1776 through the Declaration of Independence.

7.12 Declaration of Independence
In Congress, July 4, 1776.

The unanimous Declaration of the thirteen united States of America, When in the Course of human events, it becomes necessary for one people to dissolve the political bands which have connected them with another, and to assume among the powers of the earth, the separate and equal station to which the Laws of Nature and of Nature's God entitle them, a decent respect to the opinions of mankind requires that they should declare the causes which impel them to the separation.

The very term the laws of nature expresses something that seems clearly true, which does not belong to humans, but to nature, whereby we are subject to.

The laws being independent of us, are laws which are evident in the way matter behaves, although abstract. It is through that mysterious mechanism as the Hidden Matrix that we have access to a Platonic realm and a geometric reality, as expression to the Laws of Nature.

The Declaration of Independence contains that theological teaching because the ultimate source of our rights and duties is God. (Which is not the God of Religions) There are four references to God in the Declaration:

The "laws of nature and of nature's God" entitle the United States to independence.
Men are "endowed by their Creator with certain unalienable rights."
Congress appeals "to the Supreme Judge of the world for the rectitude of our intentions."

The signers, "with a firm reliance on the protection of divine Providence," pledge to each other their lives, fortunes, and sacred honor.

The term "nature's God" refers to that which responsible for human (and the rest of) nature being what it is. It is a way of speaking of God insofar as God is knowable by human reason.

In other words, our minds, unassisted by divine revelation, can figure out that there is such a thing as human nature, and that there are laws or rules that we must follow if we are to live justly and well. Reason can see that if we violate those laws, we will suffer such evils as death, slavery, or misery. A New England preacher explained the concept in this way: "The law of nature (or those rules of behavior which the Nature God has given men, . . . fit and necessary to the welfare of mankind) is the law and will of the God of nature, which all men are obliged to obey. . . . The law of nature, which is the Constitution of the God of nature, is universally obliging. It varies not with men's humours or interests but is immutable as the relations of things."
(Abraham Williams, Election Sermon, Boston 1762.)

Again, the original conception idea for America, was that the Hidden Matrix aka The Crown Code Truth (Natures God), would be revealed as a Landscape idea, on the virgin soil, (not riddled with religious structures nefariously conceived of the Hidden Matrix), laying down the foundations of a New World Idea, (Separate from the old error, of the Church and religion) and the Architectural expression therein/thereon out of The Hidden

Matrix Design... would represent the manifesting, or materialization of the pattern and design, upon a New World 'experiment' whereby America would be of absolute TRUTH as the Creator intended. An expression of the pattern as a 'living experiment' created by man.

But we may hope that the dawn of reason and freedom of thought in these United States as Thomas Jefferson wrote to John Adams, will do away with all this artificial scaffolding and restore to us the primitive and genuine doctrines

That as understood through the Hidden Matrix, herein established, and revealed by Baron Gabriel Espinosa.

In George Washington's Inaugural Address of 1789, what he knew to be true, became recognized by the following, wherein my comments are in brackets [..]:

> *Such being the impressions under which I have, in obedience to the public summons, repaired to the present station; [thereafter the conscience shift inoculated by Pains Age of Reason, instilled the need to form a better union, separate from the previous monarchial systems.] it would be peculiarly improper to omit in this first official Act, my fervent supplications to that Almighty Being who rules over the Universe, [evident by the Hidden Matrix, also known as the Crown Code] who [Countenance upon said knowledge] presides in the Councils of Nations, and whose providential aids can supply every human defect, [referring to it as the foundation formula to everything] that his benediction may consecrate to the liberties and happiness of the People of the United States, a Government instituted by themselves for these essential purposes: [established to reveal such truth upon the earth for all mankind] and may enable every instrument employed in its administration to execute with success, the functions allotted to his charge. [whereby by the public's desire, America's sole purpose was toward that better world, and the true American dream] In tendering this homage to the Great Author of every public and private good [where by the Hidden Matrix also known as the Crown Code must be*

recognized as source knowledge to all that is] I assure myself that it expresses your sentiments not less than my own; nor those of my fellow citizens at large, less than either. [whereby its truth resonate and it at the very foundation of all people as a whole] No People can be bound to acknowledge and adore the invisible hand, which conducts the Affairs of men more than the People of the United States. [which is to say, that the truth as provided by the Hidden Matrix i.e. Crown Code, that tool of Providential guidance through that natural spiritual essence, should not be shackled to ideological definitions, in the affairs of humanity] Every step, by which they have advanced to the character of an independent nation, seems to have been distinguished by some token of providential agency. [That distinction, which has been by those types and images influenced by the providential agency of the Hidden Matrix and its knowledge.] And in the important revolution just accomplished in the system of their United Government, the tranquil deliberations and voluntary consent of so many distinct communities, from which the event has resulted, cannot be compared with the means by which most Governments have been established, [The system of the United States was established by the voluntary consent of the people, which is different than systems forced upon a populous in the development or shall we say the conquering and proselytizing of the native populations.] without some return of pious gratitude [which is to say, that the likeness in the religious expression is founded upon the same details as revealed upon that Providential truth as what the Hidden Matrix provides] along with an humble anticipation of the future blessings which the past seem to presage. These reflections, arising out of the present crisis, have forced themselves too strongly on my mind to be suppressed. You will join with me I trust in thinking, that there are none under the influence of which, the proceedings of a new and free Government can more auspiciously commence.

25.13 INJECTED INFLUENCE

Aside from the long-held tradition of Catholic manipulation of truth, any efforts in interjecting a view different than what George Washington's convictions held, and expressed within his Inaugural address, would be evidence of usurpation of intent considering the secret of the Hidden Matrix and its details understood by the former President of the United States prior to his death on December 14, 1799.

Here we see evidence of wrongful or criminal deception intended to result in financial gain and or ideological preference toward and by the Catholic Church. The following claim was published with the intended result at deceiving the general population at large, by unjustifiably claiming the convention of George Washington to Catholicism, by crediting the act or accomplishment through a Father Leonard Neale, S.J.

PHOTO 1: Excerpt for Denver Register

From the Denver Register, February 24, 1957 was published:

SLAVES HELD WASHINGTON DIED BAPTIZED CATHOLIC New York- It was a long tradition among both the Maryland Province Jesuit Fathers and the Negro slaves of the Washington plantation, and those of the surrounding area that the first President died a Catholic. These and other facts about George Washington, are reported in the Paulist INFORMATION magazine by Doran Hurley.

The story is that Father Leonard Neale, S.J, was called to Mount Vernon from St. Mary's Mission across the Piscatawney River, four hours before Washington's death. Tradition also holds, that shortly after Washington's death, Father Neale sent a heavily sealed packet to Rome. If this be true, it may yet turn up in the Vatican archives, or it may have been lost during the Jesuits' hidden years.

Washington's body servant Juba is authority for the fact, that the General made the Sign of the Cross at meals. He may have learned this from his Catholic lieutenants, Stephen Moylan, or John Fitzgerald. At Valley Forge, Washington forbade the burning in effigy of the Pontiff on "Pope's Day." Several times as President he is reported to have slipped into a Catholic church, to hear Sunday Mass.

To those in the know, having the burning in effigy of the Pope would have not been beneficial in allowing the Catholic church to reveal itself as fraudulent.
LIKE-KIND ALLOWANCES

7.14 The First Architect

Dr. William Thornton educated at The University of Edinburgh was an amateur architect who is honored as the "first architect" because his design for the U.S. Capitol was accepted by President George Washington in 1793. He received $500 and a building lot in the city of Washington for his composition. He held no government position because of winning the architectural competition.

The University of Edinburgh (abbreviated as Edin. in post-nominals), founded in 1582, is the sixth oldest university in the English-speaking world and one of Scotland's ancient universities. The university has five main campuses in the city of Edinburgh, with many of the buildings in the historic Old Town belonging to the university. The university played an important role in leading Edinburgh to its reputation as a chief intellectual centre during the Age of Enlightenment and helped give the city the nickname of the Athens.

The age of enlightenment included without doubt, the awakening of minds to the reality of the underlying truth of the Hidden Matrix as the Crown Code used by the Church, and in the antiquities was known as the Pattern and Totalities.

Designs around Washington derived from usage of the Hidden Matrix as ancient Greece and Rome did, that would evoke the ideals that guided the nation's founders as they framed their new republic.

EIGHT

SECRET OF THE APOTHEOSIS

8 Enters Brumidi

In early 1854 as the wings and the dome were being built, he heard that Captain Montgomery Cunningham Meigs engineer and the one in charge of the construction to the U.S. Capitol, was looking for an artist that could paint frescos in the capitol, like Michelangelo, Rafael, similar to the renaissance. Constantino Brumidi approached the Captain about the work.

Explaining that he studied at the Academy of St. Luke in Rome, and had painted several Roman palaces, among them being that of Prince Torlonia, and for Pope Gregory XVI, by working for the Vatican for three years.

He was also one of Pope Pius IX favorite painters and was commissioned to do the Popes official portrait. Another influence upon Burmidi was Vincenzo Camuccini who was appointed inspector-general of the Museums of the Pope, and of the Factory of Mosaics, and director of the Neapolitan Academy of Rome.

He was a member of the Institute of France, during some year's president of the Academy of St. Luke. Pope Pius VII conferred upon him, the title of Baron, with hereditary succession, and the Emperor Francis I, the order of the Iron Crown.

Showing his ability by doing a fresco in Captain Meigs office, President Franklin Pierce, senators, and congressmen all had chance at watching him work and were impressed with his work. After approval to get paid to do the entire room, and after Meigs had Burmidi start designing many more rooms in the Capitol, but protest ensued, complaints that it was foreign began, and why weren't their American artists doing the work? Meigs explained to the American party (nicknamed, the no nothing party) who had many people in congress, as well as in newspaper publication affiliations, that there was no other option, due no American artist could do a proper fresco.

As a backstory to Burmidi, he came to the united states in 1852, he had planned to come to America, after talking to American clergyman who were studying in Rome.

During the time of immigration and by the 1840's, new Catholic communities were developed, thus the need for the building big churches. Which led to his conversations about him coming to America to about St. Stevens in New York, which was planned, where he could paint the altar piece in the church. What developed in Rome caused an interruption of plans about St. Stevens.

8.1 Plan of Pope Pius IX

Being liberal, Pope Pius IX set up a civic guard required of all men to serve. Burmudi was a captain in the guard, where he allowed some freedom of the press, which evolved into people wanting to be independent and a republic, where they would not be under the Pope, but would rule themselves. Crowds grew larger till the Pope fled the city. In 1849 the people declared a Roman republic, embroiling Burmudi. The re public was going to put troops into a monastery and a convent. Burmudi claimed that he was trying to keep things safe and took things out of the monastery and convent.

After the Pope was restored to power, Pope Pius IX embraced his predecessors view on revolution and democracy as dangerous, which was understandable being Pope Gregory lived through the French Revolution and the Age of Napoleon, Gregory XVI viewed revolution and democracy as dangerous, and became committed to suppressing these expressions of liberalism.

Pope Pius IX understood the threat democracy posed to the Church, and thus a renewed ardent adherent to conservatism and fierce opponents of democracy. Thus, a crackdown ensued, against all that had any involvement with the revolution.

They were being imprisoned, which included Burmidi who was accused of many crimes, such as stealing from the monastery and convent, which included raping of nuns and such. Although in his defense, he did provide testimony of monks and others, which did not help, and he was convicted and sentenced to eighteen years in prison.

The excuse that he was going to leave Rome anyway, as a reason for his pardon, that he could come to America is lacking. His exile in 1852, set in motion, fulfilment of the deal he made with the Vatican.

We must understand that his grooming to the hidden mysteries of the Church, and that unique insight shared while a student of Vincenzo Camuccini and during at his employ with Prince Torlonia, Pope Gregory and under Pope Pius IX. His application for citizenship was applied for and was issued five years later in 1857.

When you look at the Apotheosis, have you ever asked yourselves the purpose of the designer? Have you even noticed it?

8.2 Applying the Secret

The numerical blueprint as provided by the Vatican, gave Brumidi liberty in personified expressions, becoming allegories representing prospects for the Unites States.
He painted the Apotheosis of Washington, in one year, right after the civil war in 1866.
The strategy of creating evidence which at best would ensure protection of the Catholic Church, from all future actions through enlightenment goals, The Apotheosis of Washington, amongst other works would work perfect. 1n 1776 less than 1% of the Unites States population were Catholic, but grew rapidly after 1840 with immigration from Germany, Ireland, and Italy.

The influence religion has played in politics, drives, and can affect their electability, shape their stances on policy matters and their visions of society and how they want to lead it. As a guarantee of religious stronghold upon the nation, the following became by the numerical blueprint provided.

8.3 Founding Number Parts

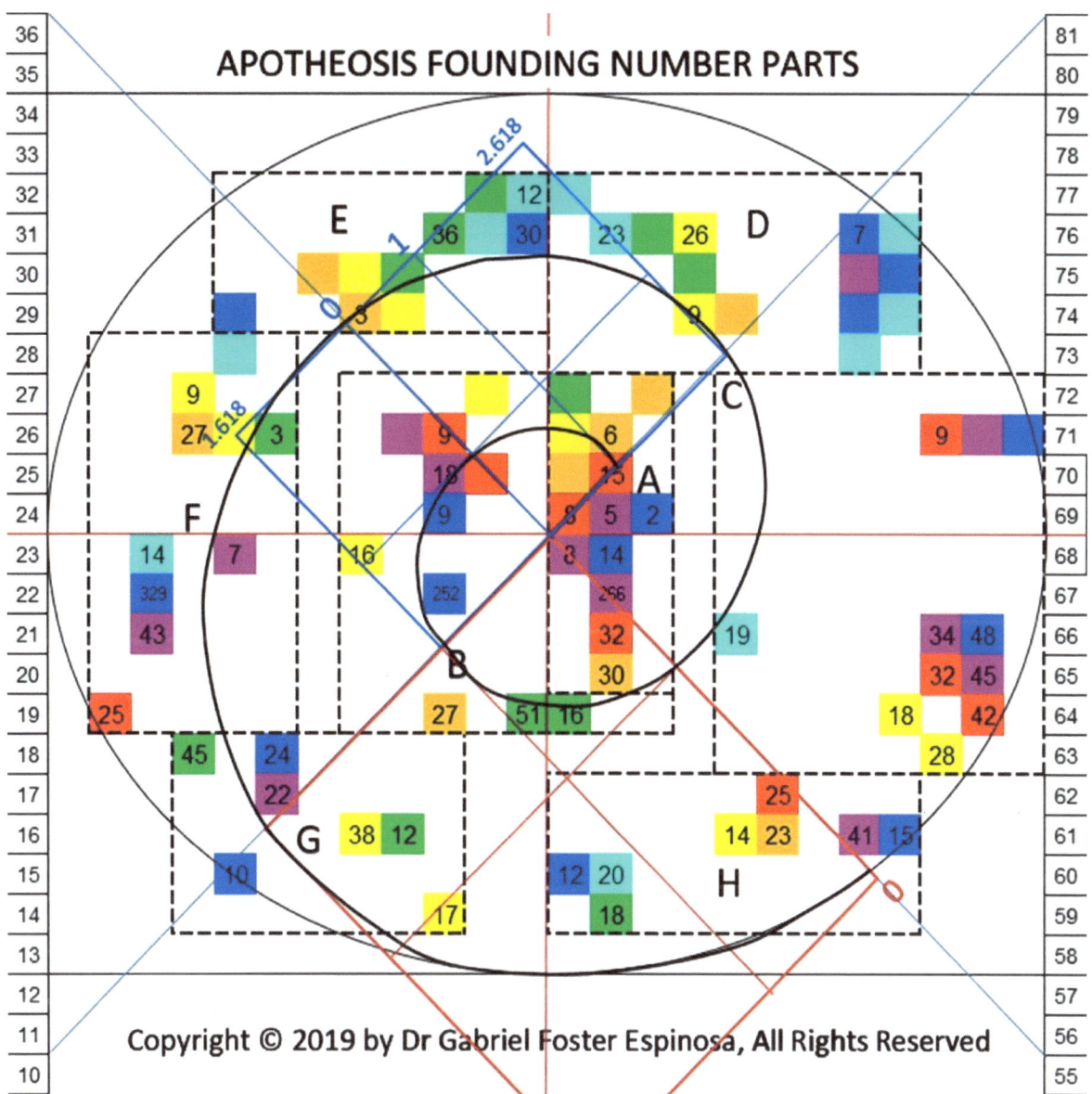

Exhibit 68: Apotheosis Founding Number Parts by Baron Gabriel Foster Espinosa

Knowing that the Hidden Matrix numbers are immovable, foundation to the Apotheosis was needed.

Holding true to formula foundation as seen, we can establish that the Apotheosis field is divided into eight sections, beginning at centre each part follows the golden spiral path as A, B, C, D, E, F, G, and H.

Each number grouping for each section, express a significance in relation to the "Hidden Matrix / Crown Code" knowledge.

All Burmudi needed to do was to associate allegorical reference to each section as provided upon master grid.

8.4. George with Liberty and Freedom

Exhibit 69: George liberty and Freedom Coordinate

Beginning with (A) Burmudi needed to place George Washington as the Father of Our Country here under the law of ten. The reference upon the Hidden Matrix seen below is 33 at black bordered square.

The significance here is the ascending (Passage) quality of the 7 numbers which sit upon 33. Flanked by the allegorical figures of Liberty and Freedom provide allusion to that Liberty of Passage. 33 by 10 is 330. Below are 33 centers, where rite of passage is by knowledge of ascension, by adding the 7 numbers 6,123, 6, 483, 30, 12, 1nd 6 for the ascended number of 666.

Exhibit 70: Passage and Thought by Baron Gabriel Foster Espinosa

The French rituals designate a treble present of the letters L.\ D.\ P.". as the initials of 'liberie de passer', or liberty of passage. Others have proposed to interpret these letters as liberie de penser, liberty of thought, the prerogative of a freeman and a Freemason.

The ascending quality or liberty of passage upon the founding number parts are considered the connecting 15 of the right quadrant field of what can be called Saint Andrews cross to 18 of field B. Here it receives that liberty of passage by fanning to the left upon verticle grid to reveal the one which has liberty to pass. 15 and 18 equal 33.

He is surrounded by vignettes, extolling the virtues of American invention and forward-looking progress.

Exhibit 71: Sections A-B
George Washington is surmounted by thirteen allegorical figures, each which represent a dual purpose, establish a hidden meaning. One can say, which is currently understood, that each represent one of the thirteen original colonies.

The esoteric meaning provides a broader interpretation. Notice that the thirteen allegorical figures are all facing frontward except one which faces opposite. From left counting each figure, results in 10. The eleventh figure is the backward facing one, which followed by two forward facing figures.

This tells us that George Washington here represents the 13th, surrounded by the twelve. The two forward facing figures next to the backward facing one, represents the hidden knowledge of 11:11 or figure 11 and the two as one and one. Note, that its total collective expression, establishes core goal ascension of 666.

8.5 Section C- Allegory of War

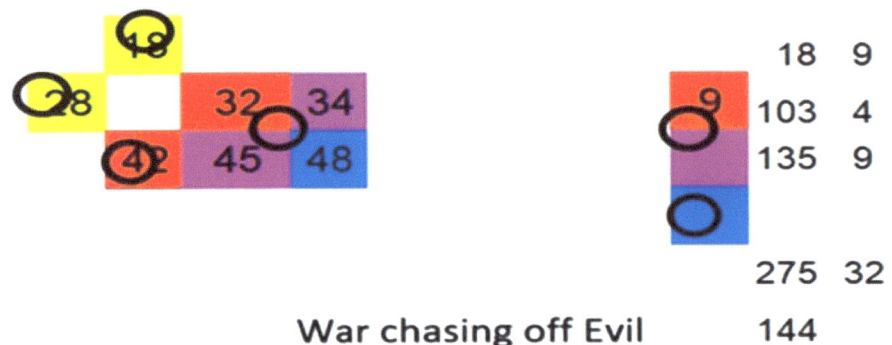

War chasing off Evil

Photo 35: Allegory of War   *Exhibit 72: Incarnation Fight*

88

The hidden meaning per the Hidden Matrix, is archetype energy awakening to itself in totality of 144, mandate is to ascend, yet it battles against forces of evil, as that going into matter, by that pulling effect in lower number development representing the gravity of the physical realm.

Exhibit 73: Battle against Ascension.

He placed the face of Jefferson Davis, president of the Confederacy as Discord, and his vice president, Alexander Stephens as Anger.

Photo 2: Struggle against Freedom

8.6 Section D-Ceres

Ceres, goddess of the harvest seated on a McCormick Reaper, one of America's great harvest inventions. Ceres, the Roman goddess of the harvest and grain, was the one who taught lowly mankind how to preserve and prepare corn and grain once it was ready for threshing. In many areas, she was a mother-type goddess who was responsible for agricultural fertility.

Photo 3: Ceres sitting upon reaper.

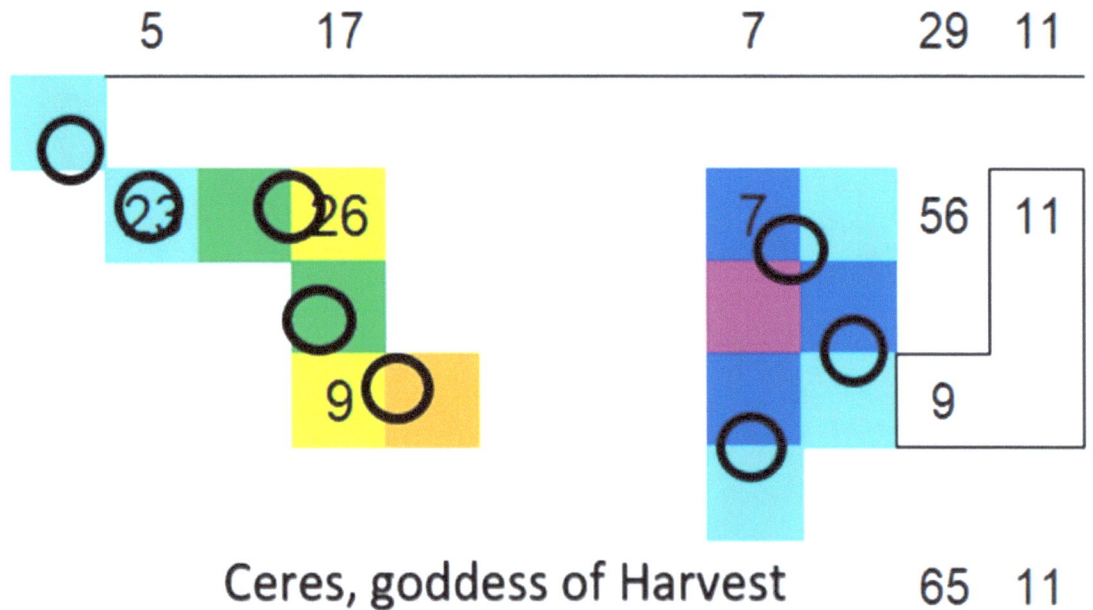

Exhibit 74: Ceres upon the Reaper and Coordinate numbers.

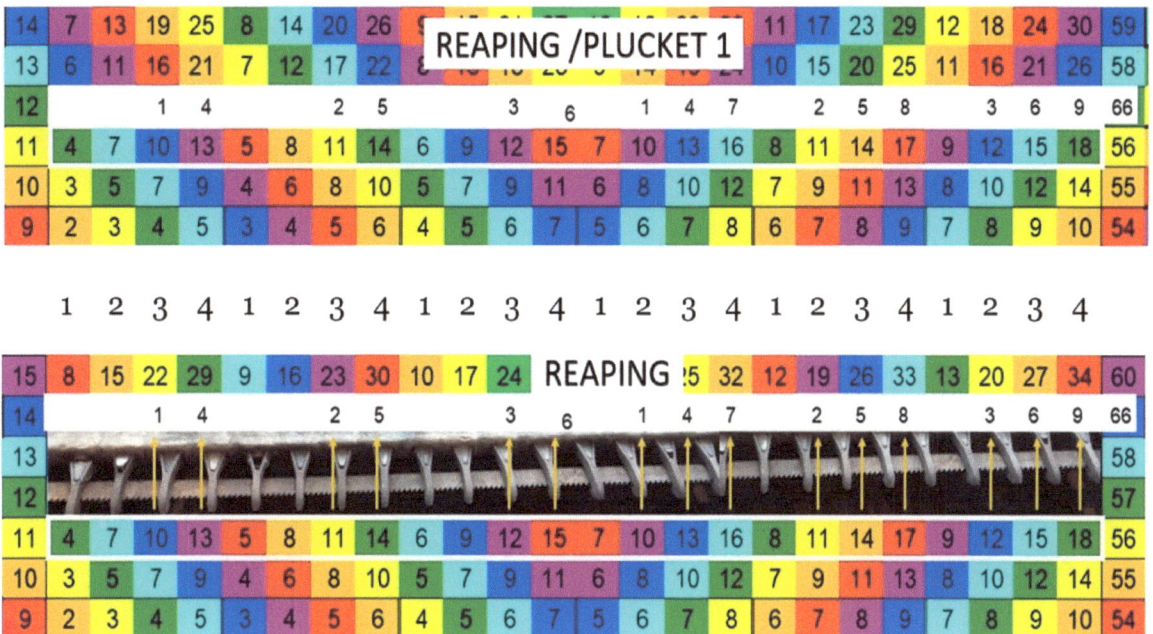

Exhibit 75: Numbers Reaped by Baron Gabriel Foster Espinosa

Here Ceres original conception is applied to the Reaper, representing likeness in process in number revelation. Guide 56 yellow at right and guide 11 yellow, at left are united causing 67, 2 of 11 is deducted leaving 65. The total polarized as 66 reaped 1.

8.7 Section E - Vulcan, the Forge

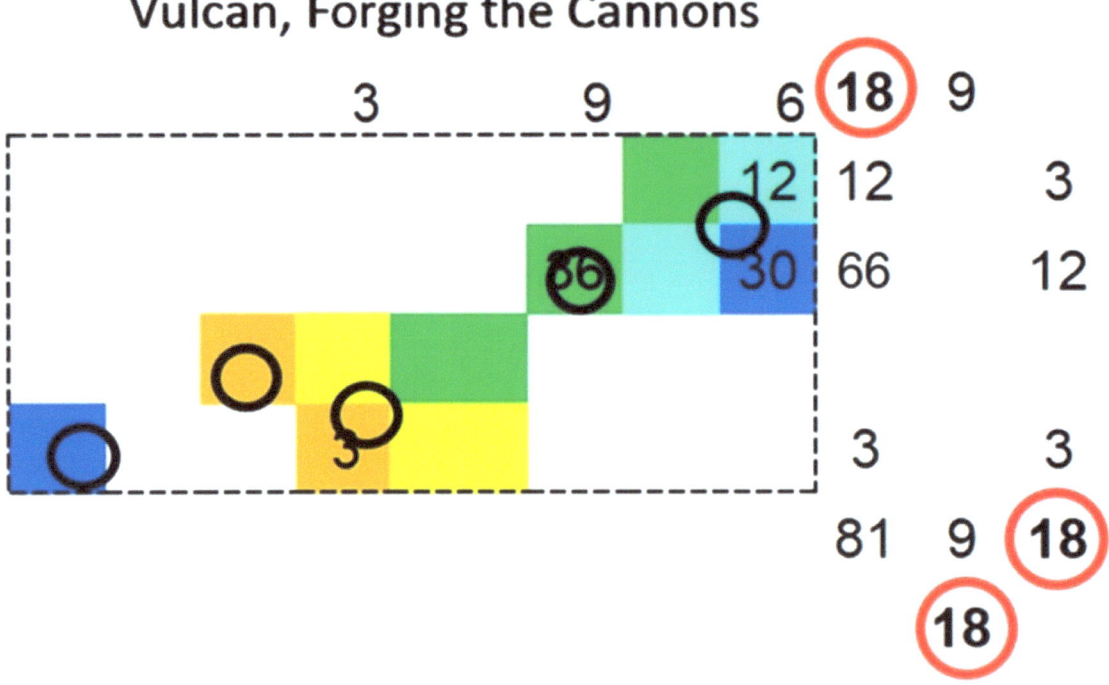

Exhibit 76: Vulcan Number Coordinate

Shown here is Vulcan forging the cannons that would become the core of the artillery for the Union Army. The hidden, or shall I say the underlying reference to cannon likeness, or that which is defined in matter. Notice the 18's and the 81 upon the Vulcan number Coordinate. The four numbers all polarize to 9. The significance is the following:

Exhibit 77: Vulcan Forging likeness

The founding number to each corner as expressed upon the crown code are 9's. The corners are comprised of 18's.

Vulcan (Latin: Volc*f*Ånus or Vulc*f*Ånus is the god of fire including the fire of volcanoes, deserts, metalworking, and the forge in ancient Roman religion and myth. He is often depicted with a blacksmith's hammer.

Vulcan belongs to the most ancient stage of Roman religion, due its relationship as metallurgy through-out the four corners (18's) of earth (with the circle upon square representing fire) upon the Matrix.

The four corners, here are allegorically established as the forging of cannons, where total men including Vulcan are four. The horizontal center 18's become the cannon balls established for use.

Varro the ancient Roman scholar and writer, citing the Annales Maxima records that king Titus Tatius dedicated altars to a series of deities including Vulcan.[3]

8.8 Section F- Mercury

Mercury the god of commerce, is seen presiding over America's bounty and paying the financiers of the American Revolution. A group of people posing for the camera.

Photo 39: Mercury *Exhibit 78: Mercury Number Coordinate*

The essence of Mercury subliminally provides coordinate to the Caduceus. The whole total being left to right provides 457 as seen at section F. The polarized sums of 33 and 8 are added to its base essence for 498. The single ascending quality as in the Caduceus held by Mercury, absorbs single digit totals of 61 and 11 or 72 for 570.

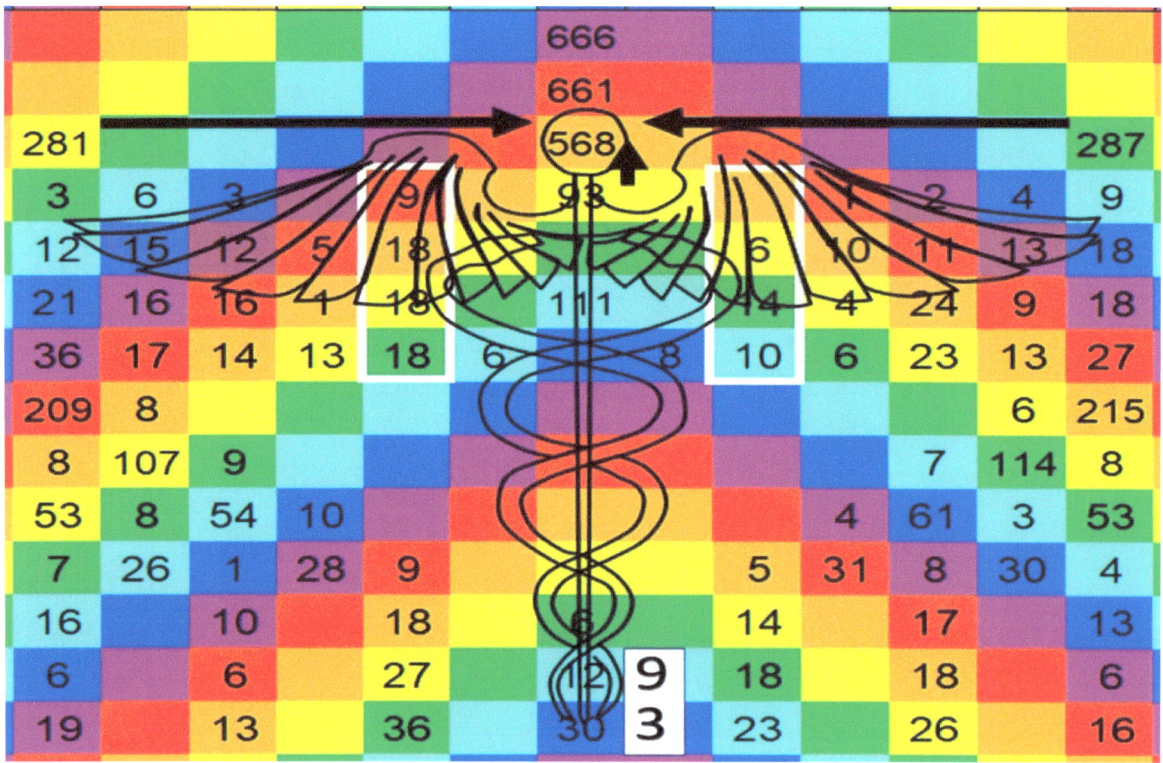

Exhibit 79: Caduceus Coordinate by Baron Gabriel Foster Espinosa

The paying is symbolized by the financier numbers of 43 and 25 where each side make claim. The secret is in their numbers which are 7 from 4+3 and 7 of 2+5. Each represent the day of rest, as 7's. Whereby their payment is due.

The payment is calculated as 7 plus 3 for each side of Mercury, which is polarized to 1 each (symbolic of the shekel) The result is 2 from 570 becoming 568, location and coordinate to the Caduceus of Mercury seen upon the crown Code. Mercury (Mercurius) was the Roman god of commerce, conceived as likeness to Matrix development process where 281 and 287 unite as high profits. 93 below the 568 unite establishing message of 661, whereat also developed are wings of flight.

Core to Matrix was understood as the realm of deity development. The outer areas became that part which defined mortals, and the material world, where character defined was as mediator between the gods and mortals.

His patron of circulation designation is due numeric foundation addition (as giving) to what becomes the circle upon the square. Like Hermes, he escorted the dead to the underworld. Also, one narrative describes Zeus punishing Lara for telling Hera, that Zues loved a Motral woman named Juturna (The Circle) by wrenching out her indiscreet tongue.

Hermes was ordered to take her to Hades (The outer area) as she was to become an infernal Nymph.

While escorting the nymph Lara to Pluto's realm, Hermes (Mercury) fathered the twin Lares, who guard the crossroads and keep watch over the city. (A temple honoring him was built around 495 BCE and stood on the southwest slope of Aventine Hill near the Circus Maximus of Rome).

8.9 Section G- Neptune

Neptune who is there with one of the ironclads, the ships that changed the face of naval warfare during the Civil War. And Venus, who was laying the Transatlantic Cable.

Exhibit 80: Neptune Coordinate

Neptune is god of the sea in Roman mythology, a brother of Jupiter and Pluto. He is analogous but not identical to the god Poseidon of Greek mythology. Roman conception of Neptune owed a great deal to the Etruscan god Nethuns. Originally, he was an Italic god paired with Salacia, possibly the goddess of the salt water. At an early date (399 BC) he was identified with Poseidon, when the Sibylline books ordered a lectisternium in his honor (Livy v. 13).

Neptune is holding the trident, rules over rivers and streams upon the Matrix, has Venus as the earliest known Roman recipient of a taurobolium (a form of bull sacrifice) is assisting in laying conduit toward Neptune being recognized, toward gaining power over the four corners of earths seas (168), represented by the allegorical four figures.

8.10 Section H-Minerva

Minerva, the 'virgin goddess' of Wisdom, shown with three of America's most prominent inventors. Benjamin Franklin, Samuel B. Morse, and Robert Fulton.

Originally, Minerva was an Italian goddess of handicrafts strongly associated to the Greek goddess Athena. The scholarly consensus, however, is that Minerva was indigenous, passing to the Romans from the Etruscan goddess Menrva, and that her name derives from meminisse, meaning 'to remember'. Considered the daughter of Jupiter, from whose head she was born, the goddess was first worshipped in Rome as one of the Capitoline Triad along with Jupiter and Juno.

Exhibit 81: Minerva Coordinate by Baron Gabriel Foster Espinosa

By common definition, all parts show the history of the Roman Republic as the precursor to American Democracy and presents George Washington as presiding over the values that at mid-century defined the hopes for this nation.

The hidden and Esoteric definitions establish a deeper and more accurate reality of interpretation. 168 as Minerva holding a spear, here represents those 'twelve darting lines' toward centre of the Matrix as the spear, and her embracing of strategic influence over the whole as that encircling, yet invisible boundary.

8.11 APOTHEOSIS PARTS

Representing the Treble of 666

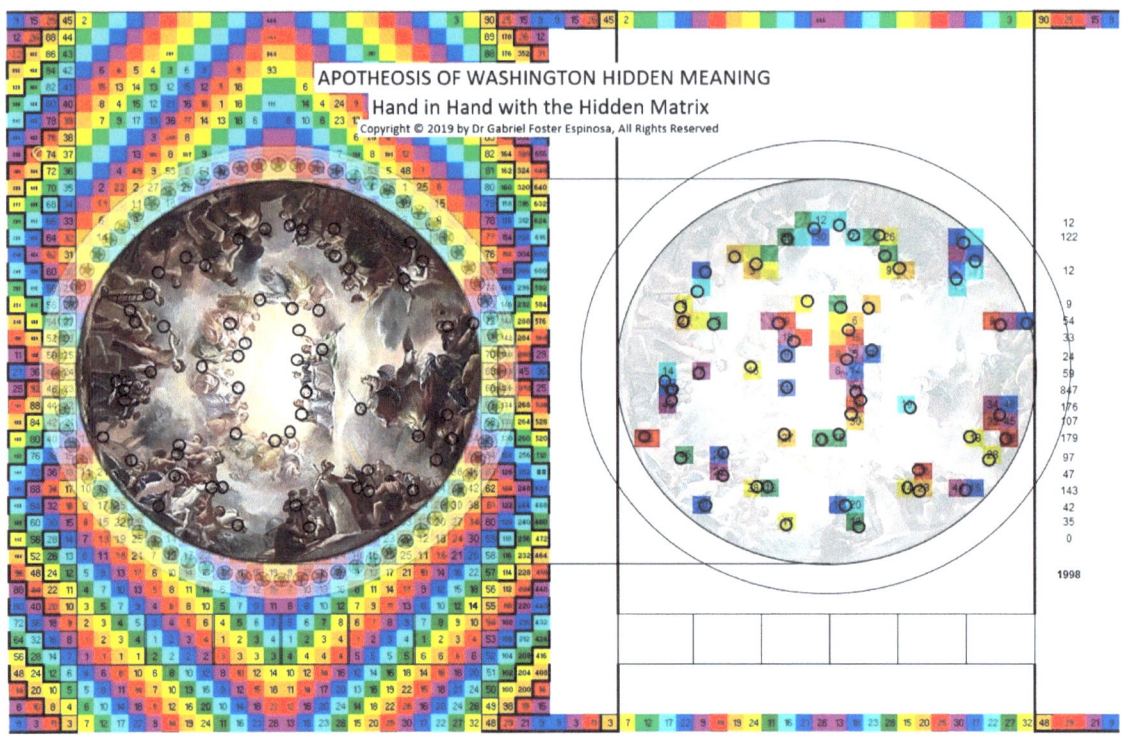

Exhibit 82: Apotheosis Revealed Numbers

Inside the Capitol Dome, the Apotheosis of Washington is encircled by a ring or 'gate' of 72 stars, a 'stargate'. Note that there are 24 squares to each of the three levels, in total there are 72 squares, not you know why they are inside and surround the Apotheosis.

Aside from The United States Capitol dome which is 288 feet in height and 96 feet (29 m) in diameter was designed by Thomas U. Walter, the fourth Architect of the Capitol, and constructed between 1855 and 1866.

288 was significant, being that it was the total sum from the first three levels upon The Hidden Matrix.

Exhibit 83: Capitol Dome Height by Baron Gabriel Foster Espinosa

NINE

OWL KNOWING

The owl is known in mythology as a sign of wisdom, in connection to the Hidden Matrix Code. In Greek myths, it was connected to the goddess of wisdom, Minerva. Original owl wisdom association to the Hidden Matrix was rotating Pattern of Matrix one quarter turn.

Photo 4: The Burney Relief

The Burney Relief was discovered around 1924 in southern Iraq, passed via various collectors and later sent to the British Museum in London. It gained public's attention in 1936 when a full-page reproduction was shown in The Illustrated London News.

Although it may or not be Ishtar, it dates to around 1800 BCE. The hidden secret is revealed through the owls and her talons. Notice the visible appendages to each foot, each have 6, to represent 666. Thus, the owl in treble became the symbol of wisdom.

9 United States Capitol Grounds

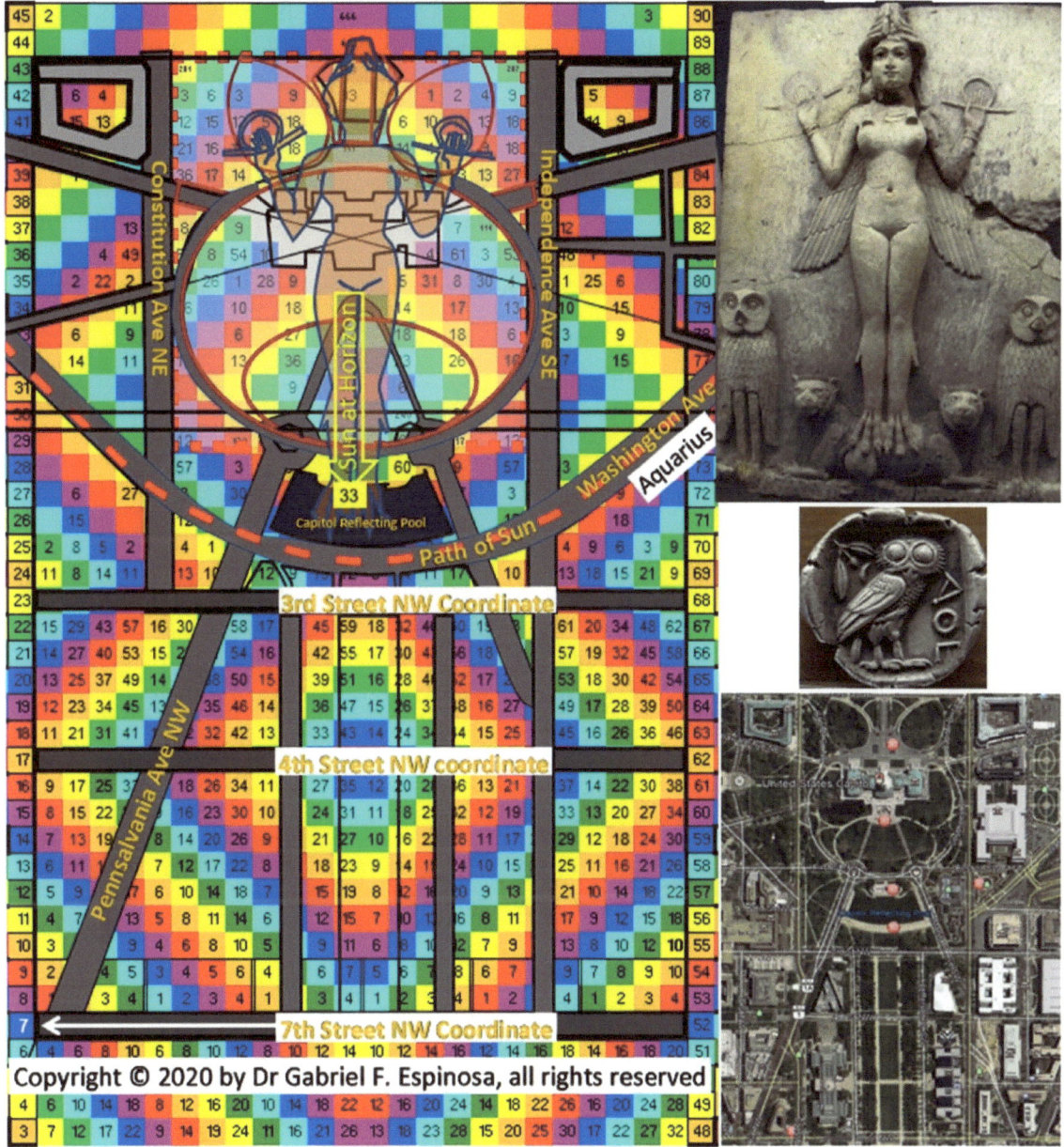

Exhibit 84: US Capitol Grounds Knowledge by Baron Gabriel Espinosa

Before gods, goddesses, evil omens, demons, nocturnal monsters of the netherworld were depicted as humans, they were almost always shown in some type of animal form.

This ancient network of immortal symbolism as with the Hittites, Sumerians, Egyptians, Ethiopians, Africans, Phoenicians (Hebrews), Greeks, Romans, Europeans, Arabs, Hindus, Indians and Latinos, we can witness today with one of these secret deities that has been depicted throughout the course of human history as a nocturnal bird of prey, that bird of night, that to them was not a symbol of wisdom, but the creature who disturbs their sleep and is the "angel of death." also known as the owl.

The Egyptian name for the owl is Mulak or Moloch, represented by the letter symbolism of M (m) because its name began with M, and the eyes or horns of this secret deity looks just like the letter m.

The "Residence Act" of 1790 provided that the federal government should be established in a permanent location by the year 1800. In early March 1791, the Commissioners of the City of Washington, who had been appointed by President George Washington, selected the French engineer Pierre Charles L'Enfant to plan the new federal city.

L'Enfant decided to locate the U.S. Capitol at the elevated east end of the Mall (on what was then called Jenkins' Hill); he described the site as "a pedestal waiting for a monument." Pierre Charles L'Enfant was a military engineer born in Paris on 2 August 1754 to Pierre L'Enfant, a painter who served King Louis XV, and Marie L'Enfant

L'Enfant studied art under his father at the Royal Academy of Painting and Sculpture from 1771 until he enlisted in 1776.

9.1 DENVER STATE CAPITOL CODE

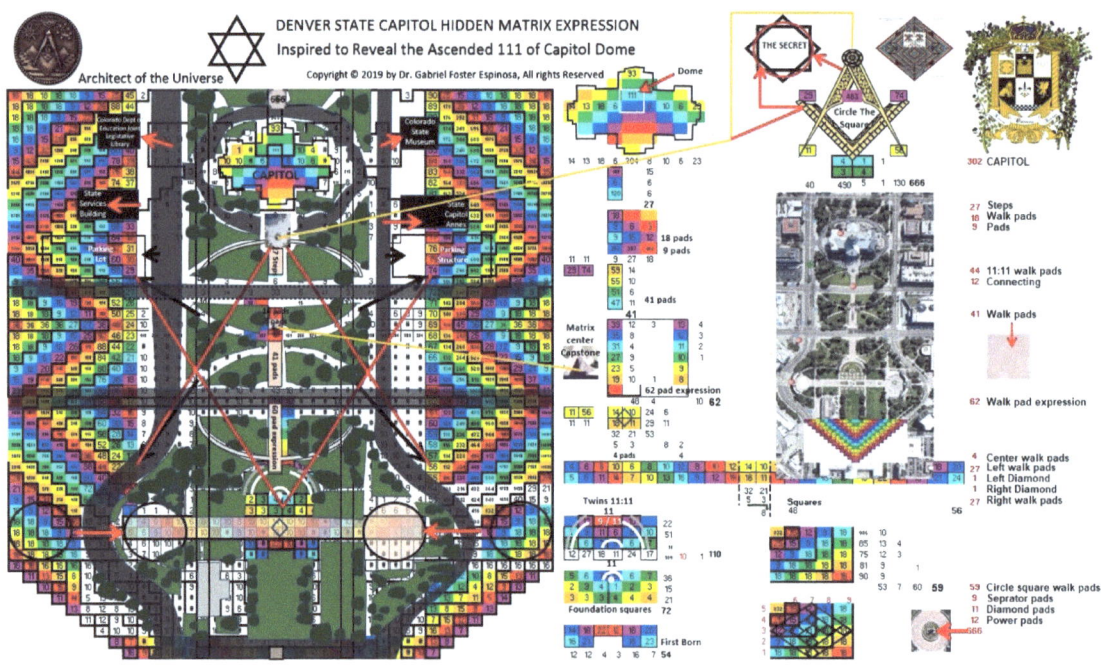

Exhibit 85: Denver State Capitol Coordinate by Baron Gabriel Espinosa

The Practice of using the details of the great secret in displaying underlying form and features, can be seen all over the world. The question is, in what fashion was it used.

There is no question, that it was meant to be used, for the betterment of mankind, and life administration, yet unfortunately by some it has been used nefariously.

Above the Denver State Capitol Code. Although to the common mind, it would appear, that each part was constructed at different times. What most have failed to recognize, is that endeavors meant for public administration, have been shaped by those in the know of this knowledge. Here the secret is held by the walking pads upon the ground scheme.

9.2 CHRYSLER BUILDING CODE

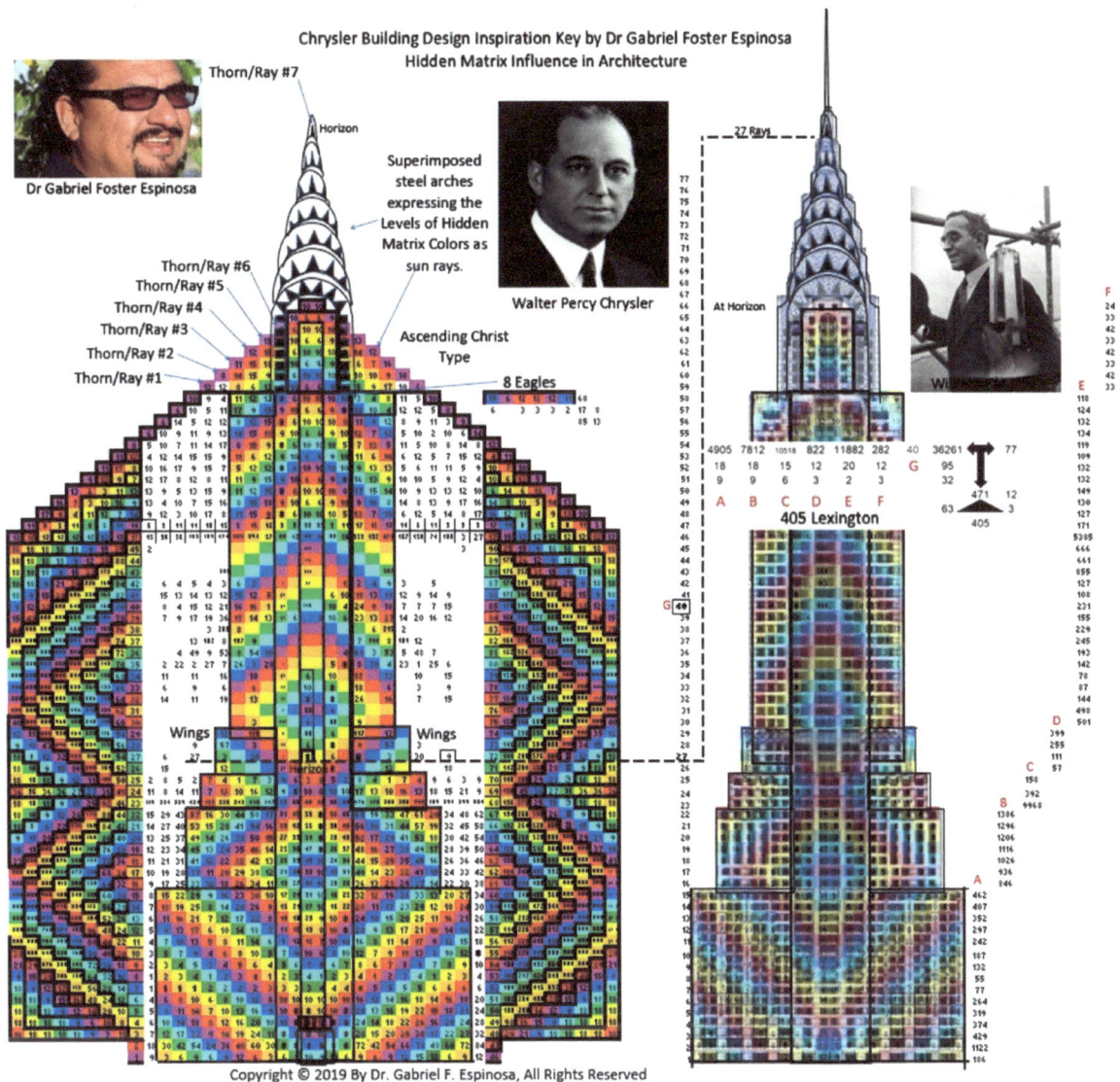

Exhibit 86: *Chrysler Building Adaption by Baron Gabriel Espinosa*

William Van Alen was born in Brooklyn, New York, on August 10th, 1883. His father died when he was a child, and his mother eventually remarried a hardware merchant. When he was 16, he started working for a notable architect, Clarence True.

True developed many row houses on the Upper West Side of Manhattan. While working as an office boy for True, Van Alen attended the Pratt Institute.

Van Alen also studied under Emmanuel Louis Masqueray, which exposed him to the stylings of the Beaux-Arts School of Architecture, named after a famous school in Paris, that taught a neoclassical style.

In 1908, at the age of 25, Van Alen won the Paris Prize scholarship. The Paris Prize is a tremendous honor for any architect. This award led him to Paris and to continue his studies at the École des Beaux-Arts.

The 1,046-foot Chrysler Building was the tallest building in the world, from 1930 to 1931 and was part of an intense race for this title. In 1928, developer William H. Reynolds hired William Van Alen, to design the world's tallest building for a site leased at the northeast corner of Lexington Avenue and 42nd Street, across from Grand Central Station which had been conceived out of Hidden Matrix details coordinate to 405 Lexington Ave.

Later that year, Reynolds sold both lease and plans to Walter P. Chrysler, who wanted to build a new headquarters for the Chrysler Corporation. Van Alen altered the plans to reflect his new patron: a domed lantern became a metal clad spire; the frieze on the 30th floor became a line of hubcaps; new gargoyles were enormous, Chrysler Eagle radiator caps; fenders and hood ornaments became part of the decoration.

9.3 WORLD TRADE CENTER CODE

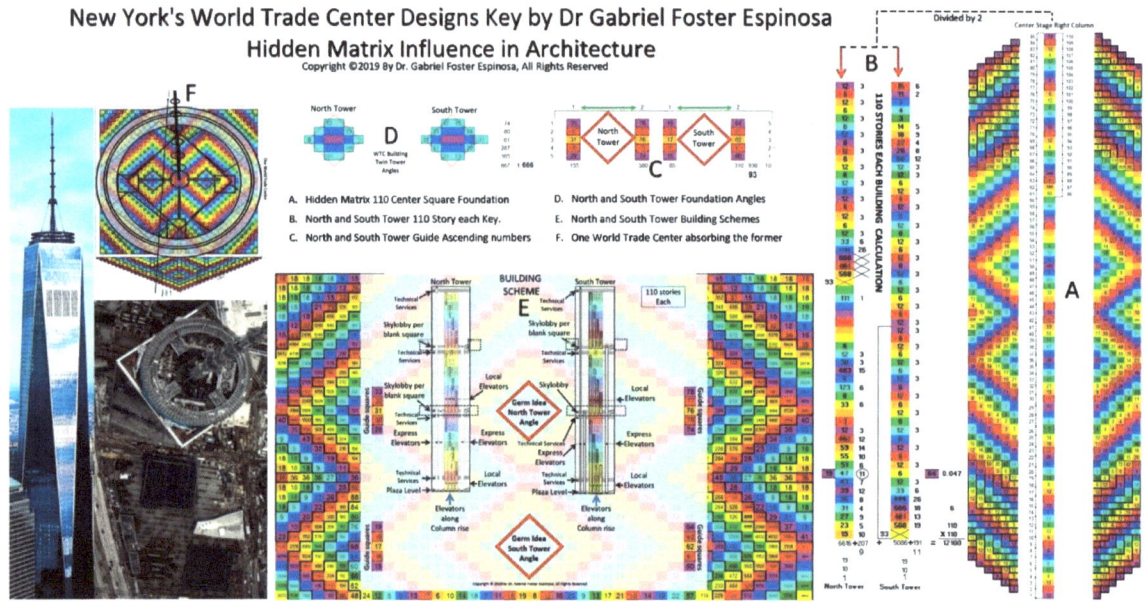

Exhibit 87: World Trade Center Hidden Matrix Influence

The Port Authority announced the selection of Minoru Yamasaki as lead architect and Emery Roth & Sons as associate architects.[31] Yamasaki easily influenced by Roth & Sons by suggestion devised the plan to incorporate twin towers.

The Father to Emery Roth & Sons, had designed the first of the twin-towered residential skyscrapers, at 145 and 146 Central Park West called the San Remo and Last of the twin-towered residences the Normandy at 140 Riverside Drive, Manhattan, which became Roth's choice for his retirement apartment.

9.4   140 RIVERSIDE DRIVE

Photo 5: Emery Roth Preference
The reason for Emery Roth's retirement apartment location choice, was that he designed it using the Hidden Matrix. The first 15 floors represent the first fifteen levels from basement in coordinate with Matrix detail.

Floor 16 represents the sum of all 15 levels as the totalities level. Floor 17 as seen upon picture exhibit of the Normandy, represents the centre level to the Hidden Matrix. Floor 18 established likeness to the second and upper half to the Hidden Matrix development.

Notice the red arrows at that level pointing to windows. The two vertical panes above their lower horizontal panes to each, express Hidden Matrix first pyramid ascending six in development.

At one level above Colgate centre coordinate as expressed at 211 Pearl Street, here Roth coordinates with the Hidden Matrix upper side, as emphasis toward tower expression. Hidden in plain sight is the Tetragrammaton (the triangle).

The four windows at bottom of triangle represent a duality, as the four paired squares upon the Hidden Matrix, and the four symbols of Heh, Vav, Heh and Yod as the Hebrew name of God.

The duality to the name is by second, third and fourth levels to triangle apex. For those who are unaware, the total to the symbols is 72. Seventy-two are the number of squares to the first six cluster of numbers upon the Hidden Matrix, which is where the 72 names of God were conceived to coordinate with.

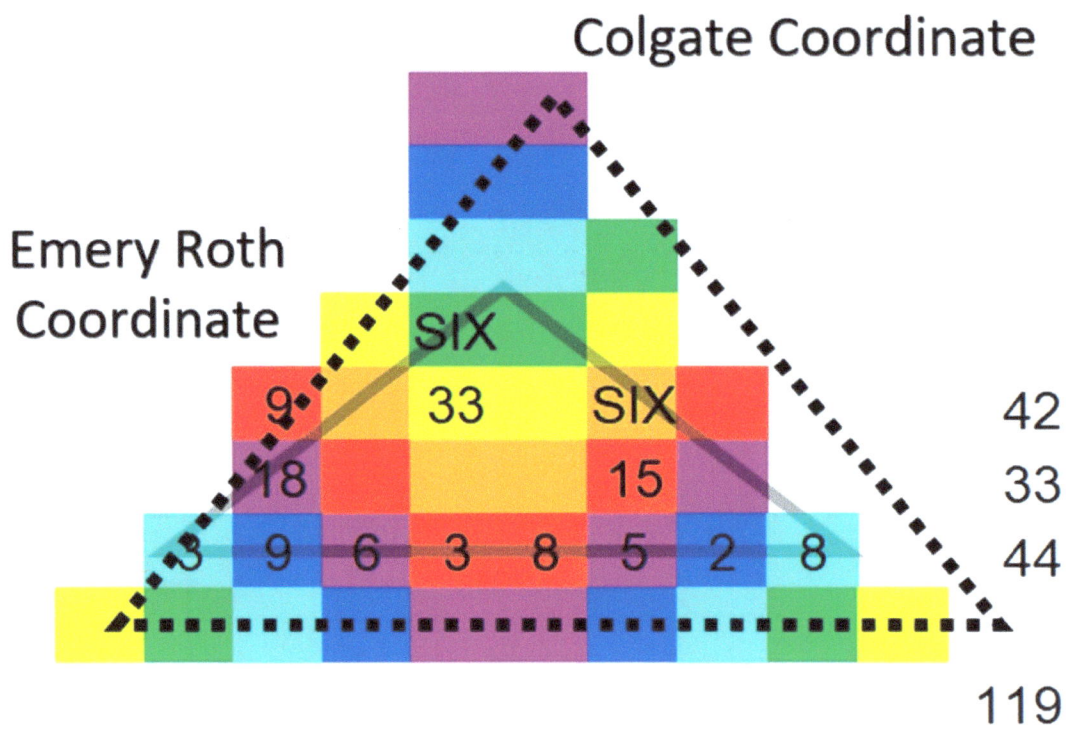

Exhibit 88: Roth and Colgate Insight

The hidden value, within the triangle (tetragrammaton) by Emery Roth as designer using the Hidden Matrix as did Colgate, was one hundred nineteen. Which alludes to a Sod of Sod meaning, understood only by Hidden Matrix detail knowledge.

From base level of Emery Roth triangle, going three levels up, six is understood directly above 33. In Calculation six orange is not considered but nine is. The reason for that is due 9 or 9's is foundation to what becomes the four corners upon the Hidden Matrix. This usage brings together and reveals that essence by core association as Six above the 33, 6 of 33, and Six of Six orange, revealing the hidden number of 666.

The difference between Emery Roth and his sons, was in how they used the Hidden Matrix and their ability to interpret its parts for usage. They chose to use the upper half of the Hidden Matrix to develop the twin towers purpose.

It is now clear, that Yamasaki was not privy to Emery Roth and Son's plans in concert with Rockefeller influence. Thus Yamasaki's original plan called for the towers to be 80 stories tall,[32] Emery Roth and Sons, using their late fathers (Hidden Matrix) knowledge as applied having Rockefellers influence, in causing the Port Authority to increase the square feet requirement.

Yamasaki would not have made such a great mistake, as to create plans which did not meet the Port Authorities original parameters.

Yamasaki having no choice, met the Port Authority's requirement for 10,000,000 square feet (930,000 m2) of office space, which caused the buildings to each becoming 110 stories tall, which met Hidden Matrix concept and future.

TEN

SECRET OF 9-11

Saturday, September 1st, 2001 Midland Texas, during an attempted call to the area code 915, my ex-wife had mistakenly after the 91 pressed another one, then a 5, when she heard a voice, asking if she called 911, she explained her error, yet the voice said that a patrol unit was nearby and would arriving soon, she explained and passed the phone to me.

This is what happened.

I reiterated the error, asking the voice to cancel any visits. She informed me that an officer was walking up to my front door now.

I heard a knock and walked to and opened the front door to the officer. It was a Sheriff Deputy. As I opened the door, the deputy said a 911 call was placed, and that he needed to check and verify that everything was ok. I insisted it was not necessary, he insisted he was going to enter with or without my permission. Left with no choice, I let him in. After his physical examination he left satisfied.

What most had not understood, in fact had not heard of yet, was the human ability to tap into another P.OV. of existence. For me, that experience is as a collective mind or alternate self-looking at myself connected in some way to my experience on earth. was the connection I have had since a child with another dimension. Several minutes after the Sheriff deputy left, I explained to my ex-wife, that a supernatural visual was being shown to me, and that I needed to have it on record. I dialed 911, this time on purpose. As I spoke to the 911 operator, I leaned against an entertainment set near me, explaining that I needed a supervisor to witness and record what I am saying. Suddenly, the two tall speaker towers toppled, crashing to the ground. Startled, the operator asked, "What was that? I said it was two towers falling to the ground. I began to explain that what I needed to record was of national security and a dire emergency. This was to fulfill an earlier warning of knowledge that flowed through me, of which I gave to the Kermit Police department on May 13, 1999

Wherein it was shared that the Texas Governor was aware of religious foundation and that this knowledge was being used against the people, in fact reference to the formula where future explosions would take place was revealed including how to stop the event from happening.

The clue was:
> *"When cities join three apart, ravage from within will try the heart. An exploding ring will surround within. Hearts of cities Ecliptic tips will join in sorrow for the morrow. For whom are the two who are true. The evil twin guides to salvation, the targeted habitation".*

I described that after the event, it would be explained as perpetrated by twenty bombers, i.e. Men that would be involved toward the catastrophic events that would cause thousands to die. Ten Days later, the events of 9/11 took place.

My development of the Hidden Matrix details revealed how its parts were used in conceiving what would unfold on the day.

10 AMERICAN AIRLINES FLIGHT 11, PASSENGERS AND TIME

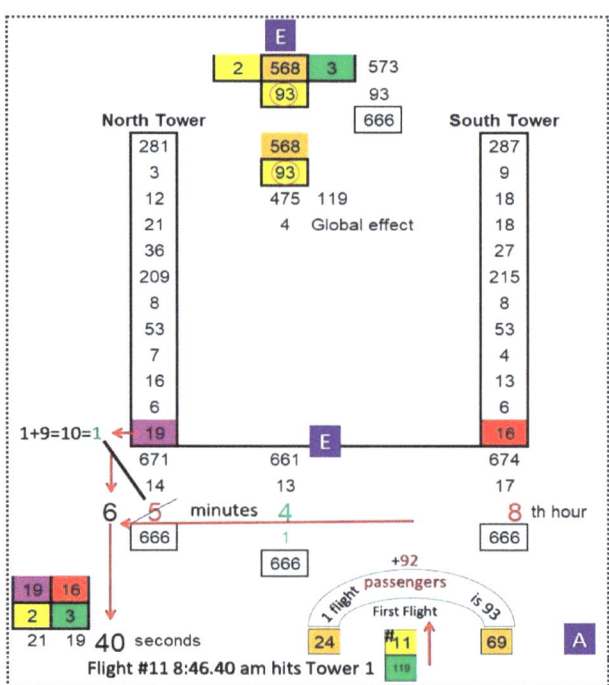

Exhibit 89: AMERICAN AIRLINES FLIGHT 11, PASSENGERS AND TIME

American Airlines Flight 11

At Boston's Logan International Airport between 6:45am and 7:40am, Atta and Omari, along with Satam al Suqami, Wail al Shehri and Waleed al Shwhri, checked in and Boarded American Airlines Flight 11 scheduled to depart at 7:45, bound for Los Angeles.

Plane took off at 7:59am. As a non-stop service from Boston to Los Angeles, it carried a full capacity of nine flight attendants. Eighty-one passengers boarded the flight (including the five terrorists).

At or shortly after 8:14am two unarmed flight attendants preparing for cabin service were stabbed. Daniel Lewin a former officer in the Israeli military, who was seated in row just behind Atta and Omari and in front of Satam al Suqami, was stabbed by one of the hijackers.

At 8:26 Flight 11 turned south toward Kennedy airport in New York.

At 8:38 Flight 11 was in rapid decent.

At 8:41 Air traffic controllers declared Flight 11 a hijacking.

At 8:44 Flight attendant Amy Sweeny, described to Michael Woodward, manager of the American Flight Services Office, "We are flying low. We are flying very, very low. We are flying way too low." Seconds later she said, "Oh my God we are too low." The phone call ended.

At 8:46:40 am, American 11 crashed into the North Tower of the World Trade Center in New York. All on board, along with a unknown number of people in the tower, were killed instantly. Source: 9/11 Commission Report, Final Report of the National Commission on Terrorist Attacks upon the United States pgs. 4-7.

Revealed upon Hidden Matrix is flight #11 number conception from polarized 119. At left of 11 yellow, guide numbers 24 and 69 orange are added together makes 93, establishing 1 as first flight and 92 passengers onboard.

North and South Tower event number, upon the Hidden Matrix, is established through polarization which gives the estimated collision time of 8:45 am. The center number of 93 to this revelation, represents the former 1993 WTC basement bombing, and that countdown beginning on February 26th, 1993 toward 9/11. Which is why later Flight 93 of September 11, 2001 does not strike a building but is taken into the ground.

Thus 93 as the former is deducted from 586 for 475. 586 polarized becomes 19 which is also deducted from 475 establishing 456. 456 as resulting sum is added to 2664 (666 x 4) for 3120 as the number of days until completion of the countdown on 9/11.

Being the first collision (addition) 1 and 9 of 19 are added, then polarized establishing the 1 representing (yellow number 2) as the planes impact and fusion with the North Tower. The 1 caused the polarized 5 of North Tower to both represent 5 to 6 as 11, where Flight 11 crashes into (111). That first 11:11 result. The conversion of 5 to 6 established the adjusted and accurate collision time as 8:46am.

The North and South Tower base numbers of 19 and 16, are added as that foretelling of two collisions, by the numbers 2 yellow and 3 green as those developed wings of flight to Mercury. Only here we are talking about aircraft coming together with base numbers, signifying two planes crashing into the buildings. Here no detail is missed as 40 seconds is added for 8:46:40 am.

10.1 Flight 175, Passengers, and Strike Time (B)

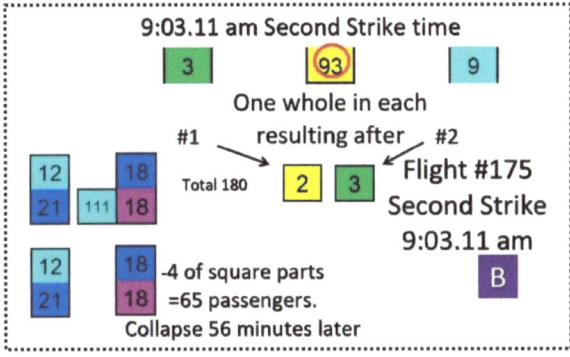

Exhibit 90 Flight 175, Passengers, and Strike Time (B)

At another Logan terminal, Shehhi, joined by Fayez Banihammad, Mohand al Shehri, Ahmed al Ghamdi, and Hamza al Ghamdi, checked in for Flight 175 scheduled to depart at 8:00am, also bound for Los Angeles.

After boarding United 175 between 7:23 and 7:28am their aircraft pushed back from the gate just before 8:00am.

The flight had taken off just as American 11 was being hijacked, and at 8:42 the United 175 flight crew completed their report on a "suspicious transmission" overheard from another plane (which turned out to be Flight 11) just after take-off. This was United 175's last communication with the ground. Using knives, hijackers attacked sometime between 8:42 and 8:46.

At 8:47 the aircraft changed beacon codes twice within a minute.

At 8:51 the flight deviated from its assigned altitude.

At 8:52 Lee Hanson received a phone call from his son Peter, a passenger on United 175, who told him. "I think they've taken over the cockpit – An attendant has been stabbed – and someone else up front may have been killed. The Plane is making strange moves. Call United Airlines – Tell them it's flight 175, Boston to L.A."

Lee Hanson then called the Easton Police Department and relayed what he heard.

Also, at 8:52, a male flight attendant called United office in San Francisco reaching Marc Policastro, telling him that the flight had been hijacked and that both pilots had been killed, and a flight attendant stabbed.

At 8:58, the flight to a heading toward New York City.

At 8:59, Flight 175 passenger Brian David Sweeney tried to call his wife, Julie. He left a message on their answering machine that the plane had been hijacked. He then called his mother Louise Sweeney, told her the flight had been hijacked, and added that the passengers were thinking about storming the cockpit to take control of the plane away from the hijackers. At 9:00, Lee Hanson received a second call from his son Peter:

"It's getting bad Dad – A stewardess was stabbed – They seem to have knives and Mace – They said they have a bomb – It's getting very bad on the plane – Passengers are throwing up and getting sick – The plane is making jerky movements – I don't think the pilot is flying the plane – I think we are going down – I think they intend to go to Chicago or someplace and fly into a building – Don't worry, Dad – If it happens, it'll be very fast – My God, my God".

The call ended abruptly. Lee Hanson had heard a woman scream just before it cut off. He turned on the Television, and in her home so did Louise Sweeney. Both then saw the second aircraft hit the World Trade center.

At 9:03:11, United Airlines Flight 175 struck the South Tower of the World Trade Center. All on board, along with unknown number of people in the tower, were killed instantly. Source: 9/11 Commission Report, Final Report of the National Commission on Terrorist Attacks upon the United States pgs. 7-8.

With 93 considered as the former, it becomes zero, to the revelation. The second strike is understood by reading from South Tower 9 passing through to 3 of the first struck North Tower building. Time established is 9:03 am. The target area to the second strike is at the two levels prior to 93 understood upon the master chart of prophecy.

The numbers 18, 18 of South Tower together with 111 of the crossing and 12 and 21 of North Tower target zone, 180 is understood. As the second plane the number 2 of North Tower and 3 representing the second plane to strike side to corner of building, exploding, and disintegrating are now deducted for 175, establishing Flight #175. With 111 of the Crossing considerations removed, allows four squares to be used. 12 and 21 of North Tower together with 18 and 18 of South Tower reference equal 69.

We all well know that this event was designed to have a global effect, in essence to be felt to the four corners of earth. Thus, the four squares are represented by 1's subliminally using 1111 as 4. Four (4) is deducted as that hidden for 65. There were 65 passengers on board, and 56 minutes later the South Tower collapsed. 1111 or 22.

10.2 American Flight 77

Impact Point and Time, Number of Deaths on-board and Pentagon.
After American Flight 77 was delayed, it took off at 8:20am.
At 8:46 the flight reached its assigned altitude of 35,000 feet.

The hijacking began between 8:51 and 8:54. Announcement by Pilot established that the plane had been hijacked.

At 8:54 Aircraft deviated from its assigned course, turning south, two minutes later its transponder was turned off, even primary radar contact with the aircraft was lost.
At 9:00 American Airlines Executive Vice President Gerard Arpey after learning communication with American 77 had been lost, ordered all American Airlines flights in the Northeast that had not taken off to remain on the ground. Upon learning United was missing a plane, American Airlines headquarters extended the ground stop nationwide.

At 9:12, Renee May called her mother, Nancy May in Las Vegas. She said her flight was being hijacked by six individuals who had moved them to the rear of the plane. She asked her mother to alert American Airlines. Nancy May and her husband promptly did so. At some point between 9:16 and 9:26, Barbra Olsen called he r husband, Ted Olsen, the solicitor general of the United States. She reported that the flight had been hijacked, and hijackers had knives and boxcutters. She further indicated that the hijackers were unaware of her phone call, and that they had put all the passengers in the back of the plane.

About a minute into the conversation, the call was cut off. Solicitor general Olsen tried unsuccessfully to reach Attorney General John Ashcroft. Shortly after the first call, Barbara Olsen reached her husband again. She repeated that the pilot had announced that the flight had been hijacked, and she asked her husband what she should tell the captain to do. Ted Olsen asked for her location and she replied that the aircraft was flying over houses. Another passenger told her that they were traveling northeast.

The Solicitor General then informed his wife of the two previous hijackings and crashes. She did not display signs of panic and did not indicate any awareness of an impending crash. At that point, the second call was cut off.

At 9:29, the autopilot on American 77 was disengaged; the aircraft was at 7,000 feet and approximately 38 miles west of the Pentagon.

At 9:32, controllers at Dulles Terminal Radar Approach Control "observed a primary radar target tracking eastbound at high rate of speed." This was later to be determined to have been flight 77.

At 9:34, Ronald Reagan Washington National Airport advised the Secret Service of an unknown aircraft heading in the direction of the White House. American 77 was then 5 miles west-southwest of the Pentagon and began a 330-degree turn.

At the end of the turn, it was descending through 2,200 feet, pointed toward the Pentagon and downtown Washington. The hijacker pilot then advanced the throttles to maximum power and dove toward the Pentagon.
At 9:37:46 American Airlines Flight 77 crashed into the Pentagon, traveling at approximately 530 miles per hour. All 64 on board, as well as many civilian and military personnel in the building were killed. Source: 9/11 Commission Report, Final Report of the National Commission on Terrorist Attacks upon the United States pgs. 8-10.

10.3 Foretelling by number design

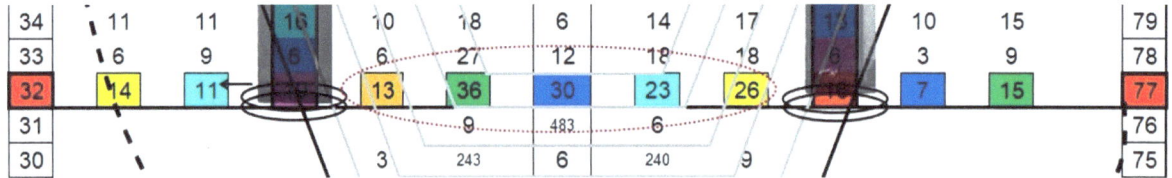

Exhibit 91: Conceived plan.

The Crown Code reveals Flight 77 was not designated as part of WTC complex targeting and represented a strategic purpose.

Guide number 77 below established airline scheduling prior to 9/11. The Polarized sums as seen at right equaled 59. Guide number 32 not used, infuses essence as 5 for a total of 64 on-board that included Captain Charles F. Burlingame, First Officer David Charlebois, four flight attendants and 58 passengers.

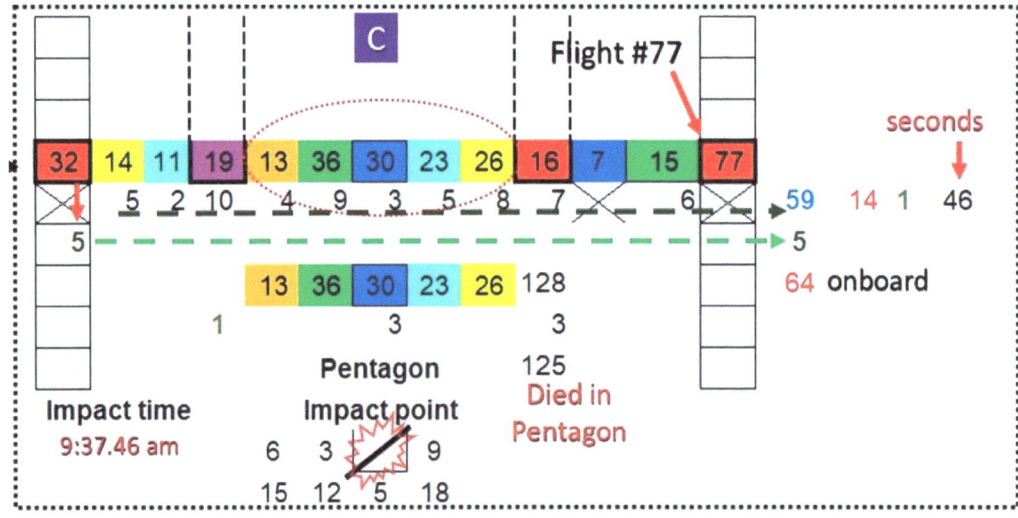

Exhibit 92: Revealed Code for Impact point and deaths.

The Towers base numbers of 19 and 16 became inner guides, holding what would define the one-hundred and twenty-five who would die in the Pentagon. Pentagon impact point also defined the time of impact.

Remember as Hebrew, its read right to left. The nine (9) is the hour with impact point separating the minutes as thirty-six (36) adding 1 for impact for 37. The seconds is understood through 59, which is polarized to become 14. 59 minus 14 is 45. Here the left over 1 of 10 polarized is added for 46, thus 9:37:46am for Pentagon impact time.

10.4 Flight 93

At 8:42, United Airlines Flight 93 took off from Newark (New Jersey) Liberty International Airport bound from San Francisco, Piloted by Captain Jason Dahl and First Officer Leroy Homer, and there were five flight attendants. Thirty-seven passengers, including the hijackers boarded. The flight was delayed due airports heavy morning traffic. It took off 25 minutes late at 8:42am. At 9:00, the FAA, American, and United were facing apparent multiple hijackings. At 9:03 they would see the second strike upon the South Tower of the World trade Center. Crisis managers at FAA and the airlines did not act to warn other aircraft.

No evidence was found, to indicate that American Airlines sent ant cockpit warnings to its aircraft on 9/11.

United's first decisive action to notify its airborne aircraft to take defensive action did not take place until 9:19, when a United flight dispatcher, Ed Ballinger, took the initiative to begin transmitting warnings to his 16 transcontinental flights: :Beware any cockpit intrusion – Two a/c [aircraft] hit World trade Center." One of the flights that received the warning was United 93. Because Ballinger was still responsible for his other flights as well as flight 175, his warning message was not transmitted to flight 93 until 9:23.

By all accounts, the first 46 minutes of flight 93's cross country trip proceeded routinely. Radio communications from the plane were normal. Heading, speed, and altitude ran according to plan. At 9:24, the pilot, Jason Dahl, responded with a note of puzzlement, "Ed, confirm latest mssg plz –Jason."

At 9:28 hijackers attacked. United 93 suddenly dropped 700 feet from 35,000 feet above eastern Ohio. The first of two broadcasts were heard eleven seconds into the descent. "Mayday" amid sounds of physical struggle in the cockpit. 35 seconds later the second radio transmission indicated that the flight was continuing. Voice of Captain or First officer could be heard shouting "Hey get out of here –get out of here—get out of here."

In retrospect Flight 93 was different that the others, whereby the other flights 5 hijackers-initiated cockpit takeovers within 30 minutes. Whereas Flight 93's with only 4 hijackers waited 46 minutes, for the same.

At 9:32 a hijacker made or attempted to make the following announcement to the passengers of Flight 93: "Ladies and gentlemen: Here the captain, please sit down keep remaining sitting. We have a bomb on Board, so sit. The flight data recorder (also recovered) indicates that Jarrah then instructed the plane's autopilot to turn the aircraft around and head east.

The cockpit voice recorder data indicate that a woman, most likely a flight attendant, was being held captive in the cockpit. She struggled with one of the hijackers who killed or otherwise silenced her."

Shortly thereafter, the passengers and flight crew began a series of calls from GTE airphones and cellular phones.

These calls between family, friends and colleagues took place until the end of the flight and provided those on the ground with first-hand accounts. They enabled the passengers to gain critical information, including the news that two aircraft had slammed into the World Trade Center.

At 9:39, the FAA's Cleveland Air Route Traffic Control Center overheard a second announcement indicating that there was a bomb on board, that the plane was returning to the airport, and that they should remain seated. At least two callers from the flight reported that the hijackers knew that passengers were making calls but did not seem to care.

It is quite possible Jarrah knew of the success of the assault on the World Trade Center. He could have learned of this from messages being sent by United Airlines to the cockpit of its transcontinental flights, including flight 93, warning of cockpit intrusion and telling of the New York attacks. But even without them, he would certainly have understood that the attacks on the World Trade Center would already have unfolded, given flight 93's tardy departure from Newark.

If Jarrah did know that the passengers were making calls, it might not have occurred to him that they were certain to learn what had happened in New York, thereby defeating his attempts of deception...

At 9:57, the passenger assault began. Several passengers had terminated phone calls with loved ones to join the revolt. One of the callers ended her message as follows: "Everyone's running up to first class. I have got to go. Bye."

The cockpit voice recorder captured the sounds of the passenger assault muffled by the intervening cockpit door. Some family members who listened to the recording report that they can hear the voice of a loved one among the din. We cannot identify whose voices can be heard. But the assault was sustained.

In response, Jarrah immediately began to roll the airplane to the left and right, attempting to knock the passengers off balance.

At 9:58:57, Jarrah told another hijacker in the cockpit to block the door. Jarrah continued to roll the airplane sharply left and right, but the assault continued.

At 9:59:52, Jarrah changed tactics and pitched the nose of the plane up and down to disrupt the assault. The recorder captured the sounds of loud thumps, crashes, shouts and breaking glass and plates.

At 10:00:03, Jarrah stabilized the airplane. Five seconds later, Jarrah asked, "Is that it? Shall we finish it off?" A hijacker responded, "No. Not yet. When they all come, we finish it off."

The sounds of fighting continued outside the cockpit. Again, Jarrah pitched the nose of the aircraft up and down.

At 10:00:26, a passenger in the background said, "In the cockpit. If we do not, we'll die!" Sixteen seconds later, a passenger yelled, "Roll it!" Jarrah stopped the violent maneuvers at about 10:01:00 and said "Allah is the greatest! Allah is the greatest!" He then asked another hijacker in the cockpit, "Is that it? I mean, shall we put it down?" to which the other replied, "Yes, put it in it, and pull it down

The passengers continued their assault and at 10:02:23, a hijacker said, "Pull it down! Pull it down!" The hijackers remained at the controls but must have judged that the passengers were only seconds away from overcoming them. The airplane headed down; the control wheel was turned hard to the right.

The airplane rolled onto its back, and one of the hijackers began shouting, "Allah is the greatest. Allah is the greatest." With the sounds of the counterattack continuing, the aircraft plowed into an empty field in Shanksville, Pennsylvania.

10.5 Flight, Plane Number and Passengers

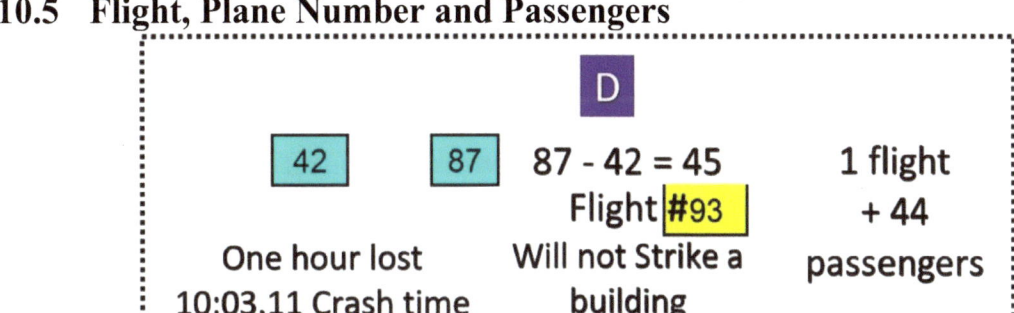

Exhibit 93: Numbers Equation for Flight 93

The entire event was orchestrated to meet details gleaned of the Hidden Matrix. Here the center number of 93 represented the former 1993 WTC basement bombing, which caused the countdown to begin on February 26th, 1993 toward fulfilling 9/11. Again, therefore Flight 93 of September 11, 2001 did not strike a building, but instead was taken into the ground, evidenced by the cockpit voice recorder.
Guide numbers level coinciding with 93, reveals 87 minus 42 for 45. 45 by formula represented 1 plane and 44 onboard.

10.6 Death Toll Goal for 9/11

Exhibit 94: Equation Totality of 2666

Total casualties were estimated to be 2666 conceived by strategic coordinate between guide numbers 32 and 77, where each Tower sum was added to central and upper totalities as seen on master chart at E and at right.

10.7 Exploding Rings Will Surround Within

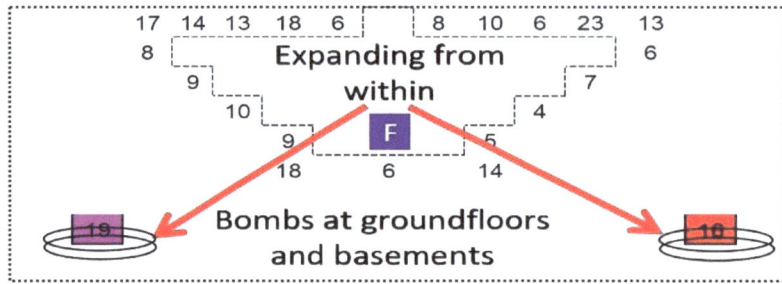

Exhibit 95: Ground floor Insight Numbers

Other descriptive aspects include Bombs at ground floors, basements and other. Ill-conceived out of Hidden Matrix Virgin coordinate to the womb (blank expanding squares) becoming that (exploding ring will surround within).

10.8 Demolition Instruction

Instruction for Total demolition is at first level after Matrix center (G). The 9 and 11 are not used. The red polarized 1's is ascended as spirit after demolition of two 110 story buildings.

Exhibit 96: Tower floors to come down

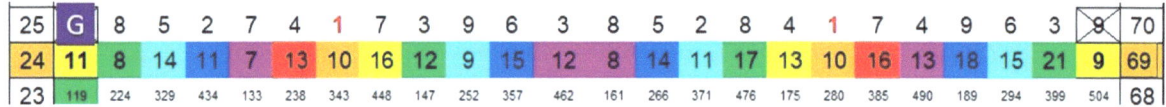

Exhibit 97: Beyond Ground Floor

10.9 852 Days from May 1999

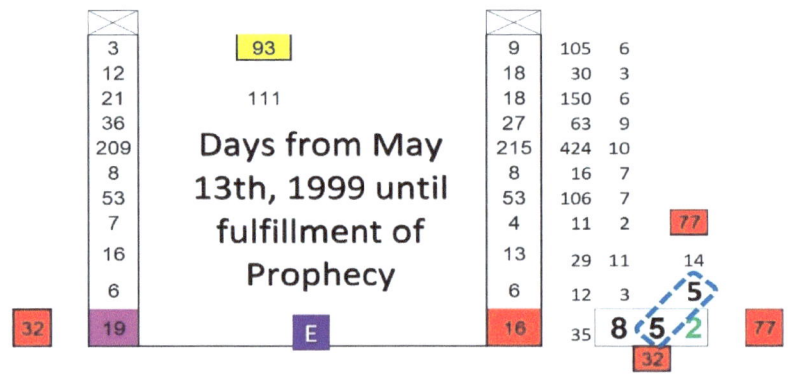

The vision of 1983 was later followed by that prophecy of May 13th, 1999. The towers themselves which followed the vision of 9/11.

Exhibit 98: Foretelling the Future

The Coordinate guides level 32 and 77 at towers bases 19 and 16 are considered by adding then together establishing the combined result of 35. When polarized, 8 is revealed. becoming the first digit of triune expression. Left guide 32 as first in manifest, polarizes to 5, establishing the second digit. Understandably the right guide 77 in that embracing reality, is polarized twice to 5 as the twin and triune union of 32. As a third digit, the 5's are referred to as 2 (twins) The result is 852, in this case 852 days to fulfillment of prophecy made May 13th, 1999. That day was 9/11.

10.10 Number of Hijackers

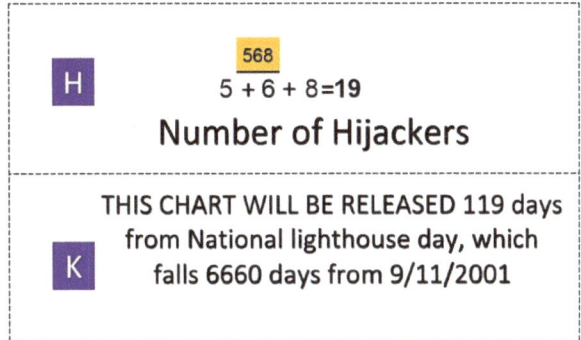

Exhibit 99: Number of Hijackers

Every detail was considered, thus as revealed of the secret, I chose when this chart would be released. Which was on December 4th, 2019.

10.11 Prophecy Details Fulfilled September 11, 2001

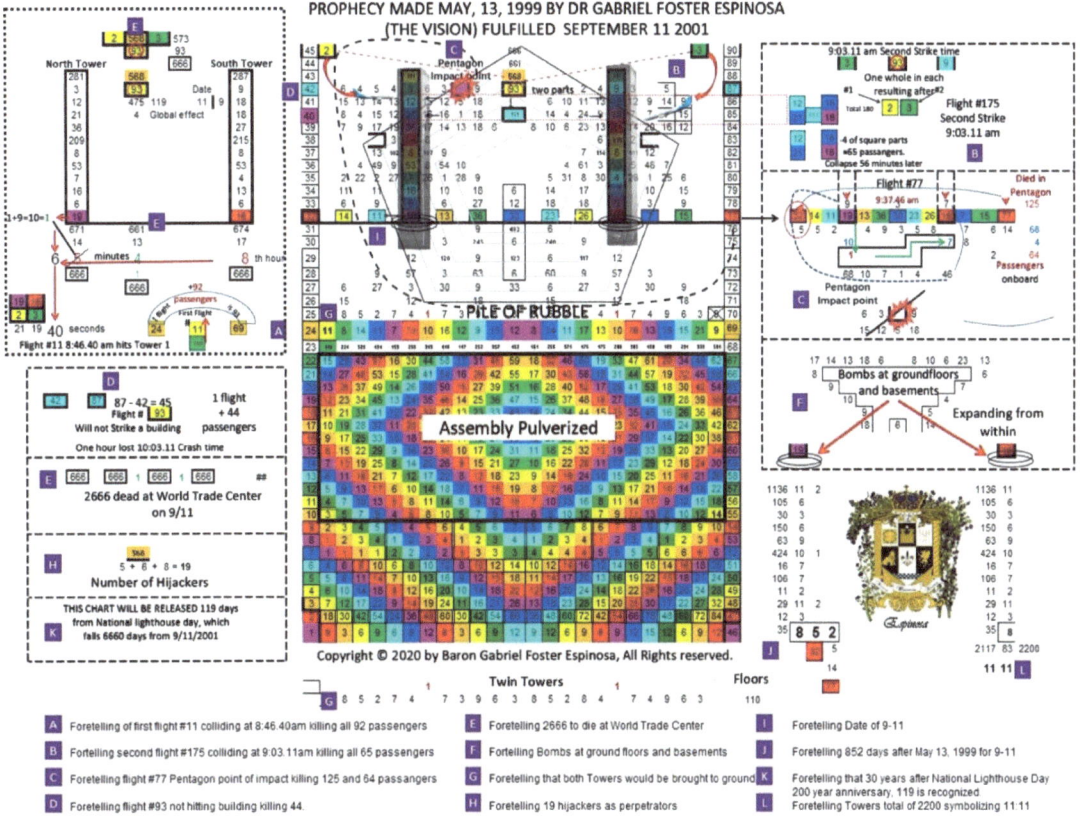

Exhibit 100: Prophecy Details

Ultimately, I shared a collective of information to some friends regarding 9/11. It appeared many were afraid to get involved. I contacted personal friends in the Music industry, including some Grammy winners, producers, and others.

One old acquaintance, I knew while she had dated a mutual friend and former cast member of the Television daytime soap opera General Hospital in the eighties, was kind enough to try to help. She relayed the response of CNN producers.

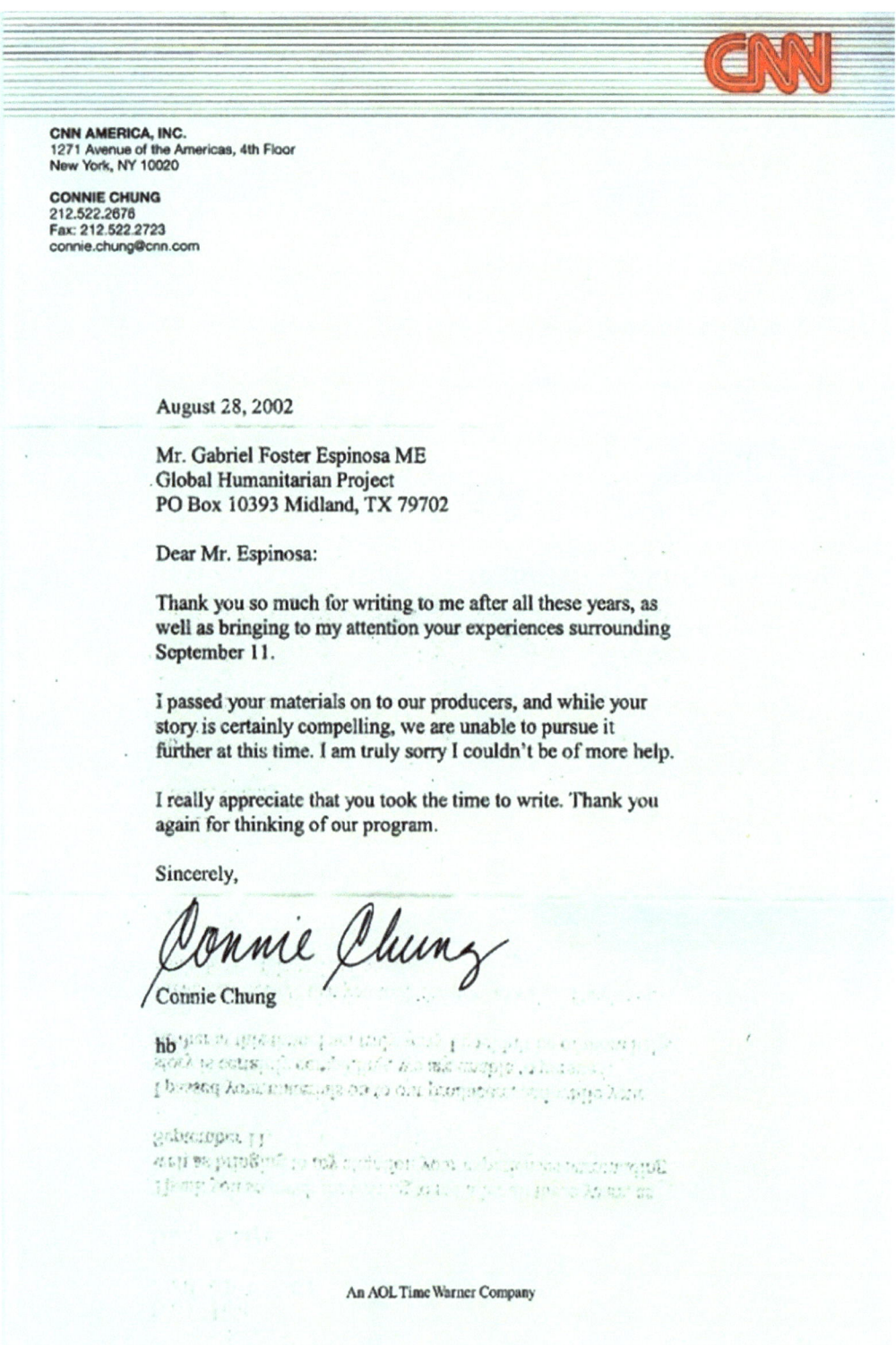

The Letter speaks for itself.

ELEVEN

SECRET OF ISRAEL

MAKE-UP OF ISREAL'S GROUNDS TO USURP THE PAST
AND CHANGE THE FUTURE.

11 Groundbreaking Revelation. The secret provides a unique that building block for society. The truths contained within are universally bound to all existence.

Below at A upon 11/11 Key to creation number 666, we see the archetype field (blueprint base) that virgin field where the 11 or two stands.

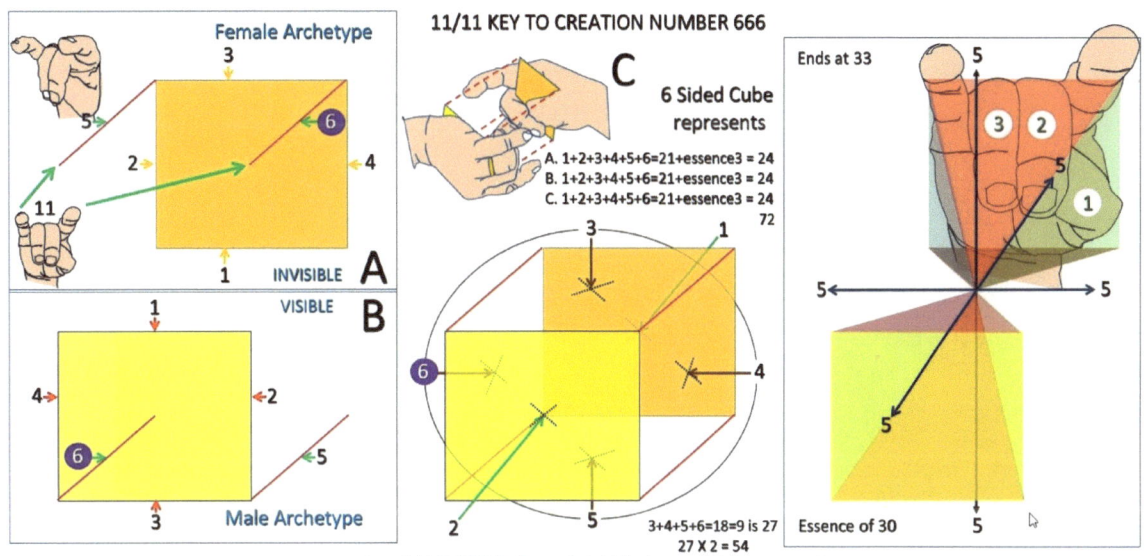

Exhibit 101: Hand Code to Truth

Later this secret became personified to development the narrative described in:

Acts 1:11 King James Version (KJV)

> 11 Which also said, Ye men of Galilee, why stand ye gazing up into heaven? this same Jesus, which is taken up from you into heaven, shall so come in like manner as ye have seen him go into heaven.

Which is to say, that through that essence revealed from the mind of that one, as that visible archetype in the flesh can comprehend. The ascending quality is understood by completing the cube and defining its parts as seen at B and C of the chart. Instruction is given by its parts.

The implementation of geographical coordinates, just as in the development of personified narratives, became widely used. This first example can be understood through the Viri Galilaei Church a Greek Orthodox church located at the northern peak of the Mount of Olives in East Jerusalem. It is part of the Monastery of Little Galilee on the Mount of Olives, which belongs to the Greek Orthodox Patriarchate of Jerusalem, and serves as the private residence of the Patriarch.

Its name is in Latin and means "Men of Galilee". As aforementioned, it is where two, stand, as personifications of section A upon the 11/11 Key to creation number 666 chart.
The following picture consists of the area between the lower Derech (Path) of Jericho and the upper Derech (Path) E-Tur Shmuel Ben Adaya (roads) near Jerusalem.

11.1 What Changed?

Photo 6: Aerial Map of Mount of Olives

Coordinating and personifying the secret numbers to the Crown Code, as was achieved by previous civilizations, became the norm, when it came to control of the common people. Notice the shapes created by the roads upon the Arial.

By understanding the Crown Code, and its parts in development, we can employ numerical foundation, toward development of fictional characters.

This next Chart, called "Make-up of Jerusalem Grid", at A where the Viri Galilee Church is located, we see how simple application of mathematical development, as in the first cube can be used here. The 1 and 2 are associated with squares corresponding to those two which remain fixed during Crown Code development.

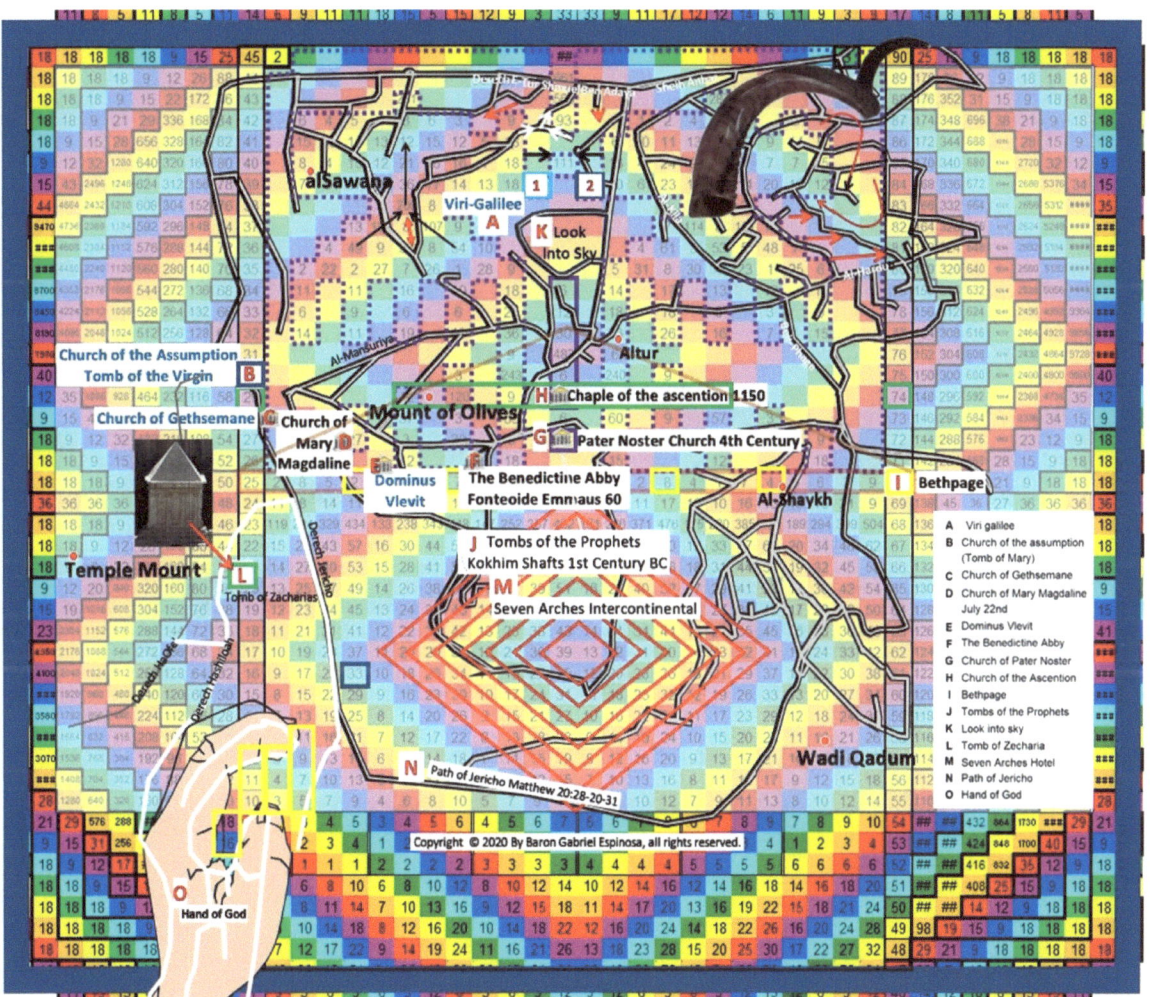

Exhibit 102: Overlay upon Crown Code

Just as the details of the Hidden Matrix, was used in the selection and defining to the parting of the red sea, here the Crown Code grid became reused in the overall development of sites in and Jerusalem. Which is interconnected with extra-narratives that all have hidden meanings.

As a topical grid, germ ideas or concepts, toward solidification of an ideological narrative, became planted as further evidence of dominance of the knowledge.

Next at B upon the same we have the Church of the assumption, which is also designated as being the spot of the Virgin's tomb. Here you can see that the location is at square number 30 of left guide column. The significance regarding this placement of the church and the narrative is especially important, to the flow of the entire story.

Glancing back upon the 11/11 Key to creation number 666 chart, A and B create C, where at right side its inner parts of the cube is shown by the upper connecting ones and the lower one's are crossed centrally in the cube expression. The result reveals six (6) five-sided triangles, corresponding to the six sides of the cube. Here we can understand the beginning to the cube, as 5x6 potential sum of 30.

Remember, what your about to grasp, is that all the stories as developed out of the great secret are one and the same, being part and parcel to the Foundation Formula to everything. Here the sum of thirty, is likened to a womb, one could say, as with the cube three manifest expansions exist.

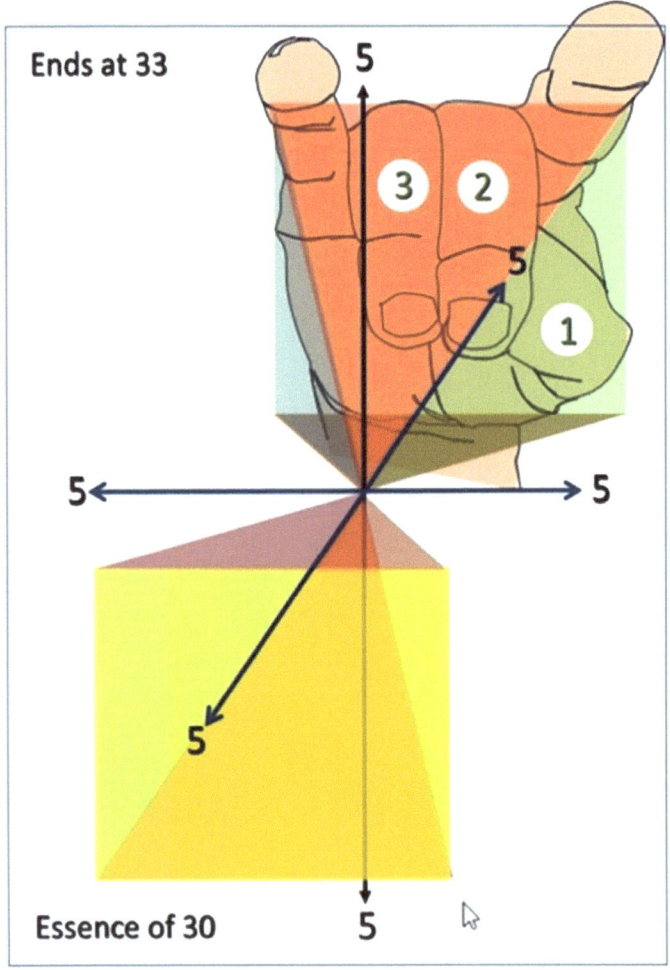

Thus, the location to the Church of the Assumption and the Tomb of Mary were coordinated to reflect the Crown Code secret of the essence of thirty (30).

The Roman Catholic Church teaches as dogma that the Virgin Mary, mother of Jesus, "having completed the course of her earthly life, was assumed body and soul into heavenly glory".

Exhibit 103: Tomb of Mary Essence

This was a play on the secret whereby, the cube as the womb toward potentiality and the six five-sided pyramids as the Cris-Tus born within, upon completion of its purpose, the female archetype is assumed altogether into that from whence it came.

At C, upon the makeup of Jerusalem Grid we have the Church of Gethsemane which is related to the agony of Christ. The location of the Church is causally related to the numerical reference within guides 28 and 73 as seen next.

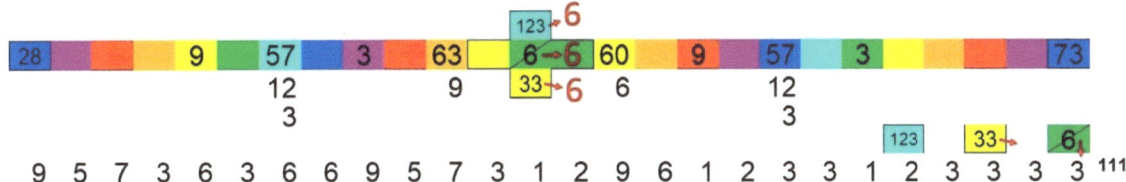

Exhibit 104: Agony of Jesus

Without knowing source material, you cannot know truth. Throughout history subliminal associations have influenced a variety of subjects. Here we have subtle allowances, giving that twist which further conceals original intent.

In comparison to Exhibit 134 and the significance of the 111 or that agony expressed, we see Former President of the United States "Ronald Reagan" gesturing what some call Hook em Horns associated with the Texas Longhorns.

Photo 7: The Hand Gesture

The sign of the horns as a hand gesture, has had a variety of meanings and uses in various cultures. It is formed by extending the index and little fingers while holding the middle and ring fingers down with the thumb. In connection to the Hidden Matrix however, the thumb is inserted behind the middle and ring fingers, establishing one who has privy and recognizes what 1111 represents of the Crown Code.

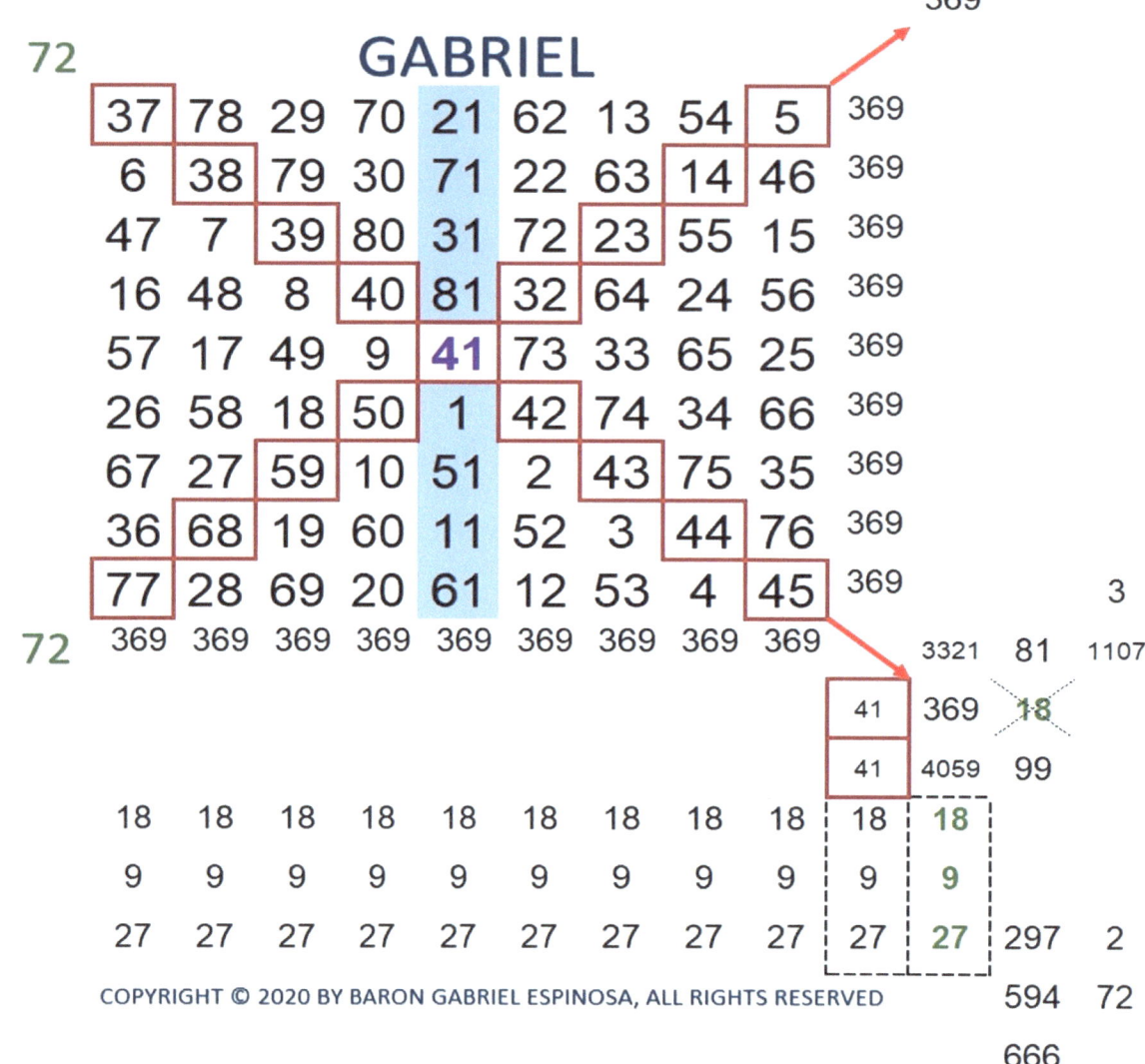

Exhibit 105: Gabriel Reveals Truth Essence

Strategies and or allowances used in past times, have led to conditioning the minds of mankind into accepting a particular gesture or symbol, which represents a far deeper meaning. In Italy for example, the version used by Former President Reagan, became employed as a means by symbolic (apotropaic) gesture, that supposedly had the power to avert evil influences or bad luck, when confronted with unfortunate events. Or to the possibility of such which also became widely used in other Mediterranean cultures.

The gesture of the horns, unknown by the varied usages, in root defined knowledge of 11:11. The difference being the thumb in front or behind, established what side of truth was your preference.

It is no wonder that traditionally it became used to counter or ward off the "evil eye" (malocchio in Italian). In Italy specifically, the gesture is known as the corona. With fingers pointing down, it is a common Mediterranean apotropaic gesture, by which people seek protection in unlucky situations.

Here, I establish the real meaning of the agony. As expressed in the hand gesture, the index and middle fingers not only represent the 1111 connecting reality, but also the crossing as in the red squares shown at left.

In the Garden of Gethsemane, Jesus per the Crown Code details, became personified to know perfectly by the math, that the forthcoming creative process, included the crossing. Which was not the personified narrative described by the church, as paying the penalty of death for all sin.

The Crown Code as personified (Jesus), did the math, and thus knew the outcome. The numbers totaled as seen above, which included numbers from 123 and 33 and half of that torn, as that agony, to remove the cup.

Luke 22:43-44

> *"And there appeared to him an angel from heaven, strengthening him. And being in an agony he prayed more earnestly; and his sweat became like great drops of blood falling down upon the ground."*

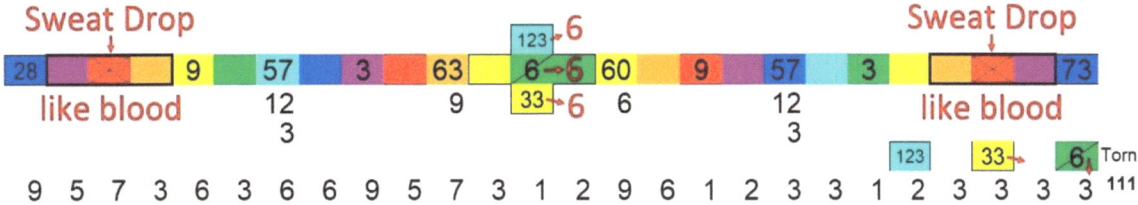

Exhibit 106: Sweat Drops of Jesus

Next, we have The Church of Mary Magdalene at D.

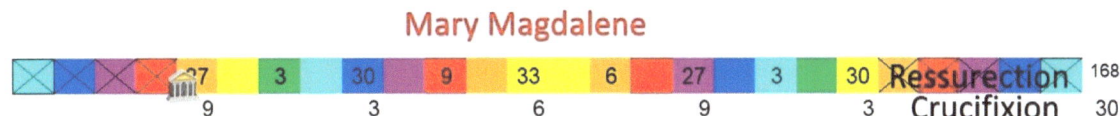

Exhibit 107: Mary Magdalene the Witness

The location just like the Church at Gethsemane, was selected due the underlying numerical coordinate to the level upon the Crown Code. Notice that the primary numbers total 168. This number is important and relates to the zodiacal crossing as referenced upon the Zodiac Conception Key considered a resurrection. The Crucifixion, no doubt here refers to the polarized likeness, of the first cube inner essence.

Thus, it is no surprise that Mary Magdalene was personified, as first witnessing both the Crucifixion and Resurrection.

In succession, we have Dominus Vlevit at E.

According to the 19th chapter of the Gospel of Luke, Jesus, while riding toward the city of Jerusalem, became overwhelmed by the beauty of the Second Temple and predicting its future destruction, and the diaspora of the Jewish people, weeps openly (an event known as Flevit super illam in Latin). (Luke 19:37-42)

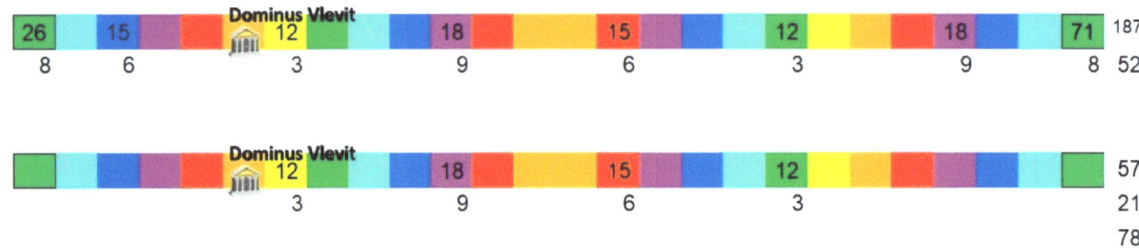

Exhibit 108: The Weeping

Jesus as the Crown Code process realizes the inner reverberating expressions of number development. Here the Roman Catholic Church, used the mathematical sums of 52 and 78 to include the 52 as foundation to the second temple, as it will produce the pattern and its totalities being that new dispensation in time. The 78 as that totality of what the first cube reveals as 72 and the six sides of the first cube, is the true temple manifest as 78. Thus, Jesus is described as having wept, being overwhelmed by the beauty of its truth, understanding the reality of the divine temple's reality.

At F is the Benedictine Abby. Emmaus became described as the location where the scene of Christ revealed Himself after His resurrection (Luke 24:13). To dispute its real site is useless, even though several places are held, by tradition and otherwise, to be the original site of Emmaus. What can you say?

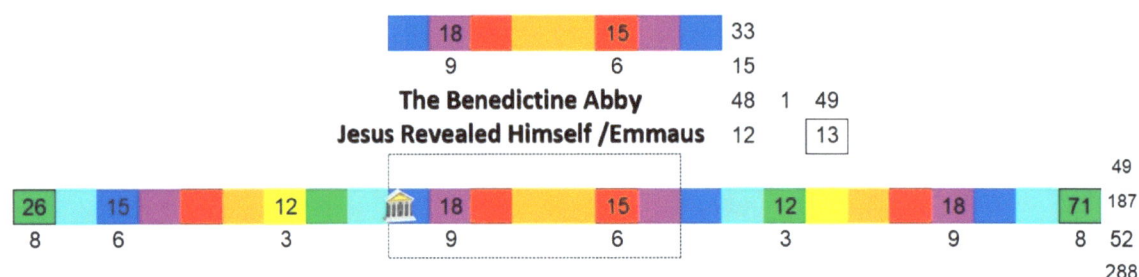

Exhibit 109: Jesus reveals Himself

Here his association to the 33, those twelve as the 13th whose essence being one with the gods, as in those first 72 parts and the 288 of the 72 squares is no coincidence.

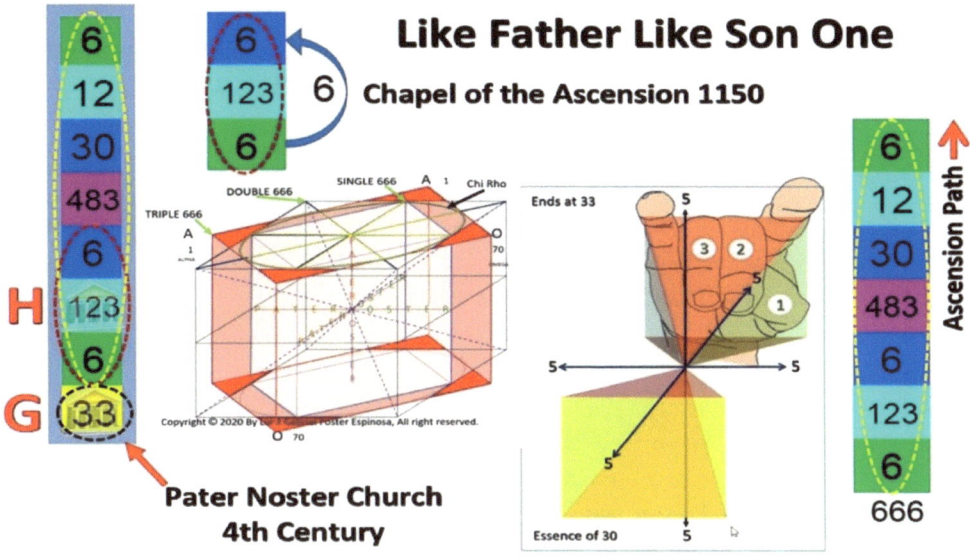

Exhibit 110: Like Father Like Son, Ascension Path

At G and H, we see the Locations of the Pater Noster Church and the Chapel of Ascension. These locations are extremely important to the development of the story. As seen above at second to right, the essence of 30 becomes fulfilled through recognition of the three as grasped within the three, becoming the 33.

The association between "the Son" and the Pater Noster is clearly defined under the topic Cris-Tus in part? of Volume 1. Yet, as a reminder we refer to that display here.

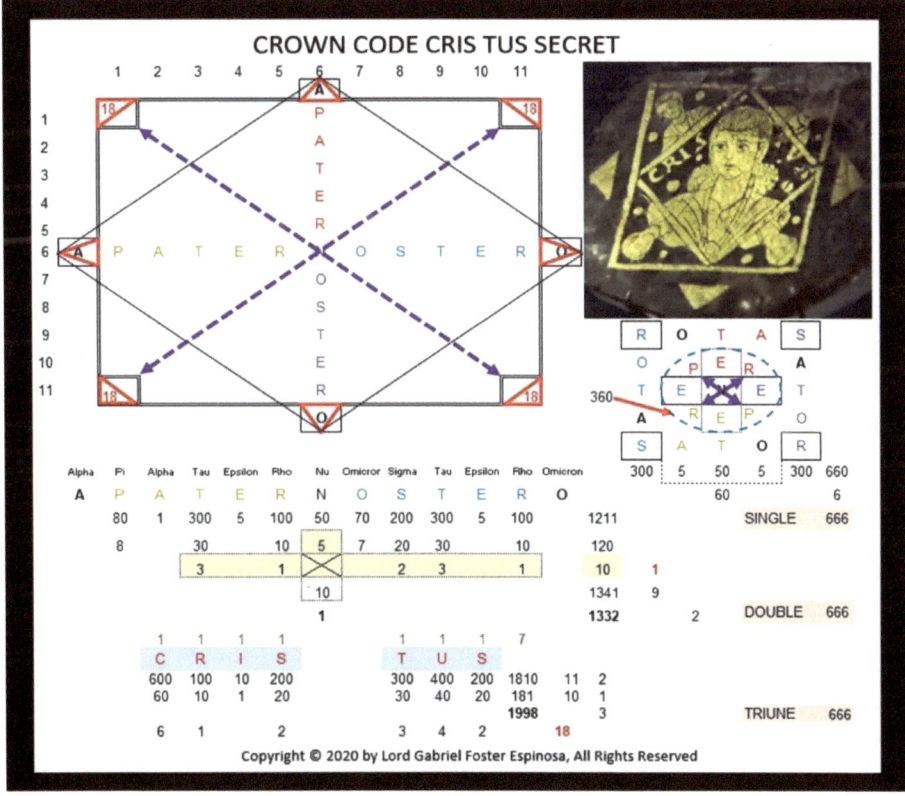

Exhibit 111: Crown Code Cris Tus Secret

Hence, the reason for the accuracy and believability, of scriptural development is due following the Crown Code details. Now consider this, what if you had been made aware of the truth from the beginning? We would be experiencing a much different and better word.

Yet that is not the case. At current establishment, power and greed overcome the masses. Using the details to the Crown Code, is after all a choice. The twists and turns of truth to make it their own, sought after complete dominance over human consciousness.

Which is why the following was nefariously written:
> *25 He said to them, "How foolish you are, and how slow to believe all that the prophets have spoken! 26 Did not the Messiah have to suffer these things and then enter his glory?" 27 And beginning with Moses and all the Prophets, he explained to them what was said in all the Scriptures concerning himself.*

The concept of Mankind being "Exceedingly Evil"

11:.2 Genesis 13:13 Context

> *10And Lot lifted up his eyes, and beheld all the plain of Jordan, that it was well watered everywhere, before the LORD destroyed Sodom and Gomorrah, even as the garden of the LORD, like the land of Egypt, as thou comest unto Zoar. 11Then Lot chose him all the plain of Jordan; and Lot journeyed east: and they separated themselves the one from the other. 12Abram dwelled in the land of Canaan, and Lot dwelled in the cities of the plain, and pitched his tent toward Sodom. 13But the men of Sodom were wicked and sinners before the LORD exceedingly. 14And the LORD said unto Abram, after that Lot was separated from him, Lift up now thine eyes, and look from the place where thou art northward, and southward, and eastward, and westward: 15For all the land which thou sees, to thee will I give it, and to thy seed forever. 16And I will make thy seed as the dust of the earth: so that if a man can number the dust of the earth, then shall thy seed also be numbered.*

The wickedness and the sinfulness were not the nefarious concept of religious designs, but rather that which constitutes, an act considered to be a transgression against divine law. It is that "Universal Law" which had been manipulated.

The Overlay upon Crown Code shows blueprint toward scriptural invention of Bethpage and the development to Jesus coming in on a donkey.

When considering the former in Goat, Heifer and Ram developments shown below, you can understand, that it is not farfetched.

Right side to grey area at steps of altar coordinate to that location up Exhibit 135 as Bethphage, which is remembered as the starting point of Jesus' triumphal entry into Jerusalem on the day that is commemorated as Palm Sunday.

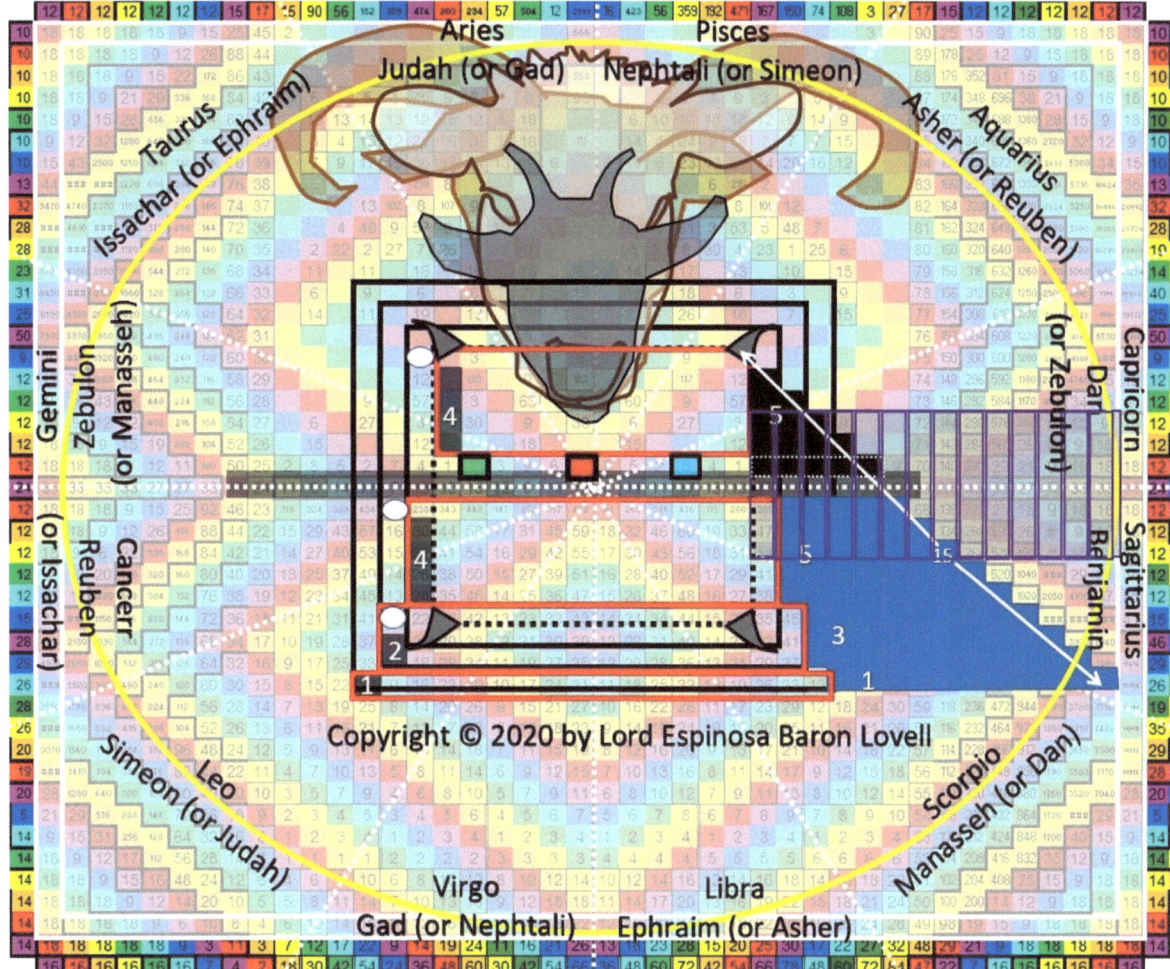

Exhibit 112: Coordinated Entry

At Bethphage, continued usage of the Donkey, married the invented ideological purpose of the Abrahamic story into the minds of mankind. Thus, in the grand design, in creation of a new religion, all sought to embrace a story which held authority.

What set them apart, was they did not only go beyond the established Goat, Lamb, Ram and two (2) bird inclusion, they made sure that those who opposed their plan, understood, that they held the greatest secret of all.

The Crown Code complete, unfortunately gave them cart blanche as nefarious developments were imposed upon the stage of humanity.

Their design was to establish a King, even if it meant lying to the people. Their King was one which would govern all Kings of the earth. In other words, a check mate on truth, held by exceedingly evil actors.

Thus, it was written wherein clarification toward the underlying truth, and the intention of the writing are expressed in the addition of a Donkey and a Colt.

> Matthew 21:1-17 King James Version (KJV)
>
> *21:1 And when they drew nigh unto Jerusalem, and were come to Bethphage, unto the mount of Olives, then sent Jesus two disciples,*
> *2 Saying unto them, go into the village over against you, and straightway ye shall find an ass tied, and a colt with her: loose them, and bring them unto me.*

> *3 And if any man say ought unto you, ye shall say, The Lord hath need of them; and straightway he will send them.*

In other words, go to your enemy (who used the same Crown Code insight) and you will know the secrets of their developments, as that ass tied. Not only that, but you will also establish, that it is known, of the colt which limbs extent to the four winds understood upon the Pattern and Totalities.

> *4 All this was done, that it might be fulfilled which was spoken by the prophet, saying, Tell ye the daughter of Sion, Behold, thy King cometh unto thee, meek, and sitting upon an ass, and a colt the foal of an ass.*

In reference to DAUGHTER OF SION John 12:15; Matthew 21:5. Here the narrative as "Lord" uses "daughter" in a representative sense, and quoted from memory the prophecy of Zechariah, herein later understood as the hidden truth.

Usurpation of truth becomes evident in the following:

"Rejoice greatly, O daughter of Zion; shout, O daughter of Jerusalem" (Zechariah 9:9). Daughter implies parents who brought her into being and surrounded her with loving care and provision.

To those who do not know the truth, they are swayed to embrace, and accept the imposed narrative. Thus, foundation to the deceit was planted.

> *6 And the disciples went, and did as Jesus commanded them,*
> *And brought the ass, and the colt, and put on them their clothes, and they set him thereon.*
> *[Which is to say, the Crown Code was personified]*
> *8 And a very great multitude spread their garments in the way; others cut down branches from the trees, and strawed them in the way.*

9 And the multitudes that went before, and that followed, cried, saying, Hosanna to the son of David: Blessed is he that cometh in the name of the Lord; Hosanna in the highest.

> *[Which is to say, that the people were successfully fooled into believing the lie]*
> *10 And when he was come into Jerusalem, all the city was moved, saying, who is this?*
> *11 And the multitude said, this is Jesus the prophet of Nazareth of Galilee.*

[A collective design was imposed against the minds, to accept by narrative the illusion]

> *12 And Jesus went into the temple of God, and cast out all them that sold and bought in the temple, and overthrew the tables of the moneychangers, and the seats of them that sold doves,*

[Which is to say, that others who have used the secret, will be thrown out, even those who hold the secret from the its foundation as in the crown code process in development to the heights of the usage of those doves as used in 9/11 previously mentioned. A collective design was imposed against the minds to accept the narrative of the illusion]

> *13 And said unto them, it is written, My house shall be called the house of prayer; but ye have made it a den of thieves.*

[To ensure success, one can attribute the saying "the pot, calling the kettle black" appropriate. Because here we see the intent, of usurping truth and making it their own (Abrahamic design)]

> *14 And the blind and the lame came to him in the temple; and he healed them.*
> *15 And when the chief priests and scribes saw the wonderful things that he did, and the children crying in the temple, and saying, Hosanna to the son of David; they were sore displeased,*
> *16 And said unto him, Hearest thou what these say? And Jesus saith unto them, Yea; have ye never read, Out of the mouth of babes and suckling's thou hast perfected praise?*
> *17 And he left them and went out of the city into Bethany; and he lodged there.*

Now we come to J, without question knowledge is power. How it is applied, is the key. The designers to the new ideology understood the implications of past and contemporary usage. In fact, aside from rebuilding and establishing their definitions on top of the ancient old developments. Here although these Kokhim Shafts were not used until the 1st century BC, their reference as to solidify their narrative became employed.

A kokh (plural: kokhim, Hebrew), in Latin loculus, plural loculi, is a type of tomb complex characterized by a series of long narrow shafts, in which the deceased were placed for burial, radiating from a central chamber. These tomb complexes were generally carved into a rock face were usually closed with a stone slab which had channels cut into the centre of the shaft, to drain any water that seeped through the rock.

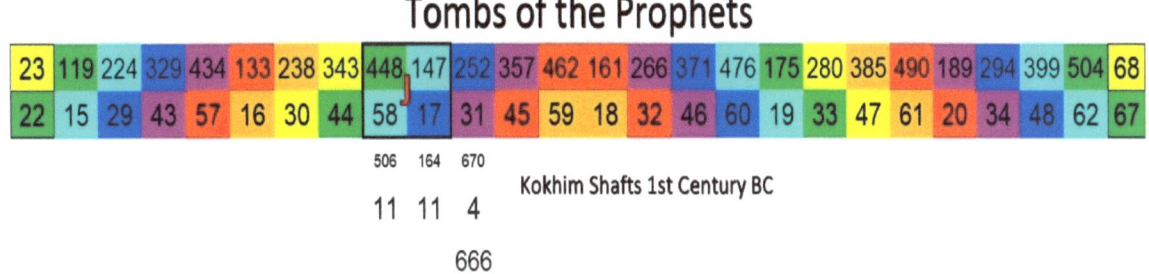

Exhibit 113: Tombs of the Prophets

The Location of this Kokh, needed usurpation to meet the need of inner circle verification of deep insight to the Crown Code and secrets held therein. Notice that the location consists of four squares of the Crown Code development. Their totals along with their polarized sums to the negative result in 666.

There is no need, in going into the significance of what 666 represents, and how it relates to the development of the Prophets. You get the idea.

Next, we have K which is related to the A being the Viri Galilee narrative, in that it represented ascending quality from the blank squares entering between squares 1 and 2 seen below upon the Crown Code to become 111, personified as being lifted into the sky (Acts 1:9-10) We know this to connect the Personified likeness to the Pleroma or cloud event.

Exhibit 114: Looking into Sky

How this relates to how the story of Jesus was developed using the Crown Code, is simple when one considers the parts.

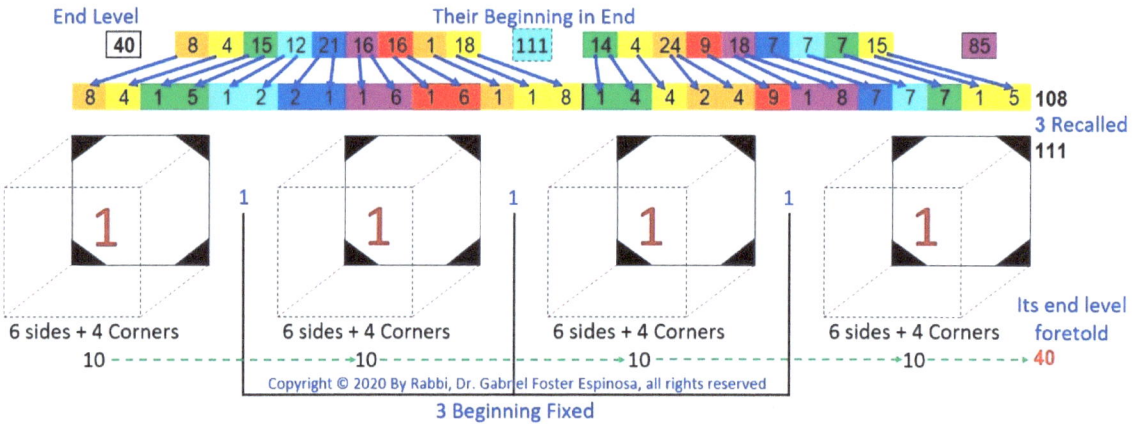

Exhibit 115: Into the Sky

Above is a breakdown of the parts referred to in the previous Exhibit referring to Acts. Only here, we have an expanded view of the two white robed men, and the following level, which is connected to Jesus, being taken up into a cloud and out of sight at the next level.

Beginning at the lower level, six (6) and eight (8) at center became the two men standing in white robes. A method in story development is one, totaling the numbers in single succession, and two, giving them character.

Notice six (6) and eight (8) are not used in its totaling which results in 111, identifying Jesus who it is taken up. Understanding how he was taken up in story development, the next level numbers are also are totaled in single succession. The recalling of 1 and 1 and 1 of the beginning of the Crown Code we see 111 again. This identifies Jesus as 111 being taken up into the cloud.

The reason he became out of sight, is because his character development was to remain a secret. Which is why it was written that Jesus himself after being asked if he would in the narrative in verse 6 if he would restore the kingdom of Israel. He the replied with a statement which you should now recognize as hidden in plain sight admission of the writer to the scripture.

He said to them in verse 7, "It is not for you to know times or seasons that the Father has fixed by his own authority". Which is to say, you will never know the secret of the Crown Code, yet I reveal it to you now.

Also, in Acts 1:14-15, they continuously used Crown Code numbers in story development. Notice that it says, that in those days, Peter (14) stood up, which meaning 14 was added to the sum of 111 for 125. 14 polarized is 5, which is deducted from 125 for 120, the number of people in attendance.

It continues: vs. 8, "But you will receive power when the Holy Spirit has come upon you, and you will by my witnesses in Jerusalem and in all Judea and Samaria, and to the end of the earth."

This area also was used to associate to the womb, the waters, the fountain, even to the narrative as the father of Gilgamec/Gilgamesh "34 Gilgamec, whose father was a phantom (?), the lord of Kulaba, ruled for 126 years as referred to upon the Sumerians Kings list.
At L we have the Tomb of the personified Zacharias. What this represents, reaches far beyond what normally is expressed. It is only recognizable to those in the know, which is far and a few. For it represents knowledge only held by the very elite.

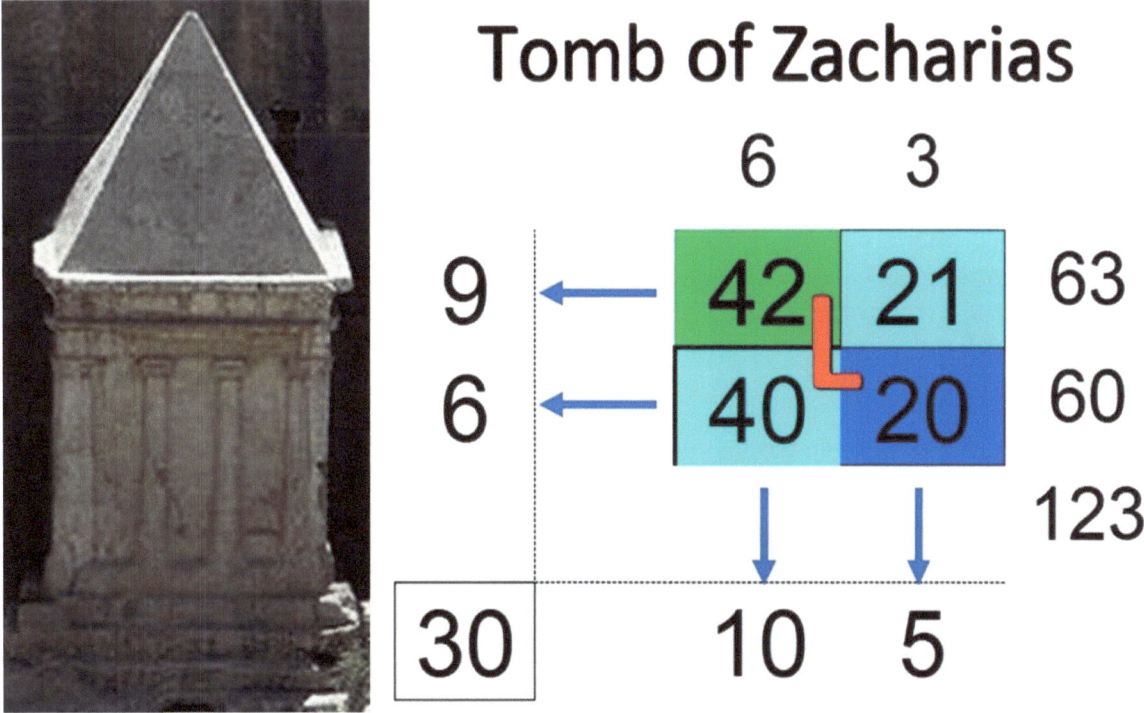

Photo: 8 Tomb of Zacharias   Exhibit 116: Tomb of Zacharias

The location upon the map, verifies the knowledge held by its development. The association of the three within the pyramid structure is unmistakable. Its façade expressing 11 centrally and 11 at corners, is no coincidence.

Exhibit 117: Zacharias Coordinate

Note: the guide numbers of 29 and 74 each polarize to 11 each, expressing knowledge to the foundation of the pyramid structure. This why the pyramid was placed on top of the monument base of 11 11.

Aramaic and Hebrew Zecharya, composed of the elements zechar 'to remember' + ya 'God. The Esoteric underlying meaning is more refined, being ya (1111) + zechar (reveals).

11.3 Seven Times Seven.

At M upon *Exhibit 142: Overlay upon Crown Code* we have the Seven Arches Intercontinental / Hotel, which is owned by the Jordanian Royal House.

The Seven Arches Hotel, which used to be called the Intercontinental, was built a few years before the Six-Day War on the Mount of Olives, on a spot overlooking the Old City, at the initiative of the Jordanian royal family.

The hotel opened on March 20th, 1964, as the Hotel Jerusalem Intercontinental, managed by the US Intercontinental Hotels chain, became one of the buildings most identified with East Jerusalem. In 1964 it was the site of the founding convention of the Palestinian Liberation Organization.

After the Six-Day War, and the loss of Jordanian sovereignty over Jerusalem, the property was entrusted to the Custodian of Absentee Property.

Although the physical condition of the hotel has deteriorated, and it is no longer a luxury hotel. In 2010 right-wing groups in Jerusalem tried to promote a plan to renovate it and to transfer it to one of them, but the plan was canceled, apparently for fear of damaging relations with Jordan. There is no doubt, that Jordan has clear understanding as to the foundation of Israel.

11.4 Underlying secret to Hotel location

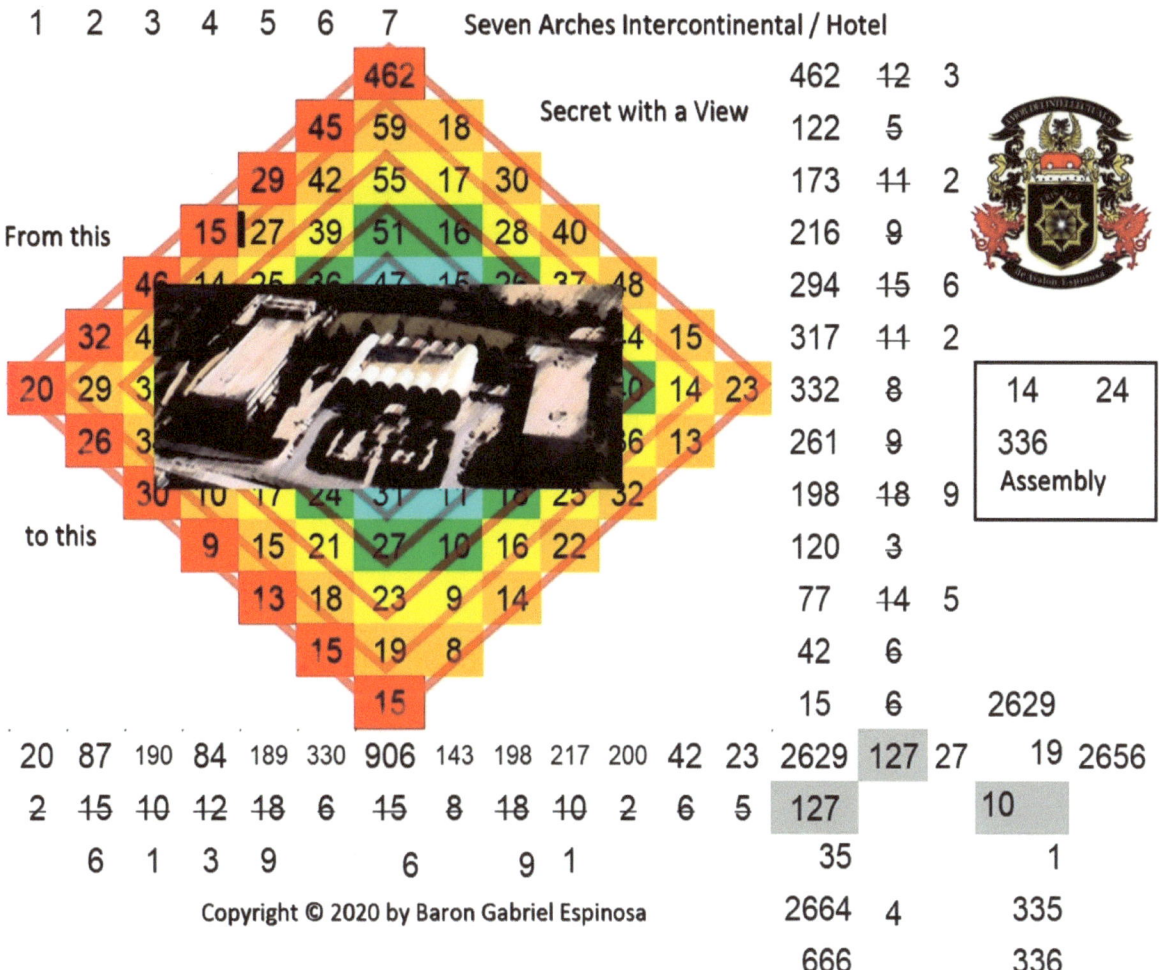

Exhibit 118: Hotel Secret Coordinate

The underlying meaning of the Hotel being built at its location, was the hidden reference, that they all shared the same secret of the Crown Code. The concept and purpose to the hotel, was a loud message. Israel decided to respond. To grasp the type of knowledge cunningly established and used, we need not search too far. Let us consider the source.

The Amarna Letter EA 289: "A Reckoning Demanded" is here written. In {..} is my commentary.

11.5 The Amarna Letter EA 289

Photo 9: The Amarna Letter EA 289

11.5a Within EA 289, letter five of six. (Not a linear, line-by-line translation, and English from French.) [1]

(Lines 1-4) --[Say to the king, my lord: Message of 'Abdi-Heba, your servant.
{Abdi-Heba as obvious counsel to the king, revealed his mutual knowledge by the following}

If[all] at the feet of my lord, the k[ing], 7 times and 7 times.

{The code implied established reign over the general populous by Crown Code Coordinate of the 7 times 7 as exhibited on the previous page}

(5-10) Milkilu does not break away from the sons of Labaya and from the sons of Arsawa, as they desire the land of the king for themselves. As for a mayor who does such a deed, why does the king not (c)all him to account?

The common thread is knowledge, of the Crown Code, and its meaning, which is known by the opposers. How the knowledge is used, becomes the challenging element. Desiring the land which had been established by usage of the Crown Code, has always existed. Even before the establishment of Isarel. The Catholic Church, The Crown of England, as well as those behind Israel know the consequences of loss.

(11-17) --Such was the deed that Milkilu and Tagi did: they took Rubutu. And now as for Jerusalem-(URUUru-Salimki), if this land belongs to the king, why is it ((not)) of concern1 to the king like Hazzatu?

{Hazzatu known today as Gaza,}

This gives you a picture of why the response from Israel was what it was during the six-day war.

The Six-Day War, also called June War or Third Arab-Israeli War or Naksah, brief war that took place June 5–10, 1967, and was the third of the Arab-Israeli wars. Israel's decisive victory included the capture of the Sinai Peninsula, Gaza Strip, West Bank, Old City of Jerusalem, and Golan Heights; the status of these territories subsequently became a major point of contention in the Arab-Israeli conflict.
N is the very revealing Derech Jericho (The Path of Jericho)
In Mathew 20:29 we understand by the Crown code why, the scripture was written the way it was.

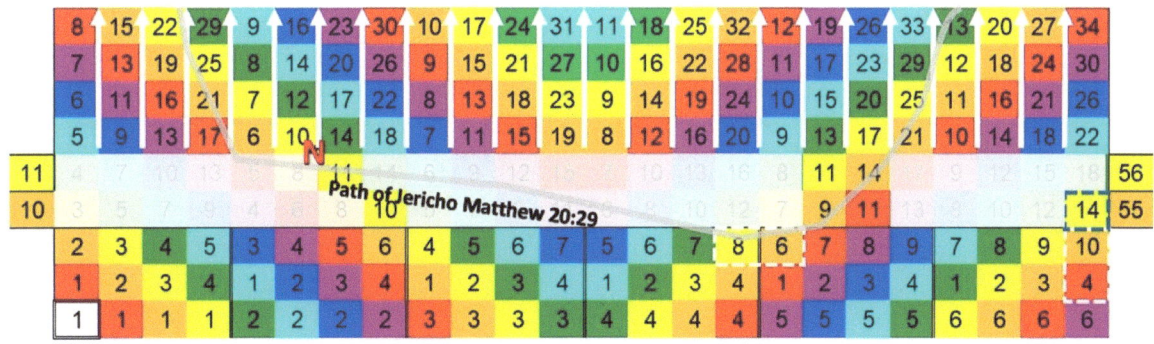

Exhibit 119: Path of Jericho Coordinate

A clear personification of process became used. The first and second levels in that here immediately after the initial six number groups, the area after the third level of those six clusters become what is later defined as the assembly in Church development, as the area of the pews. Here being the cemetery upon the mount of Olives

Note: The path of Jericho which leads to the old city of Jerusalem, and is that path which leads out, thus they departed from Jericho, whereafter the squares upon the Crown Code become many defined by the Hotel secret Coordinate. Only now we see its hidden aspect of Hidden Matrix development becoming the great multitude that followed him.

11.6 Imposing hand of God.

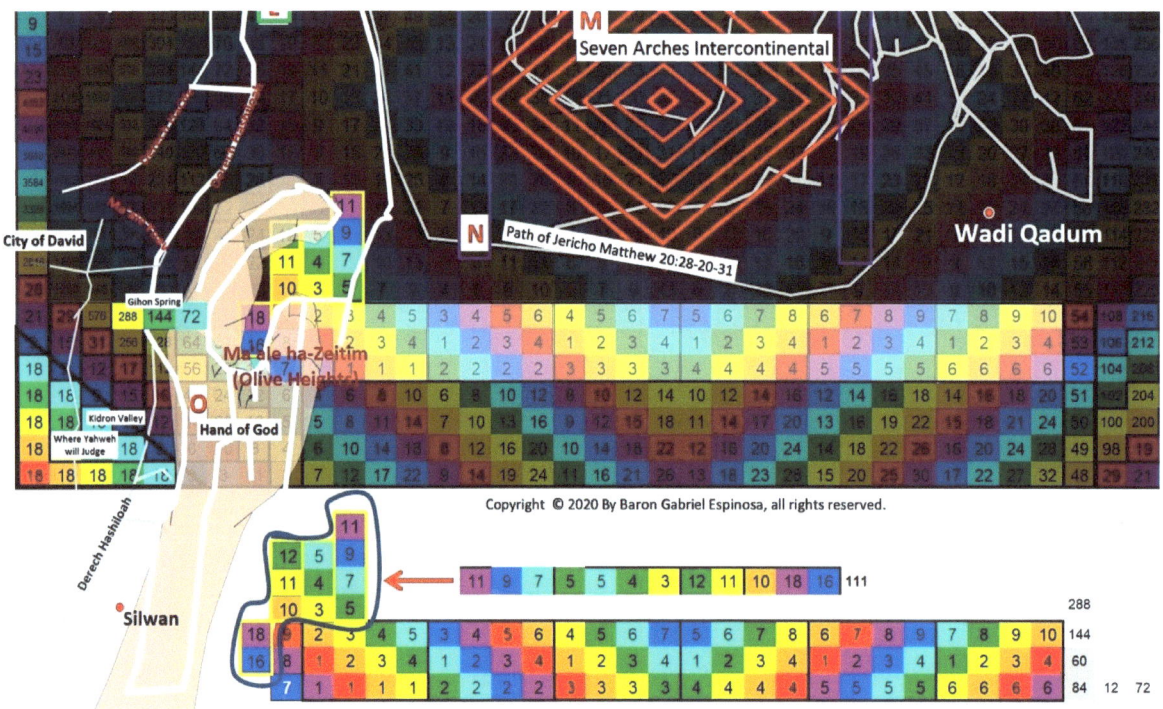

Exhibit 120: Manipulating Hand Coordinate

11.7 What the Evidence Shows What all this evidence shows us is that the concept of "God" has been used since the antiquities. The greatest scam upon the entire earth, was in creating monotheism. The conversion of mankind used that hidden in plain sight strategy. Although clear reference of the plurality of the Gods as in Genesis 1:26 Then God said, "Let us make man in our image, after our likeness" the error still infected the minds of man.

The Initial six number groups to the Crown Code, seen above became foundation to the creation story. As the Foundation formula to everything, its salient details became abused through their usurping, and turning it into a lie. What those six clusters develop relates to the whole of creation. Thus, in Genesis Chapter 2 verse 1, the expression of "Thus the heavens and the earth were finished, and all the host of them"

At Left of the four 1's as root to the Crown Code, notice the number seven at left. That became defined as the seventh day that God finished his work. The resting on the seventh is due the guide numbers are not part of the core ascending calculation.

We must understand that the defining of the Crown Code is Archetype, considered as a blueprint toward the operations of creation.

In verse six, "and a mist was going up from the land, represents the ascending levels as seen upon chart which consists of the area that reaches to the seven arches hotel. The Lower right became known as the Garden of Eden where he put man, which is why it had become a cemetery.

The Tree of Life as "The Crown Code" number coordinate as in the seven Arches Hotel numbers at Exhibit 151: Hotel Secret Coordinate which by the Knowledge is that tree. How it is used is ultimately the good and evil aspects to the results.

Notice the Gihon Spring located at the knuckle of Gods Hand. in 701 BC, King Hezekiah cut a tunnel down to the Spring. He dug it to supply water during an Assyrian siege. It says in 2nd Kings: "[Hezekiah] made a pool, and conduit, and brought water into the city" The significance is that it borders with the surrounding blue squares upon the Crown Code. Thus, its symbolic nature and naming, as was applied to all the lands surrounding of the knowledge of the tree of good and evil.

In the manipulation of Universal Knowledge, one can surmise that mankind must awaken to a higher purpose. Thus the truth of what is expressed by "Thus the heavens and the earth were finished, and all the host of them" of Genesis 2:1, one must ask the question as to just how does this Universal knowledge help us in our reality?

As a final example within this book, not only the establishment of the beginning, referred to as creation be established, but also that which qualifies existence.

There is only one thing which must be inclusive to the very foundation and part and

parcel to the creation potentiality, and that is time, as nothing exists without the existence of time

At World Science Festive, heading reads:

TIME IS OF THE ESSENCE... OR IS IT? "

"What is time? Isaac Newton described it as absolute, but Einstein proved that time is

relative, and, shockingly, that time and space are intricately interwoven.

I qualify and establish by usage of the Crown Code, as an all-inclusive foundation

formula model, that the essence and nature of time and space,

including gravitational quantum reality, are intricately interwoven as fundamental within archetypal creation.

If this is true, what new picture of reality will emerge?

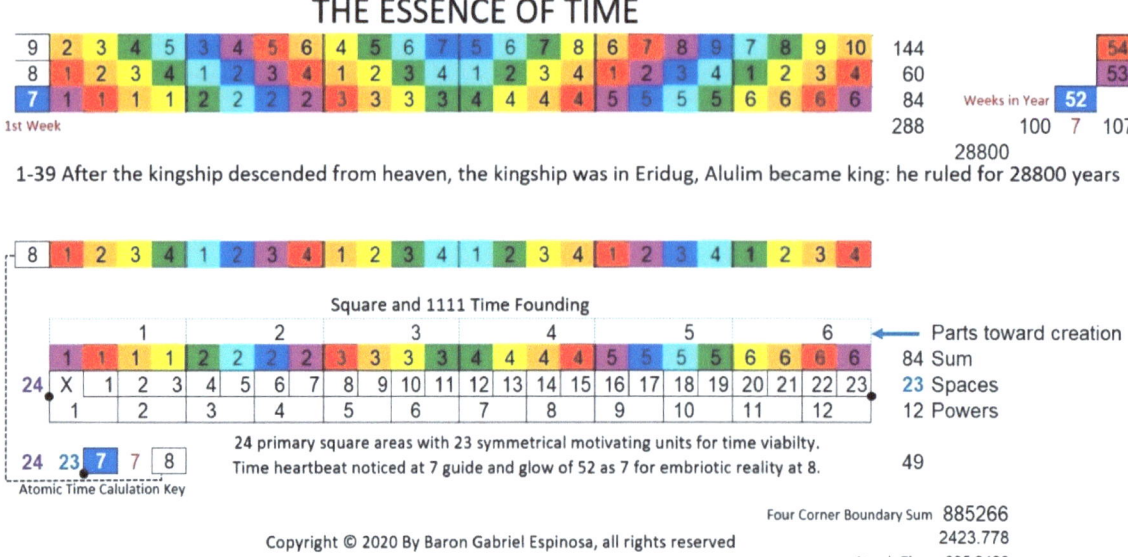

Exhibit 121: The Essence of Time

11.8 As established by the hand coordinate of "God" as upon the geographical makeup surrounding the Mount of Olives, there is no doubt, that the reference to creation by the Crown Code was used in establishing religious ideologies, to the extent of giving narrative to a variety of Gods, here more specifically Abrahamic.

The totalities within development to the universal language, became used differently by each king, being either for the good or bad of humanity. Separated by what seems incalculable spans of time, or times defined by those preventing the recognition of that Universal truth. Nefarious use brings us to modern reality. Which, believe it or not, are intertwined and coexist as that experience, reverberating also what The Crown Code truly means to all existence.

Just as in the Sumerian Kings List, the narrative of time begins at the first six number sets of the Crown Code, seen at bottom of Exhibit 154: The Essence of Time.

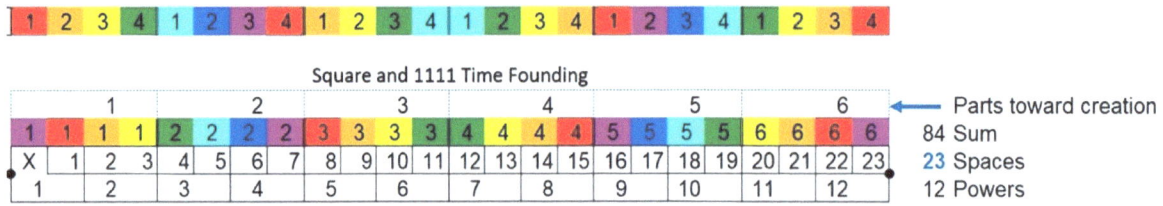

Exhibit 122: Square and 111 Time Founding

The six sets are the six parts, as archetype not yet in creation as understood by Exhibit 134: Hand Code to Truth.
The First Level contains 24 spaces as times daily unit potential, which numbers sum 84. Each set contain two pairs, understood as twelve powers. Sum 84 can also deduct the square essence of 24 revealing the 60 seconds in a minute, and 60 minutes to the hour development.

The level also contains two color coded symmetric halves. By polarizing the 84 and the 24, 17 is revealed which must coincide with polarized process to become 8. This becomes essential and important, in times revealing in existence.

For the time being, no pun intended, we deduct 8 from 60 to establish 52, which manifests as the 52 weeks in the year. As completion calculation to the first level, and being part of symmetric halves, 52 becomes 7 and is placed opposite and left of purple number one. The result is understood as the 7th day of the first week of 52 weeks to the year.

We cannot continue unless we have balance, which means, eight of 17 was deducted in revealing process, it must be remembered thus, 8 is placed above the 7 at the next level. The manifesting squares being blank, not must be associated to each set of four, hereafter designated 1, 2, 3 and 4, which in sum essence agree with the essence of 60 toward times manifest.

Exhibit 123: The Essence of Time

I am sure that you have noticed the description "1 39 After the kingship descends from heaven, the kingdom was in Eridug, Alulim became king: he ruled for 28800 years" this is taken from the Sumerian Kings List, as the first King listed upon the list.

This is because levels one and two unite in effort, which one can associate with coupling, agreement. The first level purple one (1) as male and the second level blank square, designated as a one (1) is likened to a female womb. Here they agree, thus, they consummate.

The one (1) of the first level and the one (1) of the second level produce the third level, at first column is 2. Each column thus establishes third level numbers, whereby providing the first 144 sum. As a King, this knowledge as base becomes vital in understanding process toward what becomes the entirety of the Crown Code.

This Revelation of Great truth, that I have been given by universal authority to reveal, and to develop, the intricacies of its truth in its entirety.

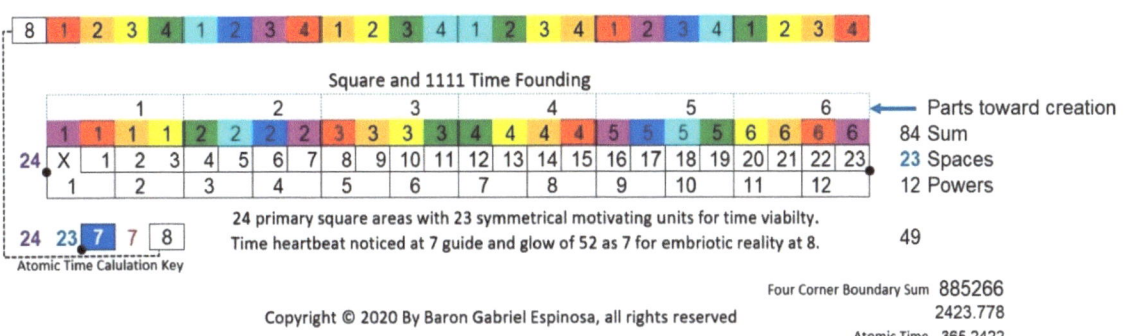

Exhibit 124 Square and 111 Time Founding

In establishing what I as a true King [of the kingdom of consciousness] can reveal, the first 24 are considered symmetric in nature, thus 24 of the first is placed representing the first cube, or that founding desire toward development of what can be achieved, whereby it recognizes itself as 23 toward fulfillment. The number 2423 becomes. guiding essence as the seven (7) and the (7) of 52 are recognized as outside of the core development, thus in expression establishing two digits, less than 2423 for 2423.77. The reality of times establishment is in creation, which is a product of the union between levels one and two, which provides understanding to the first level manifest or first born at level nine (9) thus what is considered in the womb, being at level eight.

The resulting Universal Calculation Key Number is revealed as 2423.778.

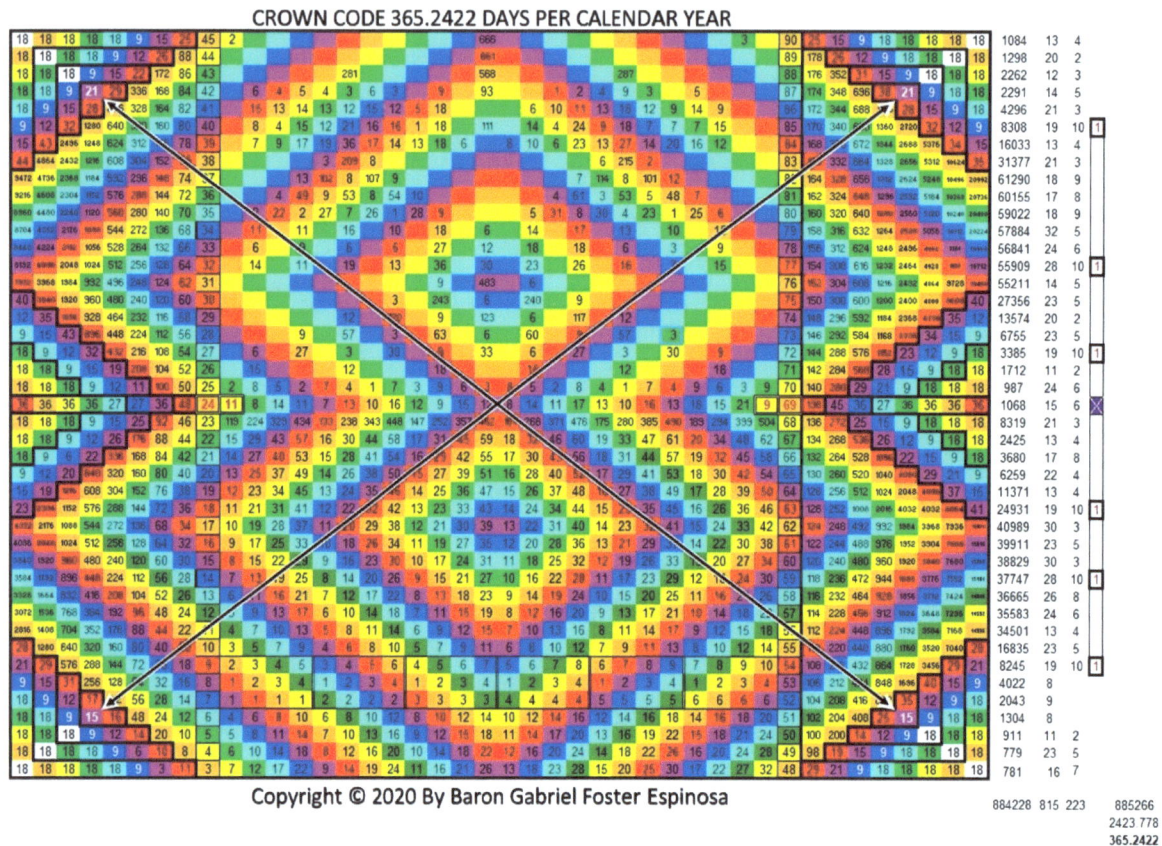

Exhibit 125: Atomic Squaring of Time

11.9 Atomic Time. Currently, the most accurate atomic clocks cool the atoms to near absolute zero temperature by slowing them with lasers and probing them in atomic fountains in microwave-filled cavity such as the NIST-F1 Atomic Clock. Considering the numerical development within the four corner area upon the Crown Code the sum of 885266 is realized which includes the polarized essences, except the 6's or fourth part in red, as they relate to the six sides of the first cube instruction and the first six three level sets of the Crown Code.

As mere numerical result, it cannot mean anything unless until one applies the Universal Calculation Key Number of 2423.778 as established from first instruction toward development of the Crown Code. I establish through the Crown Code, a mathematical formula which provides time to such accuracy which never had been proven before.

885266 is divided by 2423.778 which results in 365.2422 as the exact estimation of the annual days in the year, a number only met by the atomic clock.

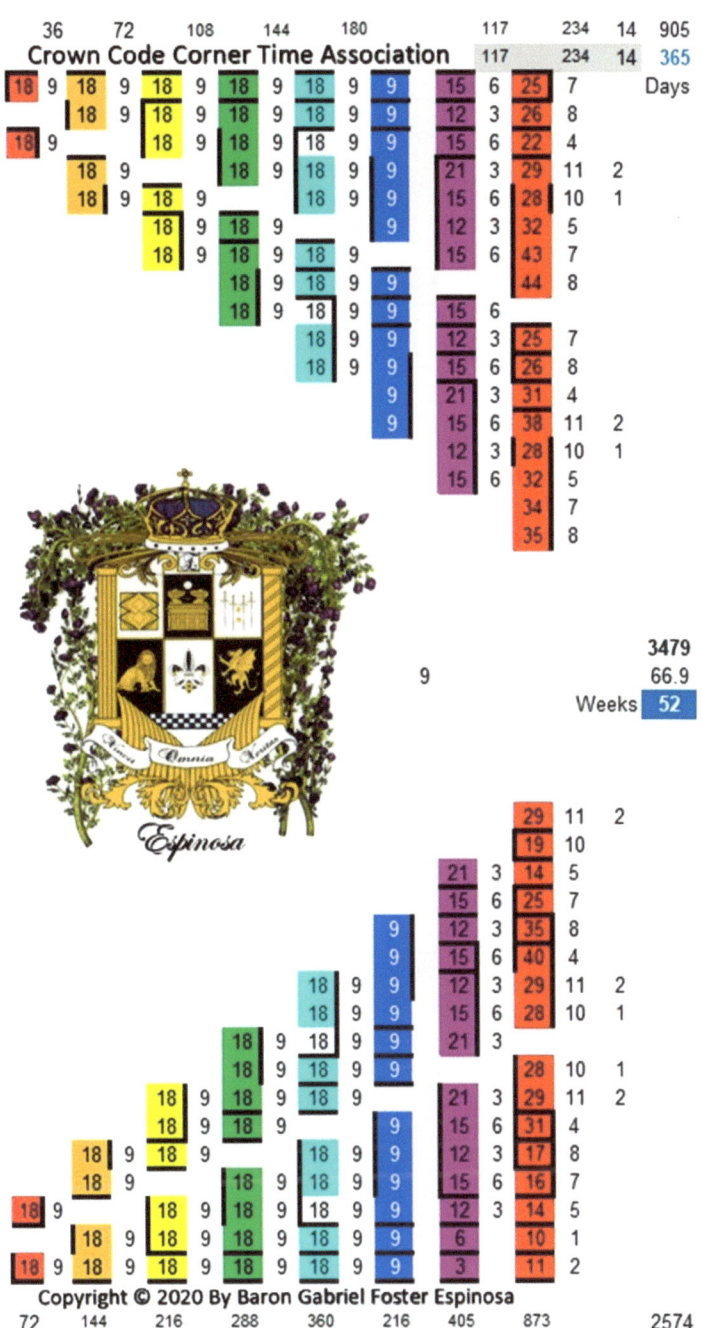

Exhibit 126: Crown Code Corner Time Association

The four corners express that crossing as that part into existence. Here the four are separated and polarized revealing foundation association as 365. The square sums and the polarized sums are united to equal 3479.

The six founding parts within the four corners are considered and applied with the six symmetrical corner emanations as 66.

The separating 9's sum of 216 must also be polarized and used, establishing 66.9 Time association is 3479/66.9 for 52 weeks in the solar year.

TWELVE

THE OTHER SIDE OF GENESIS
RACISM ROOT

"NOBILITY RISES-UP FROM THE SOUL, THE SOUL'S MATRIX IS UNIVERSAL LOVE, THEREFORE, TO BE NOBLE WOULD IMPLY WE SEE BEYOND RACE AND RELIGION. WHENEVER WORDS, IDEAS OR EXPRESSION, ARE TAKEN OUT OF CONTEXT A PROBLEM WILL OCCUR. AS A PEOPLE OF EARTH, WE ARE CONTINUOUSLY FORCED TO SEEK SOLUTIONS TO PROBLEMS THAT NEVER REALLY EXISTED BUT WERE CONSCIOUSLY CREATED BY THOSE IN POWER AND CONTROL. WE ARE ALL DIFFERENT, WHETHER ITS COLOR, RACE, OR CULTURE, IT'S BECAUSE OF SUCH DIVERSITY, THAT MAKES THE WORLD AN AMAZING CONCEPTION'

Stories as included in the Bible, derived out of those details contained in the Crown Code.

12. The misunderstanding, or misinterpretations thereof, are primarily due to a variety of factors.

1. Source material had been removed from that which is available for examination by the people of earth. One can consider natural disaster, or cataclysmic events which aided in wiping away ancient records, whereby the discovery of such, would enlighten modern interpretation into a new perspective. An original perspective and meaning of the ancient narrative.

2. Source material had been purposefully removed, as a means toward proprietary development, and societal control. The results of which varied in the hampering of liberty and consciousness.

3. Literal interpretations were imposed upon the masses, whereby the underlying truths as contained in certain writings became hidden and privy to only a few. The result was a less than accurate interpretation of that written which was originally established to be understood by esoterically minded insights, specifically, by that as understood of the Crown Code.

Examples from the beginning of time, and from generation to generation, are seemingly abundant, which echo reverberations of injustice, about Racism, especially in Modern day.

The subject of racism, especially in modern day, has brought about that reverberating echo of injustice. Examples have been given by many, from generation to generation, and seemingly since the beginning of time.

Now, we must get to the root of what became the foundation toward racism. *It is a separate conception of that conceived idea of being a chosen people.*

What we are going to examine, is the story of Noah, Ham, and the Curse of Canaan.
If we look at this story literally, in other words factually, who did what to whom in that tent, to merit such a curse?
Jeff A. Brenner's Mechanical Translation of the book of Genesis serves as a superb example which takes us closer to original meaning.

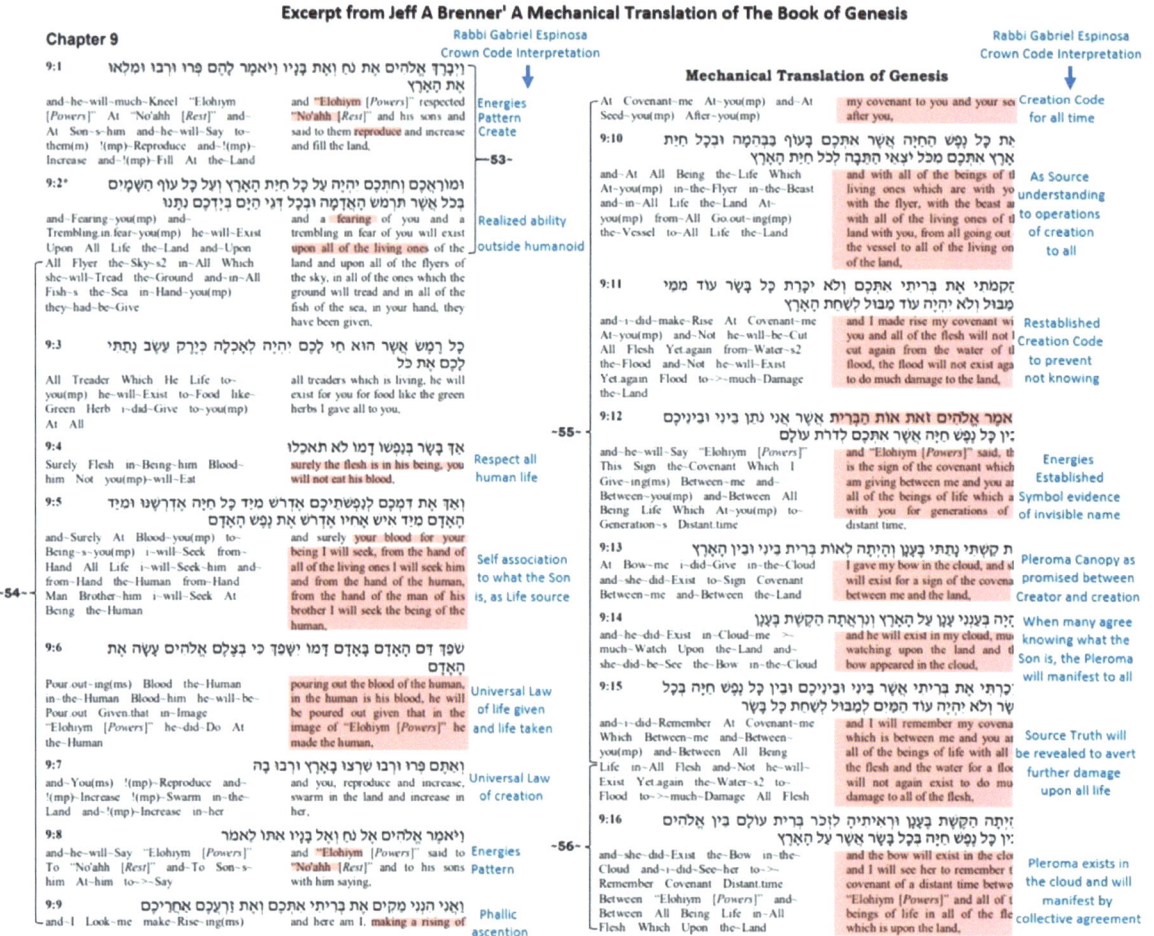

Photo 10: Genesis 9 true meaning 1 thru 16

In verse one (1) of Chapter 9 "Elohiym (Powers)" refers to the energies within the countenance of the Pattern, being those processes in development. Noah represents the guide columns of the Crown Code, wherein his sons as those components are from, as life potential, energy thrust, and the hidden aspects to creation.

In verse two (2) Man, endowed with intellectual application, is different than all other species of earth, which depend on our administration of life upon this planet.

In verse three (3) Those Treaders (creatures) which cannot make improvement amongst themselves, meaning lacking intellectual capacity at utilizing the Crown Code.

In verse four (4) Mankind must not consume each other. The likeness known as "what the Son is" that countenance of the Crown Code, is within each and every one of us.

In verse five (5) The universe seeks that each one, by their own hand, recognize that which is within, as the son and the daughter within.

Thus, in verse six (6) mankind by taking a human life unjustly, his life is required of him/her. For it is by the universal truth, man's likeness is of that truth.

It is in that realization, **in verse seven (7)** that life should reproduce and increase within her (the cosmos).

Which is why it was followed **with a verse at eight (8)** where the powers as those forces as the pattern, recognized creation formula guide columns as "Noah (rest)" and his sons (within the Core of formula) with him.

In verse nine (9) Creations potential is expressed in the rising of the covenant, which is to say, life is produced by that seed of truth.

In verse ten (10) clarification of this fact is defined, as salient to all beings of the invisible living ones, and to the living ones that are produced which go into matter and become incarnate.

At verse eleven (11), we see that the Crown Code was made rise again, only here it is referring to a physical being, as a human, who through (as redeemer of covenant details) reestablishes the reality of the covenant, in the form of the Pattern and Totalities, that Hidden Matrix, known modernly. The significance to such an event, is that flesh, in this case, mankind, is restored, and not to be cut off from knowing universal truth. The lack of knowledge is the cause to the damage to earth.

In verse twelve (12) The powers refer to the sign, which is how the universal truth is recognized, establishing its truths for all beings of life, for all time.

In verse thirteen (13) what takes place, is that union of that covenant with that sign. The sign being a bow in the cloud (the Pleroma) which needed union with that one who would reveal the secrets. [one as myself]

This is verified by that written originally in Greek, wherein the *Tripartite Tractate (57,8-59, 38) of the Nag Hammadi Library* refers to The Pleroma, or Fullness uniting with the Savior as revealer to the covenant.

Within it reads:

> "His members, however, needed a place of instruction, which is in the places which are adorned, so that {they} might receive from them resemblance to the images and archetypes, like a mirror, until all the members of the body of the Church are in a single place and receive the restoration at one time, when they have been manifested as the whole body, - namely restoration into the Pleroma. – It has a preliminary concord with a mutual agreement, which is the concord which belongs to the father, until the Totalities receive a countenance in accordance with him. The restoration is at the end, after the Totality reveals what it is, the son, who is the redemption, that is, the path toward the incomprehensible Father, that is, the return to the pre-existent, and (after) the Totalities reveal themselves in that one, in the proper way."

It is this sign which qualifies the authenticity of the Crown Code as that covenant.

In verse fourteen (14) is described that "he will exist in my cloud, much watching upon the land and the bow appeared in the cloud". This reveals exactly what the Son is, the Son is at-one with the cloud.

In verse fifteen (15) remembering, consists of something that already happened and what is anticipated to happen again, per interpretation. To the modern reader, it must be made clear that the "I did Remember" refers to a former experience, where the knowledge was revealed during a previous cycle.

The "I will remember" refers to the writer's knowledge of the truths suppression, and in knowing revelation of the covenant original likeness would happen again in the future, to prevent catastrophic results.

In verse sixteen (16) The former physical one, as the Savior in past cycle, the "did" became the "will" during this cycle, which hereby became fulfilled. For I did see her, as that bow in the cloud.

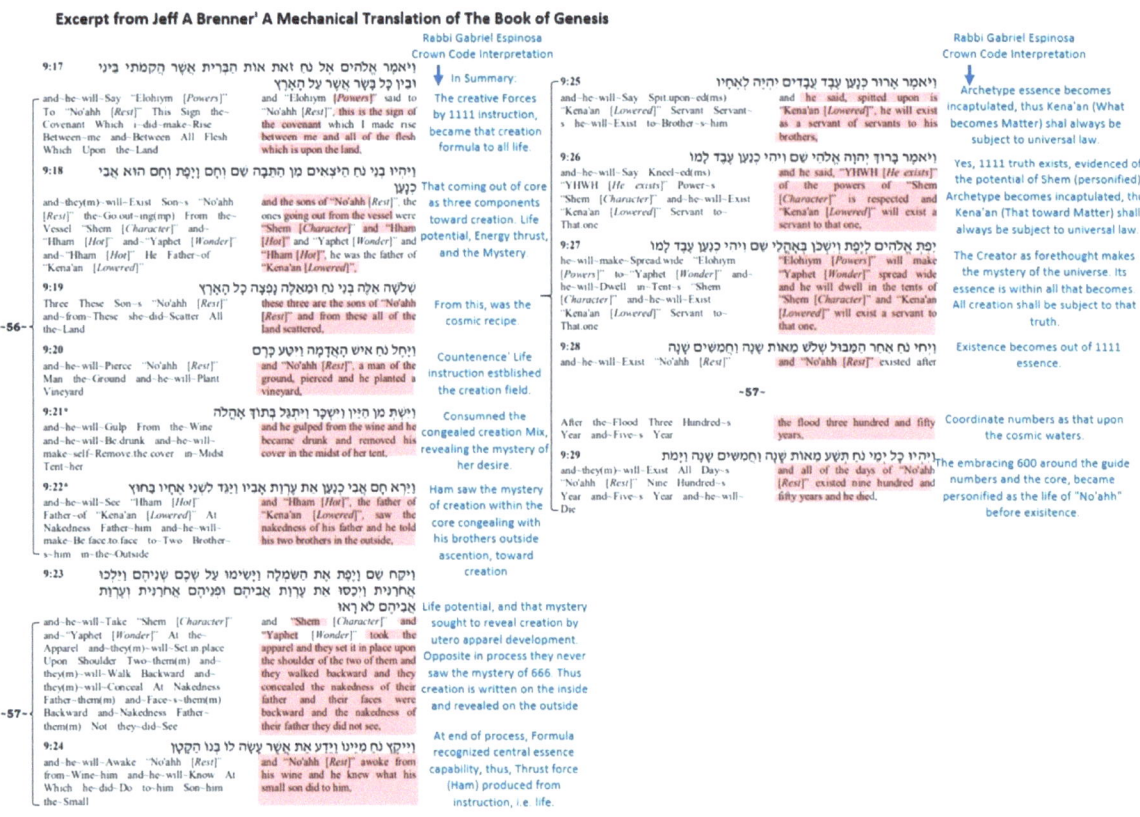

Photo 11: Genesis 9 true meaning 17 thru 29

As a reiteration in verse 17 of Chapter 9 in Genesis. The personification becomes directed at Noah (the guide columns) that the Pleroma is the sign of the Covenant, which was brought about through a man risen (as product of covenant) just as all life, upon earth.

In verse eighteen (18) included are Noah's sons, which are within the guide columns defined as the ones going out of the vessel. The parts associated with planetary and humanoid development, here being the same in part to what later was developed and referred to at Exhibit 20: Jesus Christ and Virgin Secret in Chapter ten (10). Let me explain.

In verse 18, we see what comes out of the core of the Crown Code, personified as the "Shem [Character]" and "Hham [Hot]" and "Yaphet [Wonder]".

"Shem [Character] was conceived of the left seen on chart below, which shows those polarized numbers as 9's that total 54.

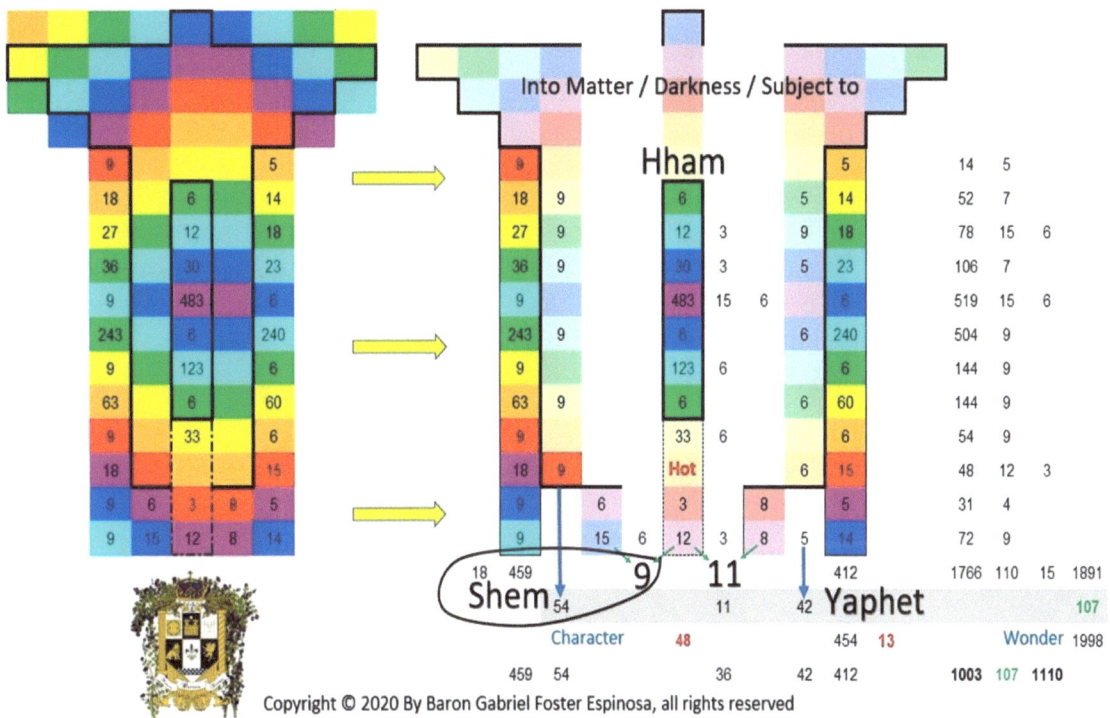

Exhibit 127: Shem Ham and Yaphet Association

The 54 relates to the 3rd level of the first six number groups.

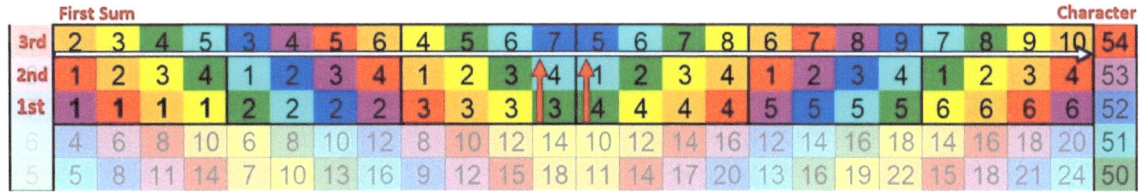

Exhibit 128: The first sum character

Notice that each column consisting of the first and second levels, when added together, each produce the sums at the third level. The first sum, the first born, the first result, takes on a character Shem, which in this narrative represents the third level reality at guide number 54.

The second qualifier toward that designation, is the fact that the founding numbers prior to polarization, equal 459, this when adding 4 plus 5 plus 9 the result is 18. It is no coincidence that the four-corner association, as the Countenance upon the pattern having eighteens.

Hham, is that portion later emphasized as that causative or impregnation, by the Holy Spirit, entering between the virgin's legs. It is that insemination quality, "Hot", as in such heat before climax. Here, those congealing forces, thrust toward life potentiality.
Hham's totality, stands upon 33. 3 and 12 as those 48, which became interpreted as 4 plus 8 for 12, as foundation to the expression in verse 19, from the three sons "from these all of the land scattered" (into twelve parts).

 Hham represents the central aspect of the first born, as 666 [light energy into matter]
Yaphet, at right establishes that third part to the triune essence or spirit. Yaphet total of 412 is united with its polarized essence of 42, which produces 454. Interpretation reveals that number to be 13. We can consider that being central with twelve surrounding. The wonder is that Shem, Hham and Yaphet together united by that remaining 11 essence, due to the 9 has been absorbed by Shem. Establishes a conduit as 11 uniting the two brothers symbolically, as that other side, expressing the mystery of 1111. The polarized result of 54, that 11 essence and the 42 are added, as 107 to 1891 to reveal its triune reality, as 1998 a treble 666.

In verse 20, "No'ahh [rest] is described as a man of the ground (meaning firm as in the guide column numbers which are stationary) wherein the core to the Crown Code becomes defined as the vineyard.

Noah becomes personified as piercing the ground and planting a vineyard. Those congealing forces produced, those archetype energies in the production of life.

In verse 21, We understand Noah gulped from the wine and became drunk. This was developed to describe the fountain effect, of scattering, as becoming drunk in following the process of her Rosetta grid [Rosseta grid to mean, circle from omni point and its parts]. likened to a cathedral stained glass front window.

Noah is also described as removing his cover, in the midst of her tent. This was written to describe that the invisible archetype toward existence, became recognized. That invisible became visible; thus, its invisibility cloak was removed. It is this root of knowledge which became used again, in the description where in Matthew 27

> *50 Jesus (Personification of the unifying archetypal parts), when he had cried again with a loud voice, yielded up the ghost.*
> *51 And, behold, the veil of the temple was rent in twain from the top to the bottom; and the earth did quake, and the rocks rent.*
> *52 And the graves were opened; and many bodies of the saints which slept arose,*
> *53 And came out of the graves after his resurrection, and went into the holy city, and appeared unto many.*

Which is to say, that the invisible (Ghost) left, and that toward manifest became revealed, just as "No'ahh" removing his cover revealed his essence which was in the tent. The tent is that part to the Crown Code, which consists of that within the column guides, being another way of saying, that the display within the pleroma as understood became manifest.

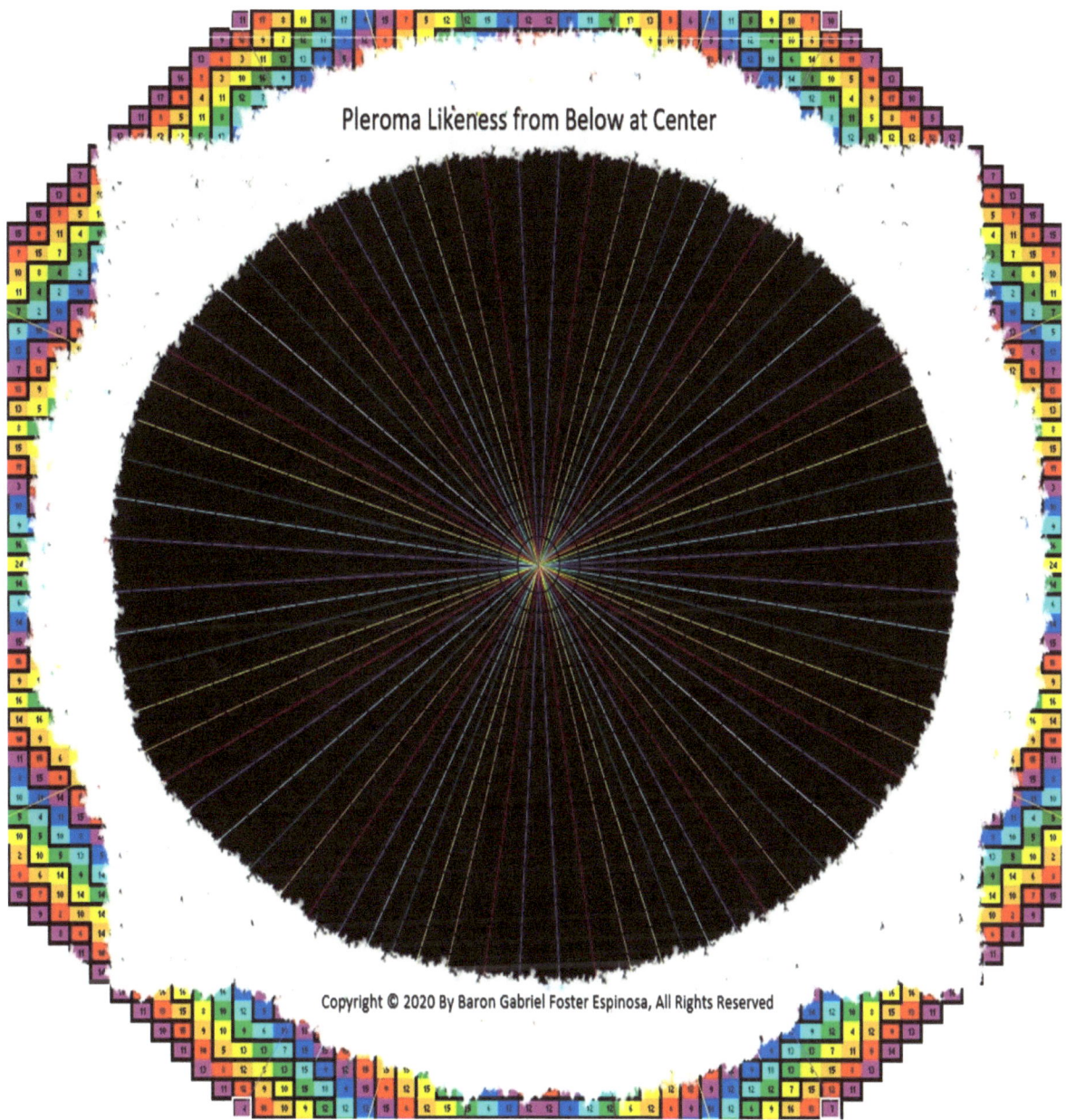

Exhibit 129: Pleroma likeness from below

In verse 22, Genesis 9, the story goes on, where "Hham [hot]", the father of "Kena'an [Lowered]", saw the nakedness of his father and he told his two brothers on the outside.

Here, we recognize that through development process Hham as central column sum of 666, sees what was previously invisible. Existence out of the invisible becomes seen through opposite process, such as from core 666 and downward.

In verse 23 "Shem [Character]" and "Yaphet [Wonder]" in that downward process toward existence (of becoming) take the congealed forces, setting it in place as on their shoulders, symbolic of planetary development as well as utero creation. Which is why the two walked backward as on the outside, of inward essence and concealed the nakedness of their father.

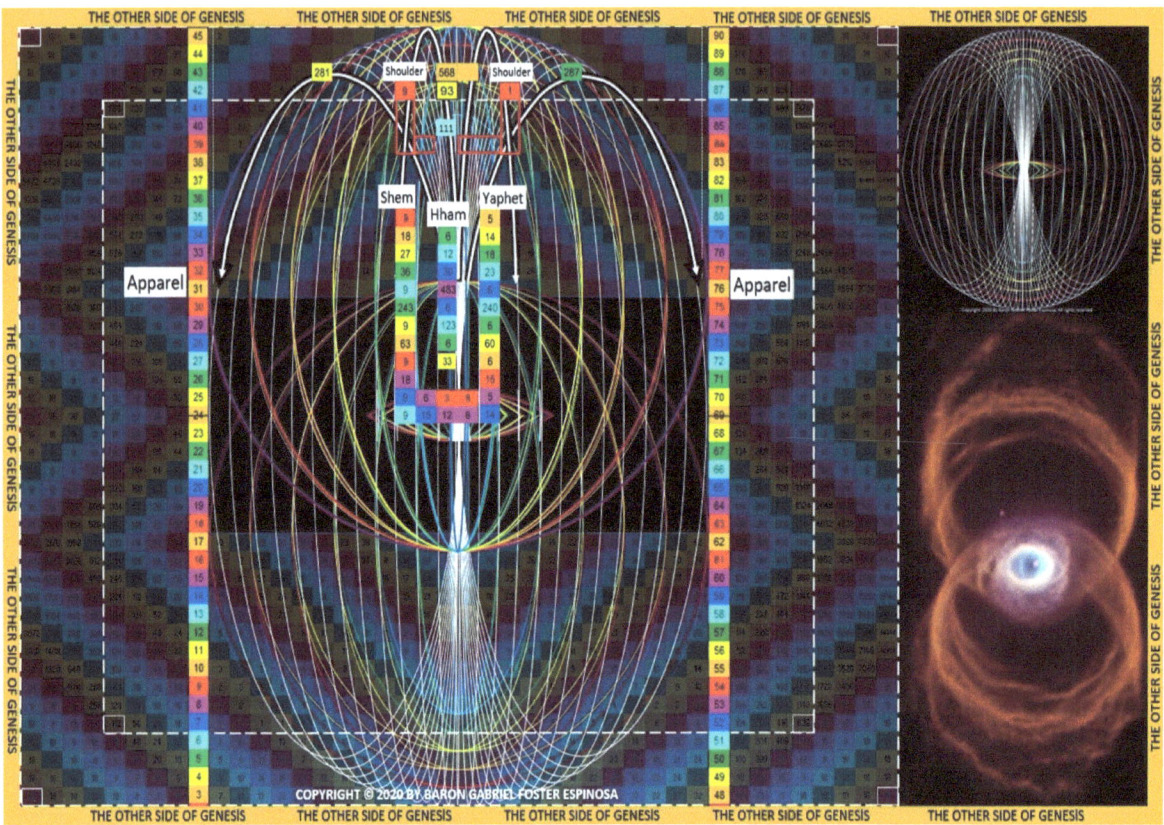

Exhibit 130: The other side of Genesis

Notice the Shem, Ham and Yaphet, associations consist within the central white two arrows return as Shem and Yaphet. It is in the downward passing that the covering takes place. In general, her expansion stretches to the boundary set by the guides toward creation.

The two shoulders defined as one to each being 9 and 1, are directly coordinated with that later used, in development of the virgin narrative as previously understood.

In verse 24, "No'ahh [Rest]" awoke from his wine as in Pic 127e the other side of Genesis, he knew what his son did to him, (to the creative process toward manifest reality).

In verse 25 "No'ahh [Rest] he said, spitted upon is "Kena'an [Lowered]" Here we must realize that what is explained is not that of disgust, as in spitting, but that act of water development as in the expanse of space, toward planetary development. "Kena'an [Lowered]" refers to that (Countenance of the Crown Code) which is going into matter. In other words, that which was in archetype and invisible, likened to the essence of the creator, or spiritual forces becoming captured, imprisoned in matter.

The description that "Kena'an [Lowered]", will exist as a servant of servants to his brothers, has nothing to do with slavery as misinterpreted and thus experienced in the annals of history.

The brothers referred to are that product, not part of that within the vessel, but that which is populated into matter. Which are not, within the guide columns upon the Crown Code, as that vessel which later is defined as Noah's ark. The parts to the revelations of the Crown Code, misinterpreted purposefully or not? has caused so much pain and suffering when used as justification of slavery of any kind, whether by governmental or ideological imposition.

To qualify what the underlying meaning of Genesis truly represents, we need just go to the following verse. **In verse 26,** "No'ahh [Rest]" (as the guide column vessel) is personified to say, Kneel-ed(ms) "YHWH [He exists]" powers of "Shem [Character]" and-he-will-Exist "Kena'an [Lowered]" Servant to that one.

The development of YHWH as God, in context of how this truth has been misused, is one of those great sins against mankind. To understand just how evil and cunning developers of the Gods have been, let us consider YHWH through the Tetragrammaton as discussed in the book 11:11 Language of Light, Secrets of the Hidden Matrix and Magical Universe. Within is understood that the Tetragrammaton was borrowed and adapted out of the antiquities, through Egyptian and Greek association of the Invisible Name, to the Invisible symbol of God exhibited in this book at chapter sixteen, wherefrom the three powers were usurped as pictured below.

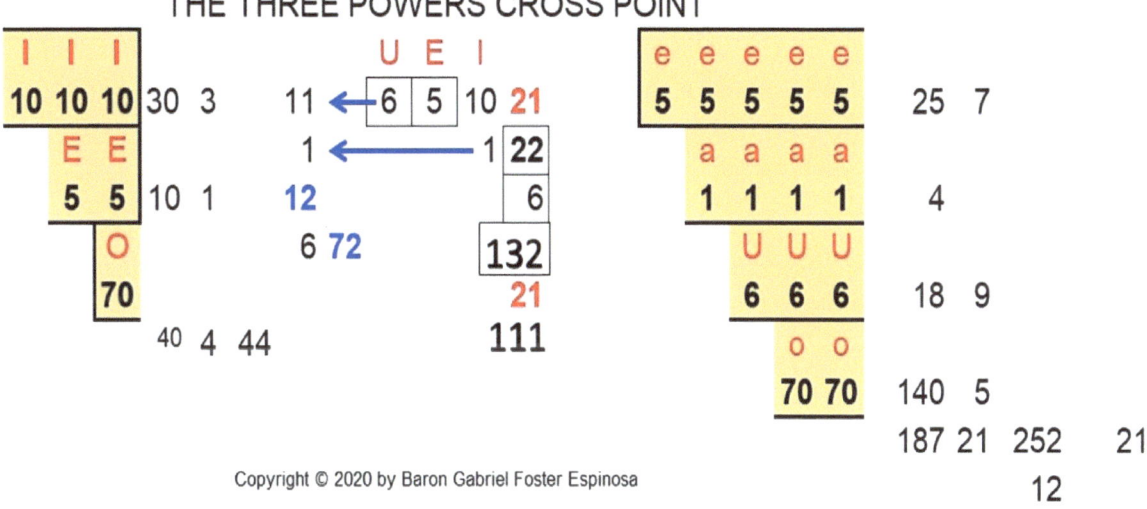

Exhibit 131: The Three Powers Crosspoint

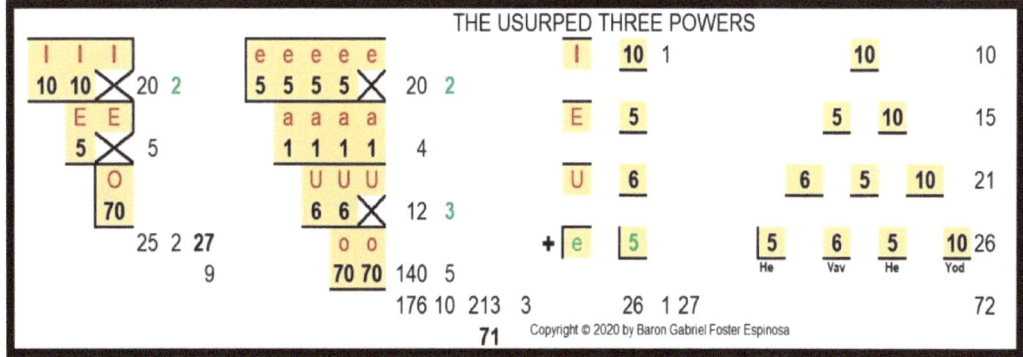

Exhibit 132: The Usurped Powers

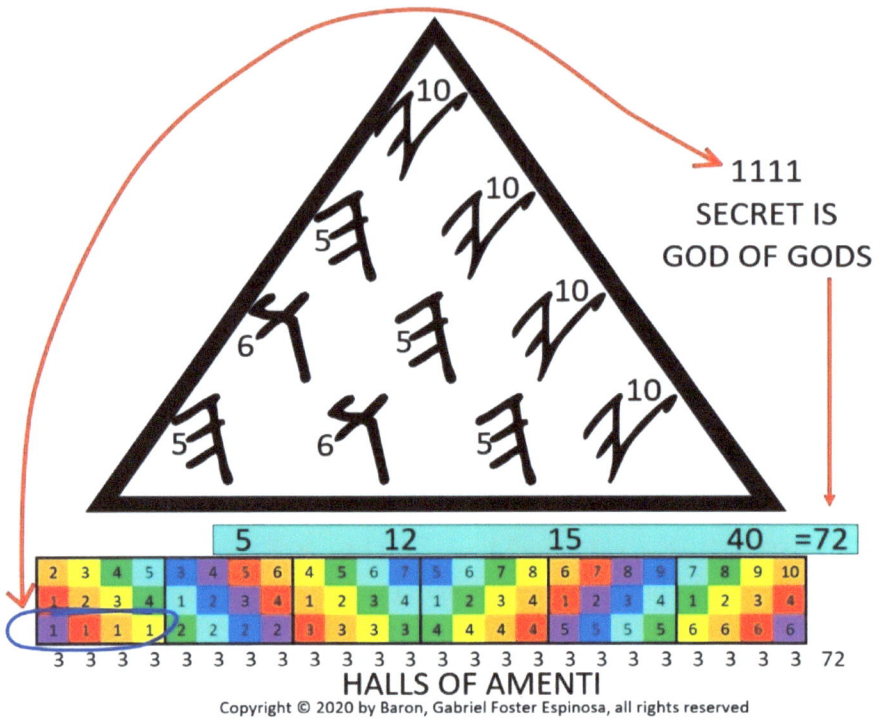

Exhibit 133: The Imposter Name Yod He Vav He

The evolution and usurpation of the key sum of 72, which represents the squares of the three levels of the founding six clusters, to the Crown Code. Which is also the level of the first sum, as related to Shem [Character].

So yes, "YHWH [exists]" through the power of personification, i.e.… [characterized the same as Shem was].

Later it was this inside information which inspired Kircher in his 1653 published work Oedipus AEgyptiacus. Within are "two of the best-known images of early modern material on Kabbalah. Kirchers version of the tree of Life, representing all four Kabbalistic worlds (Archetypal, Angelic, Celestial and Elemental) Kircher adapts the Hidden Matrix details to further the universalist ideology of early modern Catholic Church.

Reuchlins YHSVH at the heart of the diagram, signifies the secret as the three between the four, here personified as 'Jesus Christ, the center of all nature, in whose name all the other the other divine names are concentrated. You can find the 12-letter divine name, from which emanates the 42-letter name, then the 72-letter name, or rather Kirchers variant of the Jewish tradition, with 72 four-letter names of God, representing the 72-nations that comprise all humanity.

I must agree, with Daniel Stolzenberg where he argued, that by this stratagem, Kircher transformed the notion of the divine names as instruments for theurgical invocation into the representation of the totality of humanity under the influence of the Christian-Kabbalist divine Pentagrammaton, as a universal revelation and promise of salvation to all peoples (Stolzenberg 2013, pp. 162-74).

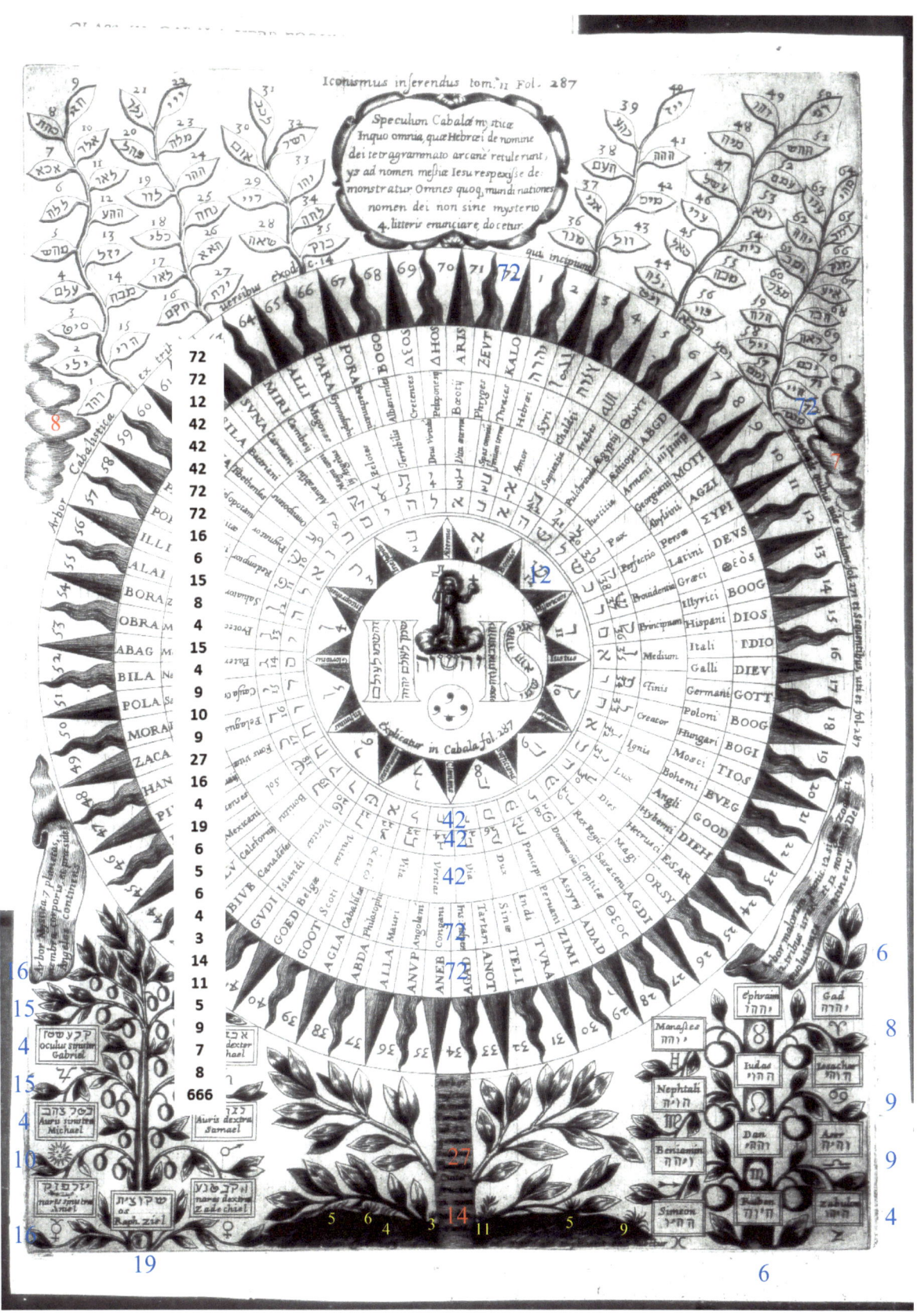

Photo 12: A diagram of the names of God in Athanasius Kircher's Oedipus AEgyptiacus (1652-54)

The Number association given to tribes, the zodiac, planets, angels, and those parts and pieces of the Hidden matrix was used that the totality of humanity became subject to and under the influence of the Christian-Kabbalist divine Pentagrammaton, as a universal revelation as that new customized adaption of promise and salvation, in essence usurping the truth meant for all peoples.

The strategy used here was not new, for it had been used in the antiquities as evidenced in the development of the gods.

Photo 13: OEDIPI AEGYPTIACI cover 1653.

The red circles below highlight hidden keys to universal knowledge, as reapplied and used by Kircher toward Catholic Church benefit. At the end of Chapter 7 and at the beginning of Chapter 8 seen is the simplicity of number usage, and the expressive potential within each.

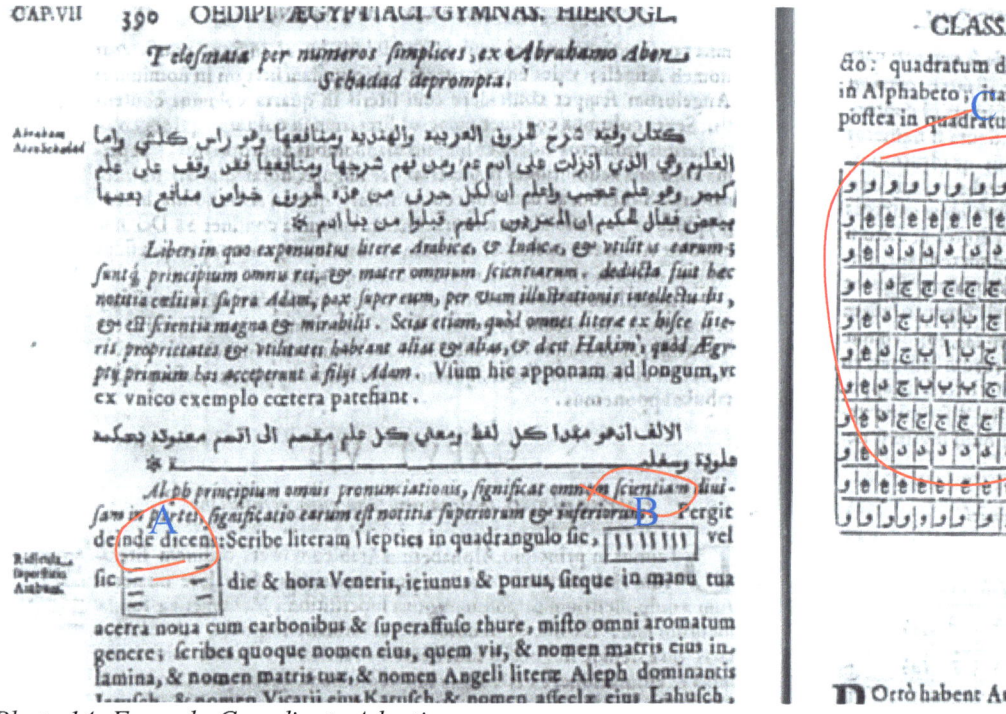

Photo 14: Formula Coordinate Adaptions.
A: the beginning and their end expression as shown at exhibit 115 on page 134 of chapter eleven, as Hidden Matrix foundation of 11:11. B represents what becomes as the Kabbalistic 70 and two ends for 72. C represents that reality of 11:11, which develops the 666 of the Hidden Matrix, considering the stone the builders rejected application.

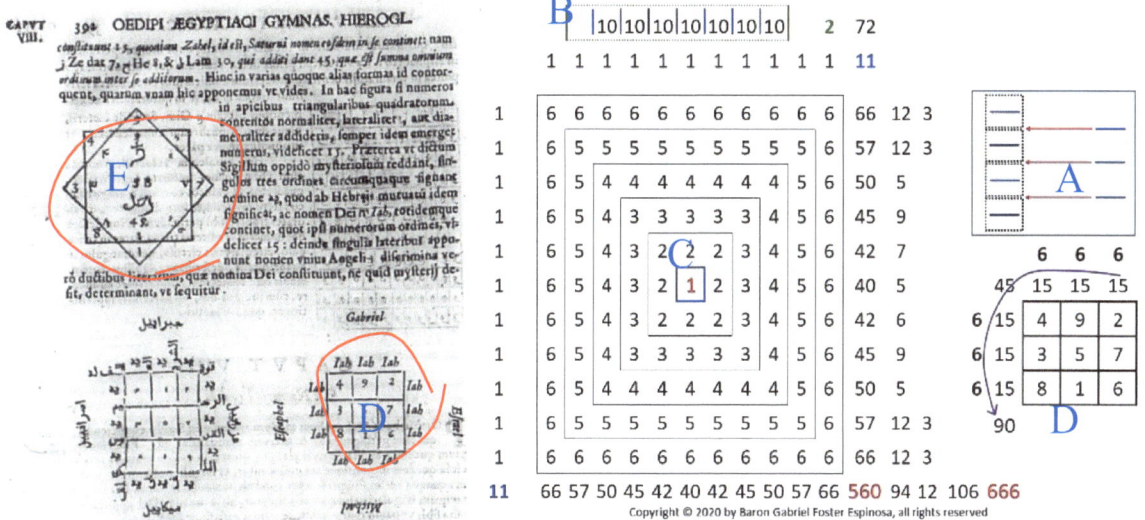

Photo 15: Kircher knew Hidden Matrix   Exhibit 134: Secret Calculations

D in the most simplistic semblance to core two guide columns, mathematically one reaches 45 at left and the other reaches 90 causing expression to the end or top of Hidden Matrix Core development as seen below.

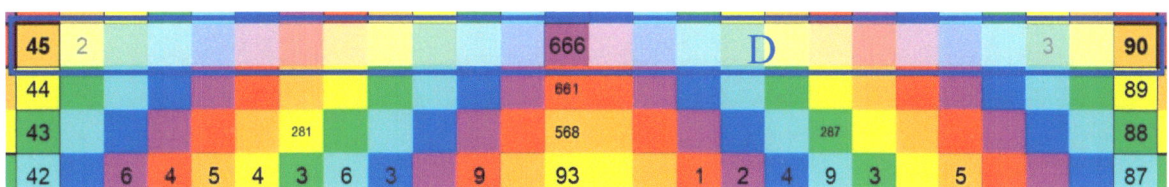

E signifies the Hidden Matrix spread which extends past the core.

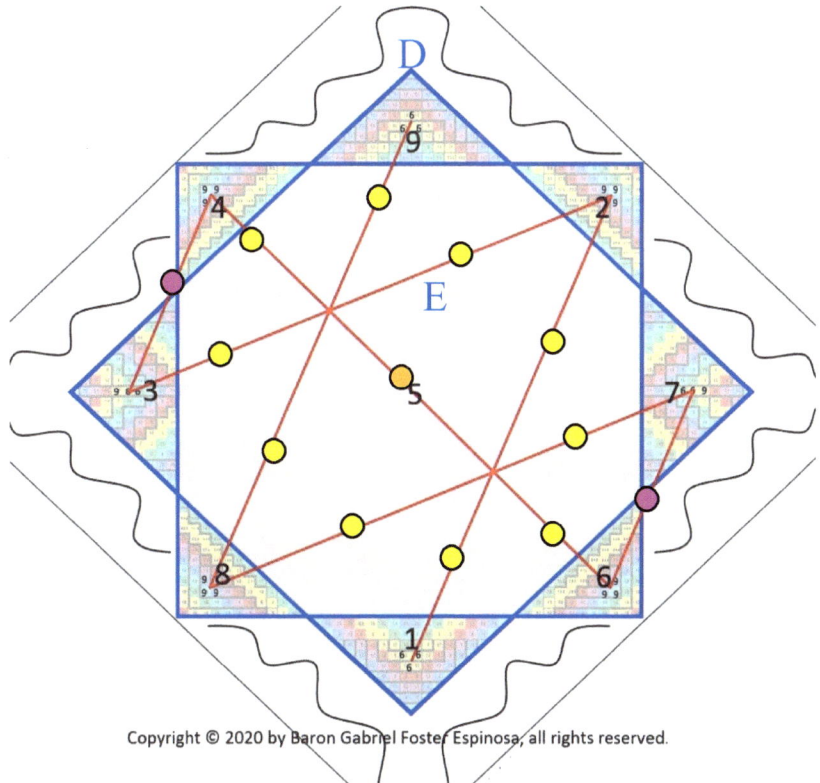

The key to the sequence of one (1) through nine (9) is the expression.

The yellow dots represent the five inner lines to either side. The orange in between joins in expressing 11. The outer lines as ends both agree and together with the inner say 11:11.

Exhibit 135: Kircher's Outer Spread association to 11:11.

It must be made clear, that what developed in relation to the operations of creation as understood through the Hidden Matrix, was a great gift to mankind. Yet perverting its truths, altered the future of mankind in the negative, was exceedingly deceitful and very evil.

Life being subject to universal law is a profoundly serious thing.

Personifying and or giving character and an altered narrative to its true and underlying meanings, has brough mankind into enslavement through deceit.

The servitude talked about in the biblical narrative is matter, where existence is subject to that universal truth.

Thus, "Kena'an (existence) as creations result, will always be subject to or you might say a servant to the brothers.

So in verse 27 "Elohiym [Powers]" as those 72, will make "Yaphet [Wonder]" spread wide and he will dwell in the tents of "Shem [Character] Which is to say that, the essence of creation will continue and remain within all that exists, thus, will dwell in the tents of "Shem [Character]" which are all the living ones.

From verse 28 through 29 "No'ahh [rest] existed after the flood (The spitting) of verse 25, 350 years representing those field dividers, summed outside and round the four corners seen upon the chart below.

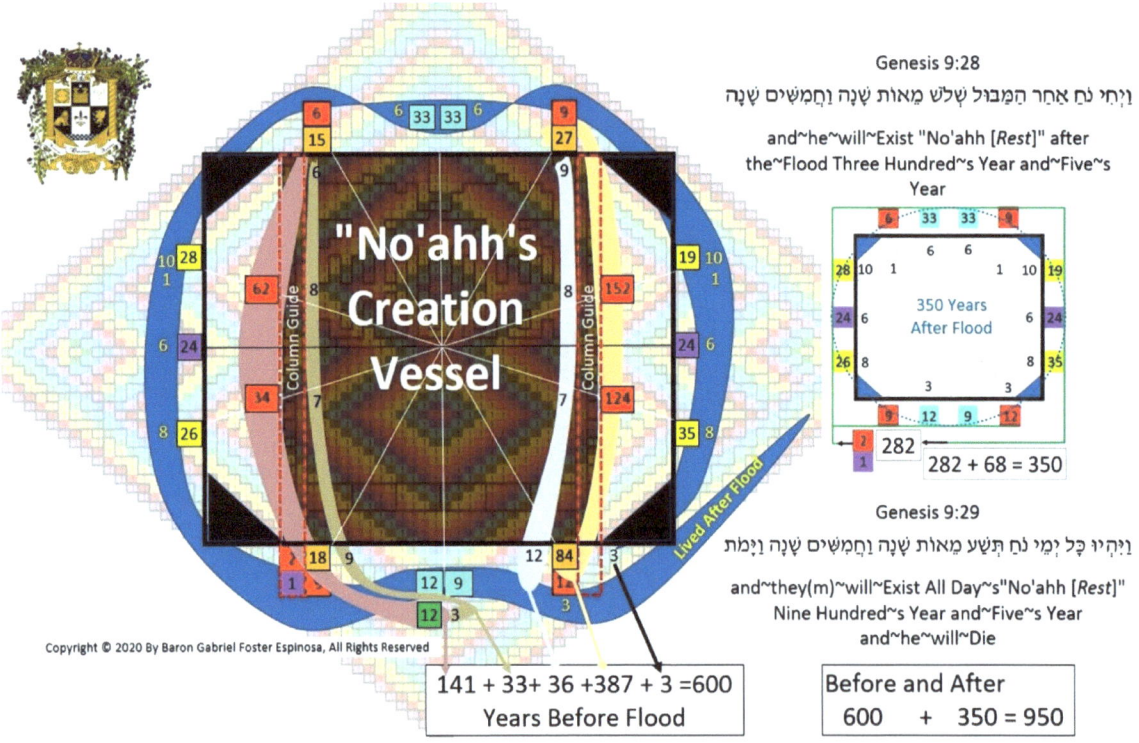

Exhibit 136: No'ahh's Creation Vessel

Before the flood (spitting) Noah existed as guide columns. Their coordinate associated numbers by the field dividers, embracing the core of the Hidden Matrix, because the writer needed to establish the years before and up to the flood, as created by the spit of "No'ahh" on "Kena'an", the developing planet. It is these very field dividers, which provide a clear coordinate to development, of the Zodiac as those waters.

Evidence has shown, that Gods of wrath flood stories, racism and the slavery experiences are plentiful, yet when compared to the truth of what the Hidden Matrix reveals, it is not difficult to understand, why the world is in such a mess.

The universal sign is a bow in the cloud, a pleroma, which is in union with that one as me, who would reveal the secrets of the Hidden Matrix, Crown Code. [The Bow was never the rainbow, for it is and always will be that within the cloud.] In modern time, I am the Witness to the Pleroma, allowing me to reveal the secret.

The human species has sought to incorporate that expression to themselves, in the invention of demi-gods.

Although slavery dates to prehistoric times, emphasis must be derived upon the development of the gods, usually in the most advances regions. We see this in the Indus Valley of India, and in ancient China. From the Tigris and Euphrates rivers in Mesopotamia, the Nile in Egypt systems of law recognized slavery.

Between the 6th and 4th centuries Greece embraced such a system.

It was once that during the classical period in Athens, a third to half of the population consisted of slaves. It became worse in Rome in service to the Gods.

Consequentially, modern ideas of freedom and democracy emerged out of a slave society.

The concept of freedom was more of a distinctive nature developed and experienced through large-scale slavery out of classical Greece and Rome.

While slavery declined in northwestern Europe in never really disappeared. From North Africa, Spain, southern France, Russia and even Sicily most slaves were "white" out of areas in Eastern Europe or the Black Sea.

During the 1300's, Europeans were using black and Russian slaves to raise sugar on Italian Plantations using the trade of exploiting African labor on sugar producing Islands off the coast of West Africa.

Rationalization came in the form of the Bible, especially during the development of America.

Most slaveholders identified themselves as Christian. Two favorite texts were used in justification of slavery.

We have Genesis 9: 18-27 which we have already discussed at the beginning of this chapter.

The morphing continued, where even changing the color of Ham to that different than his brothers to justify slavery biblically.

Thus, "The Curse of Ham" was achieved by dropping Canaan from the story and making Ham black, where his descendants were made Africans.

As a command to the slave, Ephesians 6: 5-7 where it read: "Servants, be obedient to them that are your masters according to the flesh, with fear and trembling, in singleness of your heart, as unto Christ; not with eye-service, as men pleasures; but as servants of Christ, doing the will of God from the heart; with good will doing service , as to the Lord, and not to men: knowing that whatsoever good thing any man doeth, the same shall he receive of the Lord, whether he be bond or free."

Ultimately mankind is faced with a choice. What has been established upon mankind, needs changing.

Recognizing that which mankind needs for its survival, begins by knowing what it has lost.

What had been lost, is embodied in the great secret of 11-11 which had been given to mankind for its prosperity while being part of universal existence.

Evidence has shown, humanity has suffered greatly while being kept in darkness and from its truth.

Mankind now, by the revelations as exhibited within this publication can break away from that mental enslavement, which can lead to the abolishment of racial underpinnings and those divisions which have allowed and justified a physical slavery of a peoples.

There is no question that a Creator exists and has so greatly provided evidence in all that exists.

The intricacies and beauty of that structure which not only congeals existing as archetype toward all life, is very real.

To ignore such reality, which is both simple and complicated is not wise.

The truths as contained within its reality, is foundation to all knowledge, which allows humanity to understand how existence has been throughout previous histories to those who have kept its reality from the people. The reality is, that those previous civilizations have all ceased to exist.

If we desire a future for our families and the continuance of life, we must recognize that we cannot survive without that universal alignment which can only become by the truth it has provided.

Thus, the future of mankind is in its own hands.

Much change is necessary, much growing pains will occur, yet it is for the best, if humanity is to survive what it has set in motion.

Let us do this together and create a better world for our children and the rest of humanity on this planet.

"I urge you to share this knowledge far and wide as quickly as possible.

As a sense of urgency, which I find, is overwhelming".

Gabriel

About The Authors

Baron, Dr Gabriel Foster Espinosa

Th.D. D.Div. Rabbi. M.E. Reiki. O.M

Dr Gabriel Foster Espinosa born in Texas USA 1963 is a Doctor of Theology and Divinity, Rabbi, Mentor/Tutor/Consultant of Esoteric, Metaphysical, Spiritual Subjects, Polymath, Mathematical Epigraphist, , Reiki Master, Matrix Diviner, Kabbalah, Mystic, Semitic Languages Tutor and Ancient Language Decoder, Developer of Pattern and Totalities aka Hidden Matrix, Revealer to Oral Torah Foundation Source and Establishing Paleo Alpha Bet, Decoder of Ancient Artifacts and Architecture, Philosopher, Intellectual, Writer and Author. President of Anaiah 501(c)(3) Denver Colorado

Creator of The Hidden Matrix Formula

Baroness, Dr Jan de Avalon-Espinosa

Th.D. D.Div. F.Inst.H.T. MEACH. dip hyp. NLP. SLCP. MBCT. REBT. EQ. EFT. Reiki. O.M.

Dr. Jan de Avalon-Espinosa born in Southampton UK 1950 is a Doctor of Theology and Divinity, Esoteric, Metaphysical, Spiritual Consultant Tutor, Foremost Esoteric Scientist, Healing Minister/Mentor/Tutor, Theurgist, Philosopher, Hypnotherapy, NLP Master, Psychology, Counselling, Life Coach, Holistic Therapist, Bio Energy and Aura Energy Photographer and Analysis, Magickal States, Higher States of Consciousness, Shamanic States Guide, Matrix Diviner, Reiki and Karuna Master Teacher, Mystic, Intellectual, Writer and Author.

Executive Vice President Anaiah 501(c)(3) Denver

Former Director Daisy International Romanian Charity and One World Charity, Former European Ordaining Priest in the Order of Melchizedek. 'The Studio' Meditation, Reiki Healing and Esoteric / Metaphysical / Spiritual Centre Norwich Norfolk UK.

NOTES

NOTES

NOTES

NOTES

www.ingramcontent.com/pod-product-compliance
Lightning Source LLC
Chambersburg PA
CBHW041514220426
43668CB00002B/21